After M. de Trèvise.

Day & Son Lith: to The Queen.

RESIDENCE OF THE AMBASSADORS AT TIEN-TSIN.

RECOLLECTIONS

OF

BARON GROS'S

EMBASSY TO CHINA AND JAPAN

In 1857–58.

By The MARQUIS DE MOGES,

ATTACHÉ TO THE MISSION.

[AUTHORIZED TRANSLATION.]

SR *Scholarly Resources Inc.*
Wilmington, Delaware

DS
507
. M 713
1972

SCHOLARLY RESOURCES, INC.
1508 Pennsylvania Avenue
Wilmington, Delaware   19806

Reprint edition published in 1972
First published in 1860 by Richard Griffin and Company,
    London and Glasgow

Library of Congress Catalog Card Number: 72-79818
ISBN: 0-8420-1366-0

Manufactured in the United States of America

CONTENTS.

CHAPTER I.

CHAPTER II.

CHAPTER III.

CHAPTER IV.

CHAPTER V.

CHAPTER VI.

CHAPTER VII.

CHAPTER VIII.

CHAPTER IX.

CHAPTER X.

CHAPTER XI.

CHAPTER XII.

LIST OF TINTED LITHOGRAPHS.

The two last Lithographs are copied from native tinted engravings contained in a series of volumes said to be school-books, lent by the Earl of Elgin to the South Kensington Museum.

RECOLLECTIONS

EMBASSY TO CHINA AND JAPAN,

IN 1857 AND 1858.

CHAPTER I.

Decision come to by the French Government to send an Embassy
to China.—Persons selected for the Mission.—Their departure
from Toulon.—The Straits of Gibraltar.—The Canary Islands.—
Delay at Santa Cruz.—The Island of Ascension.—Passage thence
to the Cape.

TOWARDS the end of the year 1856, events of the
highest importance occurred in China. Between
Great Britain and the Celestial Empire there had
long been differences and disputes, which, increasing
in importance from day to day, at last terminated in
a sudden rupture. The famous case of the lorcha
'Arrow' was a mere pretext in the hands of Sir John
Bowring, the Governor of Hong Kong. Important
consequences had immediately followed upon it.
The populace of Canton had burned the factories of
the foreign merchants, the inadequate force under
the command of Sir Michael Seymour had bom-

B

barded this town, and blockaded the river on which it stands; a price had been set on the heads of Europeans, more than one murder had been committed, and a general fermentation had ensued in the native population. In England, the Palmerston Ministry had indorsed, with their entire approval, the energetic measures taken by the English officials in Southern China, and had expressed their resolution to send out to the spot, without delay, a force large enough to preserve in all its integrity the high prestige of England in Eastern Asia. A numerous fleet was forthwith despatched with several regiments of the Queen's troops, from the seaports of England and India. At the same time, Lord Elgin, the able ex-governor of Canada, was appointed Special High Commissioner of Her Britannic Majesty to China, and invested with full authority over the functionaries of England, settled along the coasts of the China seas. These important disputes, which had taken place in the middle empire or kingdom of China, and the announcement of a new Chinese war, excited the deepest public interest all over Europe. The French could not remain inactive while events of such magnitude were taking place in the far East. It was proper and necessary that they should take a part both in the diplomatic and military proceedings. They had, besides, on their own account, insults to avenge and just causes of complaint for which to demand redress. The continued refusal on the part of the Chinese government to give suitable satisfaction for the barbarous murder of Père Chapdelaine, put to death by the authorities at Si-lin-hien, the impertinent and arrogant attitude assumed by Commissioner Yeh, the governor-general of the two Kwangs, towards the French Minister at Macao, the bad faith of this official, and the serious injuries sustained by our countrymen and persons under our protection during the destruction by fire of factories at Canton, afforded, independent of other considerations, ample ground for the interference of France in the struggle about to take place.

Lord Elgin set out for China in the beginning of May. On the 7th of the same month, the following note was published in the *Moniteur* :—

' Baron Gros has been appointed by His Majesty the Emperor, to proceed to China, in the capacity of Special High Commissioner. Lord Elgin has received from Her Britannic Majesty a like mission, with the same title; and the two plenipotentiaries are instructed to give each other mutual assistance in the negociations intrusted to them, which, should they be successful, will doubtless open a new field to Christian civilization and commercial enterprize.

'Baron Gros will very soon take his departure in
the frigate "Audacieuse." He will be accompanied
by M. du Chesne de Bellecourt, a first class secretary, the Vicomte de Contades, a third class secretary, the Marquis de Moges, and Count de la Tour
Maubourg, attachés to the special mission.'

A few days afterwards the names of the Marquis
de Trévise and the Vicomte de Flavigny were added
to the list of the members of the embassy and completed it. Lastly, M. de Besplas, a lieutenant in the
navy, who had served in the Crimean campaign, and
had been with Prince Napoleon in his expedition to
the polar seas, was, at the special request of Baron
Gros, added as a supernumerary to the naval officers
of the frigate.

A semi-official newspaper in the following para-
graph, summed up the services which had been rendered to the state by the new ambassador during his
long official career.

'Baron Gros,' it said, 'who now is about to proceed to China, with the title of Special High Commissioner, is one of those public men who have had
the largest experience in the diplomatic service. He
has belonged to it since 1823. Long chargé d'af-
faires at Bogota, he afterwards was intrusted with
several important missions, more especially with one
to the republic of La Plata, and with another to

England, whither he went on the occasion of the expedition to Rome. It may be recollected, moreover, that he was sent on a mission to Athens as Commissioner of Mediation and Minister Plenipotentiary of France, in the settlement of the dispute pending at the time between the kingdom of Greece and England.

' Baron Gros has been since then our plenipotentiary in the settlement and demarcation of the frontier between France and Spain. This important negociation resulted in a treaty signed at Bayonne, on the 2nd of December last (1856). This treaty now lies before the Spanish Cortes for their approval, and it has by its stipulations formally put an end to difficulties which have awaited solution for centuries.'

Both the Russian and American governments had important political as well as commercial interests to protect in Eastern Asia, and they had also redress to seek for serious injuries sustained at the hands of the Chinese government. They were therefore invited courteously, by the Cabinets of Paris and London, to combine in the demonstration about to be made by the maritime powers, so that their weight might be added to the pressure necessary to bring the obstinate Son of Heaven to a due sense of his real position in this world. But they refused to take any part in the coalition however desirable its object might be. They could not share, they said, in any measures destined to coerce the Chinese government.

In point of fact the Russians had in the Pacific at the time only one vessel of war, and that a very small one, stationed at the mouth of the Amour. Those in command of the fleet of Petropaulowski, chased about from place to place by the enemy's cruisers, were glad to leave the Pacific. They had returned to the European seas, where, by the way, while *en route* for the Baltic, they had met with a good-natured welcome on the Channel and Atlantic seaports of France. The Russian navy had been well nigh destroyed by the Crimean war; nor could ships be built and sent from Cronstadt by a long and circuitous route down the Baltic and round the Cape in time to take a part in the meditated demonstration. The Cabinet of Saint Petersburg therefore simply appointed Vice-Admiral Count Poutiatine its Envoy Extraordinary and Minister Plenipotentiary in China, prohibiting him from taking any coercive measures, but giving him distinct instructions so far as it lay in his power to make common cause in his negociations with the ambassadors of the allied powers.

The American government had quite a different motive for non-interference. The 'Mississippi,' the

'Powhatan,' the 'San Jacinto,' all fine war-vessels, were already in the China seas. But President Buchanan explained in reply to the communication from the Ministers of France and England, that it was an invariable principle of policy adopted by the United States, never to become bound by treaty with a European power, and always to maintain an entirely separate and independent position. On this ground he positively refused to combine with the allies. He stated, however, that a distinguished citizen of the republic, entrusted with a pacific mission to the Court of Pekin, would leave shortly for Hong Kong; and accordingly Mr. Reed, one of the members of the American senate, chosen by the legislature of Virginia, soon afterwards set out from New York for the scene of action.

The French Embassy now hastened their departure. On Wednesday the 27th of May, at 7 o'clock in the morning, his excellency Baron Gros, accompanied by his suite, went on board the 'Audacieuse,' then lying in the harbour of Toulon. Two hours afterwards the frigate, under all her power, steamed in gallant style into the blue waters of the Mediterranean. It was a day of bright sunshine. The sea was calm. The coast of France soon disappeared on the horizon. We set out for these distant China seas, full of pleasant expectations, not unmingled however with an anticipation of the pleasure we should feel in descrying once more at our return the dim coast line which had just before faded in the distance.

The 'Audacieuse' was now to be our home for some time to come. She was a large screw frigate, which had been built not long before by the celebrated engineer M. Dupuy de Lhôme. She had a crew of 550 men, carried 56 guns, and was propelled by a steam engine of 800-horse power. Her rigging was a perfect model of grace and simplicity, but she was too broad over the bow, and this want of a tapering shape diminished her speed, and indeed almost stopped her progress in bad weather.

The commanding officer was M. d'Abeville who previously had been captain of the 'Napoleon.' He was an excellent seaman, and most agreeable man. The chaplain on board was the Abbé Fournier, a clergyman long connected with the military hospital of Therapia. His devotedness to the sick, and his reserved and gentlemanly bearing at once prepossessed us in his favour. He reads prayers twice a day to the whole ship's company assembled uncovered on deck. Every Sunday afternoon after inspection, mass is said on the lower deck. A commander, six lieutenants, three surgeons, a paymaster, and ten midshipmen form the equipment of officers belonging to the frigate. There is besides a Norwegian officer on board, lieutenant Petersen. Why he should make his appearance among the officers of a French ship of war is explained by the fact, that it is the practice of the three Scandinavian kingdoms to send a certain number of their officers to serve in tho French navy, with the view of completing their education and of gaining experience in distant seas not much frequented by their own ships of war.

Our accommodation on board was not quite up to the mark. In the hurry of our departure there had been no time to fit up a poop. Into each cabin are packed two of us, and a thirty-pounder to boot. The ambassador is cooped up in the same quarters with the commander, and to console us they also enjoy the society of a piece of ordnance.

We cleared the Isles d'Hyères, coasted along the Balearic Islands, and then came in sight of the Spanish coast, with the mountains of Granada and Malaga, the gigantic snow-clad chain of the Sierra Nevada. It was cold, it rained, it blew fresh and the sea began to heave. The embassy felt slightly indisposed. Under these circumstances Baron Gros, whose six-and-thirtieth voyage this was, stood out with his imposing stature and firm tread, a marked man among subordinates, who it must be confessed had lost somewhat of the spirit and fire with which they had embarked at Toulon. With a stiff breeze in our favour we cleared the Straits of Gibraltar through a crowd of ships entering and leaving the Mediterranean. Some were tearing along under a fair wind, while others were beating up patiently through the narrow channel with a high breeze right ahead. Our commander was every now and then forced to slacken speed, lest he should run right into one of these ships.

On the third of June we entered the trade winds; the fiery clouds far overhead, the flying fish, and indeed every aspect of the sea and sky told us of the torrid zone. At a distance of thirty-six leagues we came in sight of the famous Peak of Teneriffe. Making a circuit of the island, we cast anchor in the harbour of Santa Cruz. While we awaited the permit of the medical board of the place to go on shore, we amused ourselves in scanning the scene before us through our spy-glasses. We could see the town stuck down coquettishly on the water's edge, its whitewashed houses with their green verandahs glittering in the sun. We could see the palace of the Captain-General of the Canary Islands, the Franciscan convent, the dusky flanks of the mountain with a small fortification projecting from them like a crag; the last but not the least interesting object in the view, we could see long files of camels drawn up along the coast. There was not much delay. We had scarcely set foot on shore when we were surrounded by a crowd of beggars, wearing cloaks and smoking cigarettes, a characteristic product of the Spanish colonies in their decline. Behind the window-blinds we could catch a glimpse of the graceful mantillas and black eyes of charming señoritas. It was not long before our midshipmen found a way to get into animated talk with the pretty damsels. We were invited to balls and evening parties, and every Frenchman in Teneriffe considered it a bounden duty to entertain us while we stayed. We wished on our side to make some suitable return for all this kindness, and accordingly we decided to give a ball on board. Now the roadstead of Santa Cruz is exposed to squalls. It is imperfectly sheltered. The swell is as much felt in it as in the open Atlantic. Hence the people of Santa Cruz don't care much about venturing to sea. We engaged our fiddlers beforehand, but when the time came we found that they refused to come on board. They would not run the risk of a tempest. But what obstacle will deter a Spanish girl when a dancing party is in the wind? Our fair guests did not disappoint us, they made their appearance punctually at the hour appointed. We improvised an orchestra. The deck was cleared, and with waltzes and polkas in quick succession, we danced, and danced with spirit too, until darkness fell. There were among

the Spaniards present two gentlemen of the name of
Béthencourt, descendants of Jehan de Béthencourt,
the Norman knight who conquered these islands for
the king of Spain in 1402, and who returned to die
at Granville, his native place, in France. His descendants still reside in Teneriffe.

The Canary group is composed of seven islands·
The largest is Teneriffe, the next is Grand Canary;
another is Ferro, through which used to pass the
meridian from which the French and other nations
formerly estimated their longitude. The Spaniards,
in conquering this archipelago, have completely
destroyed the indigenous race, the famous Guanches,
who are said by tradition to have been descendants
of the Carthaginians or Phœnicians, to whom these
islands in ancient times belonged. Sad to say,
the Fortunate Islands—the Fortunatæ Insulæ—have
wofully fallen from their by-gone splendour. Every
where the canary weed supersedes the grape. We
saw the inhabitants rooting up the vines to make way
for the prickly pear. What little activity remains to
the colony, is concentrated at Santa Cruz and along
the coast. Laguna, the capital of the island, is now
deserted and lifeless. Grass, which is scarcely to be
met with in country places, grows luxuriantly in the
streets, where groups of camels kneel lazily basking
in the sun. Here and there the visitor may perceive,

on the ruinous houses, sculptured on stones black with age, the shields of the old knights who conquered the islands.

The Marquis de Trévise, Petersen, and I took a long ride one day along the road leading to the Peak. We stopped to breakfast about ten or eleven miles from Santa Cruz, at the way-side inn, or posada of Sauzal. From the upper part of the house where we sat down to look about us, we had an admirable view of the famous Peak—the Pit of Hell, as the Guanches called it; we could see the lava streams; the summit, which was still covered with snow; and the small town of Orotava, nearly hid among the fig-trees, cactuses, and bananas, which grow in rich luxuriance along the skirts of the mountains. We returned to dine on board of the frigate, after having, in the early part of the day, crossed Teneriffe in its whole width, and seen the open sea and the two Canaries from the crest of the island.

Every day, in spite of the heat, we took an excursion into the environs of the town, to escape for a time the monotony of the ship. The funda Guérin, where we could get an ice made of snow from the Peak, at this time played a most important part in our daily life. But alas! the country was pleasant only while the sun shone. At night it swarmed with creeping things; some of us, having made an attempt to sleep on the ground, were well nigh devoured—literally devoured—by the insects.

After a delay of four days, we bade adieu to Santa Cruz. On the 10th of June, under a lowering sky, at 11 o'clock in the morning, we crossed the tropic of Capricorn; and on the 20th of June, at one o'clock, we passed the line, with due regard to all the burlesque ceremonies appropriate to the occasion.

Thursday, June 25.

Petrels, sea-swallows, and a flock of large sea-fowl of various kinds, from an early hour this morning hovered round the ship. They indicated our approach to land. Accordingly, about eleven o'clock, the watch gave notice of a shore a-head; and at two o'clock, after having coasted along the island of Ascension, we dropped anchor in Sandy Bay. In the same anchorage-ground there were already four English vessels of war. Among them was the steam-transport, the 'Assistance,' which had seen service in the Crimea, and which was now conveying to China the 82nd Regiment of the line, eight hundred strong. We anchored alongside of her. The band on board, by way of salute, struck up 'Partant pour la Syrie;' and during the whole evening we could hear the fife and drum playing to the tars and red coats, who kept up a boisterous jig on deck.

In Bouillet's dictionary, Ascension is described as having 'a frightful aspect, and a sterile and volcanic soil.' In fact, it scarcely does exhibit the smallest trace of vegetation. Nothing is to be seen but volcanic masses heaped upon each other, and sand-hills.

The island is eight miles long, by six in width. There is not one stream in it. The inhabitants derive all their water from cisterns. There is no population engaged in agricultural or mercantile pursuits. It is inhabited exclusively by soldiers, and the officials of the English government. It is to all intents and purposes a military establishment. On our arrival, Baron Gros and the commander made an attempt to go on shore, but the surf was so high, and the landing-place so bad, that they were compelled to return without being able to effect a landing. Next day they were more successful. They got on shore, and the governor showed them all the attention possible in his little colony, which is treated by the English Admiralty as a vessel at anchor in the ocean. He presented the commander with some pintado eggs and two sea-turtles. There are, some of the fowls, called pintados, and some wild goats among the rocks; but the great curiosity of the island is its turtle-bed on the beach. These turtles are of enormous size; each weighs 300 pounds, is worth 2*l.* 10*s.* on the spot, and will make a meal for 35 men. Twelve

are killed every week for the use of the garrison.
The English government makes a monopoly of them.
Neither fruit nor vegetables grow on the island;
nothing meets the eye in any part of it but lava,
and pumice, and volcanic dust. The unfortunate
defenders of their country who are compelled to take
up their abode for three years on this rock, in the
absence of other excitement, betake themselves to
strong drink to wile the time away. Accordingly,
wherever the visitor goes, be it into the streets, to the
crags, or down within the very crater of the Peak, he
is sure to find broken bottles. No one seems to call
in question the propriety of getting drunk at Ascension. Habitual intoxication is legalized and recognised. A narrow and rugged island not being a safe
place for persons in liquor, parapets have been judi-
ciously built at intervals along the foot-paths to
the fort; and whitewashed, so as to guide in safety
when intoxicated her Majesty's privates of the line
in their uncertain course over the crumbling lava.

Ascension is the first in the long string of the mili-
tary posts of England, lying along the route to her
Indian possessions. In one direction, are Gibraltar,
Malta, the Ionian Islands, Perim, Aden, and Ceylon;
in the other, Ascension, Saint Helena, the Cape, the
Mauritius, Paulo-Penang, Singapore, and Hong Kong.
As we proceed, we shall touch at several of these places.

We abandoned all intention of using coal, in consequence of the badness of the landing-place. It would have been necessary to take off our fuel in lighters; and we were anchored at a mile and a-half from the shore. When we landed, we ran the risk of getting our boat staved in, seeing that she struck twice violently against the ground. We were obliged to get out by means of ropes thrown to us from the beach. The long-boat, which came to take us back at three o'clock, was thrown by the breakers far up along the rock. We thought at first that our sixteen men were drowned in the surf. Nothing of the sort, however, had happened; and although the long-boat was none the better for the shock she had got, two hours afterwards we all went back to our ship, safe and sound, drenched to the skin, but glad to be quit of this most inhospitable spot. We left at six o'clock.

Saturday, July 4.

We could neither get out of the trades, nor enter the zone of the variable winds which were to carry us to the Cape. We were nearer the South American than the African coast; and yet, it was nine days since we had left Ascension! The waves began to swell, their crests became broader, and their troughs deeper. The fore-topsail yard, strained

C

by the blast, snapped. This was the first accident we had met with since our departure from Toulon. To the intense heat a fresh gale had succeeded, and so cold had it become that we had to muffle up in our top coats, and put on our cravats as we would have done at Paris in midwinter.

Wednesday, July 8.

At last we quitted the zone of the trades and entered the region of the variable winds. A smart gale from the south-west favoured our course to the Cape. It rained, hailed, and blew, the sea all the while getting rougher and more stormy. The 'Audacieuse' outrode the storm gallantly. It was pleasant to see our little frigate, with not a bit of canvas spread but her main and fore topsail, breasting the foam-crested waves, and plunging down fearlessly into the yawning hollows. When we walked about on deck, we saw the huge waves rolling past us mountains high. On every side of the ship there rose a wall of water, bounding the horizon a few yards off. A number of large sea fowls, among which we noted the albatross and spotted petrel, followed the ship.

We were advancing in the right course at the rate on an average of ten knots an hour. But alas! we regretted already the pleasant trade winds!

Our engineer ascertained our larboard roll to be 57°, while our starboard was 20°, the mean being from 30° to 35°. The larger waves were from eighteen to twenty feet, the smaller ones about nine feet in depth.

Tho frightful rolling and pitching of the vessel prevented us from either working or walking about on deck. We were fully occupied in preventing ourselves from being tripped or thrown down. When on deck we held fast by ropes in passing from place to place. The chairs were upset, everything was turned topsy-turvy. It was no easy matter to breakfast and dine. One of the sailors, jerked from his hold by the roll of the vessel, fell and broke his collar bone. Every seam creaked incessantly. All the port-holes were closed below as well as above; which, however, did not prevent the water from penetrating into our berths, and the waves from lashing over the deck. All was damp, dark, and dreary. But it was not till the night of the 6th or 7th, that the pitching began in all its glory. Nobody was prepared for it. About two o'clock in the morning there was heard a frightful din of tumbling chairs, broken crockery, and of trunks pitching hither and thither in all directions. Every one in the darkness, and at the risk of being precipitated he knew not where, strove to make fast his chattels, and prevent their being tossed about upon the floor. That night not one of us closed an eye. In short, for two days we were at the mercy of a fierce gale of wind. We made upwards of two hundred miles in twenty-four hours, with scarcely a sail spread!

Monday, July 12.

For the last three days we have had calm weather again. It has been cold, it has often rained, but there has not been a breath of wind stirring. Our crew, which consists chiefly of young Bretons, were in very low spirits when we left Toulon, but now they have begun to exhibit a little more animation. Groups will gather on deck round a loquacious mess-mate, to hear his yarns, while in the evening the men on watch favour us with a song or two in chorus. To encourage this good humour the commander dis-tributes rations of wine among the principal per-formers. We are now little more than six hundred miles from the Cape.

The lamps are lit at five o'clock. The evenings after dinner hang rather heavily upon our hands. To wile away the time, however, and vary the monotony of the long night, every passenger on board has agreed to give an account of his travels. M. Riche has described La Plata and the government of Rosas; M. Domzon gave us an account of Otaheite and Queen Pomaré; M. Lespés of the fortifications of Sebastopol; M. de Labarrière of the court of Soulouque, the West Indies, and our back going colonies in that part of the world. M. de Vautré gave us a narrative of his sojourn at the Sandwich Islands and Lima, and M. de Besplas recounted his voyage to the Polar seas, where he had been, as I stated, with Prince Napoleon, while the doctor told us what he had witnessed in his time on board a cruiser long stationed off the coast of Senegal. Pleasantly the time passed, and when we had flavoured our tea with a drop of rum, sipped a cup of the exhilarating beverage, and eaten a ship biscuit, we popped into our berths very well contented with ourselves and all about us.

CHAPTER II.

Arrival of the 'Audacieuse' at Simon's Bay.—Departure for Cape
Town.—Cape Town.—Table Bay.—Table Mountain.—Sir George
Grey, the Governor of the Colony.—The English Colony of the
Cape of Good Hope.—The Caffres.—The Boers.—The French
Villages in the interior.—The small Republics of the Orange
River.—Wynberg, the paradise of the Cape.—The Mountains of
Constantia, and the Cloëte family.—Contrast of Civilization and
Barbarism at Cape Town.—Mildness of the Climate.—Dearness
of everything.—Our stay at the Masonic Hotel.

Simon's Bay, Tuesday, July 21.

AT last we have doubled the Cape of Good Hope.
The first part of our voyage is over. We have taken
fifty-six days to make a passage of 2,500 leagues,
which is our distance from Toulon, and twenty-five
days in coming from Ascension to Simon's Bay.
Simon's Bay, which is sheltered from the north-west
winds, is the winter anchorage in this colony; while
Table Bay, which is sheltered from the south-east
winds, is the anchorage in summer. These two roads
are about twenty miles from each other. At all
times, but more especially in winter, it is no easy

matter to double the Cape; for us, it so happened that there was no difficulty or danger. In place of the dense fog which at times surrounds the Cape of Storms, we had a bright sun and clear atmosphere. Albatrosses and cormorants winged their flight playfully in flocks over the waves; the cold weather of the last few days had given place to a more genial temperature; the sea was smooth as a lake; not a breath of wind stirred. With all our steam up we moved on at the rate of twelve knots an hour. The Table Mountain, the Lion's Head, and the Lion's Rump stood out beautifully against the cloudless horizon; and of course we were all in extasies with a mountain top which is altogether unlike anything of the kind to be seen elsewhere.

We deserved this luck. Good fortune had deserted us at Ascension. At this last-named and detestable place, we had got neither coals nor provisions, and since we left it, excepting during the terrific gale of the 9th, we had been at the mercy of contrary winds, which had drifted us towards the American coast. For some days back most unexpectedly the breeze from the south-east had freshened into a gale coming in sudden gusts, so that we could neither advance by steam or wind, and as the ship laboured a good deal the commander decided to put in at the Cape. We had been there then for some days within sight of land, pitching and rolling about, and every now and then catching a gale of wind without being able to tell when this state of matters was to come to an end. On the morning of the 21st, the wind having fallen suddenly, the commander, without losing time, ordered our eight boilers to be fired, in order that we might escape from this fatiguing and most tiresome situation. Eight hours afterwards, we cast anchor in Simon's Bay. An English transport-ship, covered with red coats, was alongside of us ; we were at first afraid that it was the ' Assistance,' our neighbour at Ascension, but it turned out to be the ' Adventure,' another British war steamer, which was conveying to China the 23rd regiment. The band was not playing, and there was no dancing on board. Sad news, no doubt, had been received from India ; the Sepoy insurrection had broken out in Bengal, and a minor calamity, the total shipwreck of an English frigate at Macao. In the roadstead an English war frigate lay at anchor, displaying the colours of rear-admiral Sir Frederick Grey. Farther off we could see a charming little screw yacht of six guns, named the ' Emperor,' on its way to the Emperor of Japan as a present from Queen Victoria. Strange it seemed to us that such a tiny bark could survive these terrible seas ! Only one French ship is in the roads, the ' Bayadère,' belonging to Nantes, homeward bound from India, having on board the master and mates of the 'Duroc,' which was shipwrecked last year on Mellish Island. We fired a salute in respect of the English fort and the admiral's flag, and in reply the English frigate hoisted French colours at the mainmast, and acknowledged by the customary discharge the presence of the ambassador on board the 'Audacieuse.' We went on shore after admiring Simon's Town, which is prettily situated at the foot of the lofty hills which surround the bay, delighted to have escaped the roll and pitch of the ship. We soon retired to our apartments to make arrangements for leaving next day for the chief town in the colony.

Cape Town, July 29.

Next day, at six o'clock in the morning, we were on our way to Cape Town. We had two conveyances. In one were La Tour Maubourg and Flavigny, in the other Trévise and myself. The ambassador and Messrs. Bellecourt and Contades were to join us in the evening. The route was rather dreary at first, although very picturesque. We kept close by the water's edge over a smooth clean beach; we forded several brooks, and at times kept so close to the sea-margin, that the sheet of a wave would rush up to us, and beyond the horses' feet and carriage wheels. To the right we saw the vessels riding at anchor in Simon's Bay ; to the left the landscape was closed by a long chain of lofty and precipitous hills. We saw cormorants plunging into the water as we approached, herons busy catching fish, and in great numbers a kind of bird with a hawk's beak and a white ring round its neck, which is called in the colony, the 'Cape Crow.' Whales are not uncommon on these coasts, and indeed it is one of the occupations of the inhabitants to capture them. We passed through a whaling village. Huge ribs with one end stuck into the ground as mark stones and mark fences, and by way of decoration in the garden, were everywhere. The gigantic bones thus brought into juxtaposition with man and his habitations, recal vividly to the mind the immense size of the larger cetaceæ. Such is the thought suggested by day. By the pale moonlight a visitor might be puzzled by more than one fantastic apparition. We stopped half way to breakfast on country fare by way of reaction from the regimen on board ship. Milk, eggs, bread and butter composed the repast, of which we partook with overflowing spirits. We soon afterwards left the beach and its marshy brooks for a well cultivated plain. The road, at the sides of which run Australian poplars, and old oaks planted in the Dutch times, led us through a number of charming villages. Indeed, from the inn where we put up to

Cape Town, the whole road is one long street dotted
with pretty cottages, with verandahs, white-washed
walls, and green outside shutters. There is an air
of elegance about the smallest cot. It is English
tidiness engrafted on Dutch cleanliness. Few houses
are roofed with slates, but the thatch is admirable.
Nowhere do we see the work left in the rough style
of our villages. The thatch is not only laid down in
a business-like way, but it is carefully attended to
afterwards. Not a straw is to be seen out of its
place, not one spot or cushion of moss catches the
eye on the roof. A bright sward overshadowed by
lofty trees surrounds each house. Among them are
planted all the fruit trees of Europe, excepting
cherries, which do not succeed in the climate of
Southern Africa. We met on our way the large-
tailed sheep of the colony, high spirited little English
horses, and herds of Dutch cows with black and
white skins. We passed through Mobury, Wynberg
the paradise of the colony, and at last arrived in the
capital. Cape Town is now a town of thirty thousand
inhabitants, built at the foot of the Table Mountain
with Table Bay for its roadstead. All the streets
run at right angles or parallel to the sea. The
museum is the chief sight. There, are exhibited all
the animals of Southern Africa, lions, tigers, leopards,
hyenas, and venomous serpents innumerable. These

animals once abounded near Cape Town, but they have been pushed farther and farther into the wilderness by advancing civilization, until it is now necessary to advance far into the interior before reaching the territories where they still roam at large. Among the curiosities we observed a portion of a stone cross brought from Portugal by Bartholomew Diaz, and put up on the land which he discovered, and named with such propriety the Cape of Storms. A pair of big boots form part of the collection. They are described on a ticket underneath, as '*the boots of a French postilion.*' We felt puzzled to know what entitled these boots to their position in a South African museum, whether they really had some interest for the inhabitants of these parts, or whether the whole thing was a joke at somebody's expense. From the museum we took a stroll to the quay. Fourteen vessels had been driven on shore there by the great blast of the 6th of July, which had overtaken us while at sea. Seven wrecks still lay high and dry near the houses. They were all English trading vessels. We went next to the Dutch Botanic Garden, where twice a week all the fashionable society of the town assemble to hear the regimental band. One of the aides-de-camps of the governor, Major Bates, took us to see some Caffre prisoners confined in the fort. They had killed cattle be-

longing to the colonists, and committed other outrages on the frontier, on account of which they had
been deprived for a year or two of their freedom to
range the wilderness. Among them there was a near
relation of one of the chiefs. These Caffres whom
we saw were superb blacks, with athletic forms;
they had all beautiful white teeth, a feature, which,
unimportant as it was, strikes one on seeing them,
from the contrast with their dark skins. Their prison
fare was that of sailors on board ship, but they were
not at all contented with it, and declared that they
could not make a meal on less than a leg of mutton
a piece. Last year a prophet made his appearance
among the Caffres, and wandered all over Caffraria
preaching that if the inhabitants would only cease to
cultivate their fields, and kill their cattle, their dead
forefathers would come back again, and they themselves would grow stronger and be able to chase the
white men into the sea. Of course fools were found
among them to believe this rubbish, who did not
sow their corn, who slaughtered their oxen, and who
now, as might have been expected, are starving of
hunger.

It is a singular fact, that there are few English
missionaries among the Caffres, although there are
among them several French Protestant clergymen,
sent out by the Reformed Church of Paris. Two of

them, M. Arbousset and M. Pélissier, who claims kin with the Duke of Malakoff, called upon the ambassador. They have been settled for five and twenty years in the country, and reside among those very tribes which some years ago were engaged in deadly struggle with General Cathcart. One of the Caffre chiefs can bring into the field as many as six thousand warriors. Besides their long spears, which they throw with a sure hand and good eye, they make use of gunpowder, which they obtain, no one can tell how. At present all is quiet among them. But, just as with us in Algeria, war is at all times ready to break forth, and the mother country is compelled to keep up an army of ten thousand men to protect the colony from invasion. Among these is included the German legion which after the Crimean war was sent to the Cape. These Germans are barracked at a distance of five hundred miles in the interior. The government has set apart land for them. They are still bound to three years of military service, after which they are to be considered as colonists.

The Protestant clergymen to whom we referred, are not however the only Frenchmen settled in the colony. At a few miles from Cape Town there are several villages, such as Fransche-Hoeck and la Paarl, which were formerly exclusively inhabited by Frenchmen who emigrated at the Revocation of the Edict of Nantes. These men of French blood have however been completely metamorphosed into Dutchmen. In a few generations they forgot their native tongue and lost all recollection of their native habits. French family names however still abound. We meet with Hugos, Rousseaus, Malherbes and De Villiers. There is one old gentleman who bears the name of Du Plessis-Mornay, whom it is said the great Napoleon wished to bring back to France, but who refused the imperial offer, preferring a farm and the quiet life of a husbandman to the country of his forefathers, and the position which would have been open in France to the descendant of one of the heroes of the Henriade.

It was these French emigrants who introduced into the country the cultivation of the vine. Almost all the young plants are still brought from France. Cape wine is excellent, and like that produced on the Canaries it takes in commerce the name of Madeira. The only wine produced at the Cape which derives its name from the place where it is made is Constantia, which enjoys a well merited reputation all over the globe. One fine morning we made arrangements to pay the customary visit to Groot Constantia. Mr. Cloëte and his family gave us a hearty welcome. They invited us to lunch. By way of expressing our sense of the hospitality shown us, Besplas, who had his photographic apparatus with him, took a sun picture of the Villa with the Cloëte family in the foreground. The work done, he presented the photographs to old Mr. Cloëte. This gentleman was very attentive to former French visitors and more especially to the suite of M. de Lagrené. After passing an hour in the drawing-room in pleasant conversation with Mrs. and the Misses Cloëte, we descended into the cellars. We tasted four kinds of wine—Frontignac, Pontac, white Constantia and red Constantia. From the cellars we went to the vineyard. The whole extent of the ground which produces Constantia is only thirty acres. Mr. Cloëte is not at all satisfied with the black labourers whom he employs. He thinks of bringing vine dressers from France. Although the house has externally a very unostentatious appearance it is surrounded by long lines of noble oaks. Behind rises the mountain or hill of Constantia, which the ambassador, who is an enthusiastic admirer of natural scenery, considered to be almost as picturesque as the Table Mountain. From the terrace we could see the ocean and the roadstead of Simon's Bay.

Mr. Cloëte is not the only producer of Constantia, Mr. Van Reynet and Mr. Collins share his good luck in owning part of the soil which produces the right grape. But Mr. Cloëte, who is obliging, and partial to the French, gets the custom of everybody connected with our navy and diplomatic service. Each of us on this occasion laid in a little store from his cellars, which we took on board with us.

From Constantia one can ride on horseback to the very summit of the Table Mountain.   Contades and Maubourg, who did not know the fact, set out one day on foot early in the morning from Cape Town, with a Malay guide, hoping to kill a few monkeys before getting to the top. They had walked about two hours when they were caught in a dense fog and obliged to retrace their steps, for the summit became hid in clouds,—or, to use the phrase of the country, 'the tablecloth was laid.' From sea this mountain has a picturesque appearance. It astonishes the beholder by its immense bulk and massiveness. The town, situated upon its lower slopes, seems to rise in terraces, and has consequently a fine effect from the sea. Trévise, who sketches better than any of us, went off one day into the bay to make a drawing of it.

We find ourselves very comfortably put up at the Masonic hotel, which is the best place of the kind in the town ; and we cannot complain, considering where we are, of being exorbitantly overcharged. Everything is dear at Cape Town. The ambassador was

D

asked a pound for the hire of the conveyance which brought him from Simon's Bay to the capital. One of us paid half-a-crown for getting his hat ironed. It takes a fortune to live at Cape Town, even in the style of a private citizen, so dear are all the articles of primary necessity. An ordinary hen's egg costs twopence-halfpenny, and everything else is charged for on the same scale. Here production does not meet the consumption. There is a ready market, but there is a want of labour to supply it. The Cape supplies with food Saint Helena, Ascension, the Mauritius, and the English Station in Western Africa. It is necessarily the victualling place of all ships going to and coming from India. Hence the efforts made by the colony to attract the current of European civilization by funds voted and set apart by the legislature to assist emigrants. At this moment the tide has set towards California, the United States, and Australia; towards the latter more especially, Table Bay being now deserted for Melbourne and Sidney. Yet the climate of the Cape is delightful; endemic diseases, such as cholera and yellow fever, are unknown. The forest trees and the fruits of Europe flourish luxuriantly, as well as the productions of the tropics. The atmosphere is so transparent, that Herschel fixed upon it as the most suitable region in the southern hemisphere for his astronomical observations. It is now the depth of winter, yet so genial is the weather that were the trees not bare and leafless, we might fancy ourselves in the heart of a European summer.

Some persons predict that the colony of the Cape will one day throw off its connexion with England. In my opinion that day is far distant. The colony is now no doubt in a great measure independent. The inhabitants elect their own parliament. They have their lower and upper chambers, and all the machinery of a separate government. The local legislature authorise or prohibit the construction of railways. They do many other independent acts. But the colony is deficient in population and capital, and cannot subsist without direct assistance from Great Britain. If the English regiments were withdrawn, it would fall a prey to the black population of the interior. The direct loss to England by a declaration of independence would be small, as, notwithstanding an extensive trade in wool, the colony costs the mother country more than it brings. But what England wished to secure in annexing the Cape to her colonial empire, and what she will spare no effort to preserve, are the roadsteads at Table Bay and Simon's Bay, maritime stations of the very highest value, which during a time of peace protect her trade, and during a time of war establish for her an over-powering preponderance in this part of the world.

How can the French cope with England while they have no possession in these seas save the little island of Bourbon, which has neither harbour, anchorage ground, or sheltered shore to serve as a refuge for vessels?

The Masonic hotel, at which, as we said, we had put up, overlooks the Parade, a large square enclosure, surrounded by a triple row of fir trees. We amused ourselves in looking down from the windows of our apartment on the crowd passing in the streets below. There could be no scene more picturesque or curious for a stranger to contemplate than the population of Cape Town, as seen in this way. There are Dutchmen, Englishmen, Malays, Negroes, Hottentots, Coolies, and an incredible mixture of all these races. For one white person there are ten blacks or tawny persons in the crowd. Tawny is however the dominant complexion. The Malay women are ugly; they dress frightfully, being fond of gaudy colours, and besmearing their hair till it drips with oil. The most refined civilization is, at the Cape, brought into close contact with barbarism or a society in the earliest stage of infancy. In the afternoon, equipages which might grace Hyde Park are met with in the streets. In the morning lions are sold by auction in the market-place. There are cab stands at the street corners as in a European city,

and there are heavy waggons suggestive of primitive
life, constantly pouring in from the interior, drawn
by fourteen, sixteen, or even eighteen long-horned
oxen. These lumbering machines are always accompanied by two drivers, one of whom holds the reins
while the other carries in his hand a long lash or
whip of bamboo, with which he can urge on the first
horse as readily as the sixteenth. Sometimes these
waggons are drawn by horses or mules, and then the
smallest team consists at least of six of these animals.
No one who wishes to be considered a personage of
importance should be seen driving less than four
horses at Cape Town. The governor offered to give
Baron Gros a drive in his travelling waggon into the
environs after the fashion of the country, that is to
say with a team of eight horses, which he said he would
increase to fourteen if the ambassador wished it—just
to show how travelling is conducted in South Africa.
Flavigny and I, satisfied with a humbler equipage,
one fine day took a charming drive to Constantia in
an open carriage, to which we had yoked four spirited
little English horses. To make amends for the
smallness of our equipage, La Tour Maubourg, Trévise, and Contades returned to Simon's Town quite
in crack style six in hand. The thing, however, at
Cape Town is to have on the coach-box a Malay
coachman in national costume. We observed that

almost all the private carriages were driven by men
belonging to this foreign population. But what gives
its particular and special stamp to the colony are
these lumbering waggons of which I have just
spoken, which are met with in all the roads, and
which, crossing through loose sands and fording
streams, convey far into the interior of the continent
the products of Great Britain.   These oxen, different
in every respect from the English Durhams, are of
Dutch origin, and have horns which in length far exceed those of any European breed.

We made the acquaintance of our Consul at the
Cape, M. de Castelnau, the celebrated South American traveller. He is a remarkable man. Setting
out from Rio Janeiro, this gentleman crossed the
whole South American continent, and in two years
reached Lima. He was accompanied by a few
French seamen and Brazilian soldiers. He returned,
again crossing the Andes, the great table-lands and
wild tracts inhabited by the Indians; and descending the Amazon through the Brazilian forests. In
this great scientific journey he lost two of his companions, one being drowned in crossing a river which
was flooded at the time, while the other was murdered by the Indians, who wished to get possession of
the instruments through which they had seen him
looking at the sun. The son of M. de Castelnau is

ambitious of following in his father's footsteps. He
has just made a seven months' journey from the Cape
to Port Natal, a distance of seven hundred miles,
accompanied by a Hottentot guide, and driving a
small caravan of three horses. He crossed the desert,
chasing the herds of antelopes before him, fording
the rivers and proceeding in this way from one Boer
farm to another. The habits of these Boers, who have
lapsed from a state of civilization to a condition little
better than that of savages, might furnish a novelist
with a few good scenes. They live in the midst of
extensive farms, in houses miles from each other,
alone with their wives and children, servants and
herds. They have large families, the ordinary number of children being from fifteen to eighteen. They
have enormous herds. The Caffres sometimes carry
off their cattle. Then the Boers mount on horseback, load their guns, and start at once in pursuit of
the robbers. They are such excellent marksmen,
and their skill in this respect is so well known to the
natives, that the latter run off the moment they
come in sight, leaving their booty behind them. It
is a remarkable fact that these wild herdsmen, living
far in the wilderness and altogether beyond the pale
of civilization, had all heard of the Crimean war. In
the evenings, when the day's work was done, nothing
pleased them better than to hear about the war from

M. Ludovic de Castelnau.   They know absolutely
nothing of politics.   They hear little of what is going
on in the world.   They read their Bibles and abuse
the English.   Round these two pivots turn all their
thoughts.   Dutch to the core, in all their feelings,
hatred of the English constitutes their nationality.
It was this feeling which led them to emigrate to the
outskirt of the colony and caused the exodus from
Port Natal, a phenomenon full of interest in the
history of humanity.   This event has been recounted
by one of themselves in the style of the historical
books of the Old Testament.

There is another remarkable fact connected with
those Boers ; and that is the recent formation in the
north of the colony of two small independent Dutch
republics.   Till very recently Cape Colony extended
much further to the north.   But the English Government, finding it useless to penetrate so far into the
interior, and preferring a well-marked geographical
boundary to an uncertain line nowhere distinctly
marked in nature, and always exposed to the inva-
sions of barbarous tribes, abandoned a whole region
which had previously been annexed, and fixed the
Orange River as the northern frontier of the colony.
It was within the limits of the territory so deserted
and left without any government, that the two small
communities to which I refer above were formed.

They have their own government, and are entirely self-dependent. The King of the Netherlands has opened a correspondence with them recently, and has expressed the interest he takes in their welfare. The origin of these states is as yet quite recent; and their resources are very uncertain. Lying far in the interior, they have no harbour; and in consequence, the inhabitants are obliged to dispose of their products, and purchase the European articles they require, at Cape Town. If these small states prosper, the fact will be a curious one in the history of African colonization. No one can fail to take a deep interest in this white population of Dutch origin, which, settled on the frontiers between African barbarism and English innovation, strives, by dint of patient toil, to re-construct in the wilderness a shadow of nationality.

The present governor of the Cape is Sir George Grey, who has the reputation of being an able administrator. He was previously in New Zealand; and he still suffers from a wound which he received there from a spear thrown at him by a native, in the course of an expedition into the interior. He invited the whole embassy to an official dinner, to which were asked all the leading people of the colony. The Government House dates from the Dutch times, and has more the look of a gentleman's seat than a public building. The oaks in the garden are magnificent. Gazelles, antelopes, and ostriches roam about within its enclosure, and remind the visitor that he is in Africa.

During our stay in Cape Town, we everywhere met with the kindest reception. We went to a ball, given by the colony, which came off in a large room belonging to the Bank. The doors were hung with French and English flags. 'Crinoline' had not found its way to Cape Town; but to make amends, the 'Galop' was in high favour. Between dances, the gentlemen walked arm-in-arm round the ball-room with their partners. Nearly every day we spent the evening at the house of Madame Mozenthal, the wife of the Austrian Consul, where, besides the family, we met with very pleasant people—among whom there were always a number of pretty young English women. And in this agreeable society we enjoyed ourselves very much.

In the walks we took about the neighbourhood to Constantia and to Green Point, on the road to the interior, we were struck with the variety of the vegetation. There were an infinity of different shrubs. There were proteas, finer than our rhododendrons; silver trees, geraniums (those of European flower-pots), growing wild; aloes, with long bare stems, and beautiful heaths, bright with rose-coloured blossoms.

Excepting two or three species, it is remarkable that all the heaths are indigenous to the Cape. They abound everywhere in this country.

The utmost religious liberty, of course, exists in the colony. There are at Cape Town ten different sects, and ten churches or chapels. Unfortunately the Wesleyan Methodists predominate—whereby a puritanic character is given to the town. They approve of neither theatre nor café; and Sunday is kept as strictly as it possibly can be in any place in the United Kingdom. There are two thousand Catholics and a bishop at Cape Town. The church, which is a modern Gothic building, is a very handsome one, although rather bare in the interior. Irish priests officiate. At Simon's Town, which contains five hundred souls, there are no fewer than four churches—one English Episcopal, another Dutch Calvinist, a third Wesleyan Methodist, and a fourth Roman Catholic. There are only four Roman Catholic families in the place, numbering in all thirty persons; and accordingly the church is very small. It is nicely situated half-way to the beach. It overlooks the roadstead; and from the deck of the 'Audacieuse,' its white-washed walls, as they glitter in the sun, have a very fine effect in the landscape.

While we were spending the time pleasantly at Cape Town, our sailors were profitably employed in casting their nets. They brought on board daily great quantities of fish. Among these was a small animal which distends itself at will, which is common in the bay, and which discharges a mortal poison. The English, in respect of its venom, call it the toadfish; we can see them, constantly swimming close to the vessel. The doctor has had one brought to him for examination. He intends to make it the subject of a scientific dissertation.

CHAPTER III.

We leave Simon's Bay.— The Aiguilhas Bank.—The Indian Ocean.
—The Island of Amsterdam.—We re-enter the Trades.—The
Island of Java.—The Straits of Sunda.—The Straits of Banca.—
Arrival at Singapore.—The English colony of Singapore.—
Diversity of Races, Religions, and Costumes.—Great Freedom of
Trade.—The European, Chinese, and Hindoo towns.—Arrival of
the ' Audacieuse ' in Canton river.—Reception of the Ambassa-
dor by the French squadron and the English authorities in China.
—The Earl of Elgin, Sir Michael Seymour, Admiral Rigault de
Genouilly, M. de Bourboulon, Count Poutiatine, Mr. Reed, and
Sir John Bowring.—The Island of Hong Kong and Castle Peak
Bay.

At Sea, August 13.

IN spite of the heavy swell which had sprung up, and
the inconvenient distance at which we lay from Cape
Town, we had managed to lay in our stores of fuel
and provisions. We had on board 12 oxen and
50 sheep. It was high time to depart, for in place of
a week we had remained more than a fortnight at
Simon's Bay. On Saturday the 8th August we
made preparations for getting under weigh at four
o'clock in the afternoon. Two days before we had

seen the East India Company's transport ship the
'Madras' arrive in the harbour. She had come with
the news of the general spread of the mutiny among
the Sepoy troops and the massacre of the English
officers. She had hurried to the Cape under her
whole steam power to ask immediate assistance. She
had taken only sixteen days to come from Ceylon.
The governor was to despatch two regiments and a
company of artillery-men. He is afraid to go farther,
lest he should expose his own frontier to the Caffres.
Similar transport ships had been sent to Mauritius,
Ceylon, Singapore and Australia. All the troops on
their way to China will now be diverted from their
route to India. It is very fortunate indeed for the
English that these events have occurred at a time
when preparations have been made for a great war in
the East. The assistance required in India is already
on its way to the spot. We left the Cape under the
painful impressions produced by this unexpected
intelligence, which in all probability would exercise
a very untoward influence on our own mission.

What are we to do if the English, preoccupied
with their own concerns, should delay to a future
occasion the settlement of their disputes with the
Middle Empire. Certainly the Chinese question no
longer possesses the same importance. Are we to
be recalled, or is the business of the mission to be

restricted to a treaty with Japan? Such were the reflections which passed through my mind in leaving the Cape of Good Hope, and entering on the long voyage which, with favourable winds, was to bring us in six weeks to Singapore.

At Sea, Ttesday, August 18.

Before setting sail the 'commander hoisted on board all the small craft belonging to the ship, fastened tight the masts and tackle, closed the port-holes, and made all ready for the heavy seas and sudden squalls of these latitudes. We have now cleared, without accident, the redoubtable Aiguilhas bank, and the swell, subsiding opportunely, has permitted us to keep the 15th of August. At sea, the Emperor's holiday of course cannot be celebrated in the way customary among vessels lying at anchor in a roadstead, with banners fluttering from every mast-head, and salvoes of artillery booming from dawn to dusk. In the morning, however, mass was said on the lower deck; and in the evening the commander entertained us to dinner. Double rations were given out to the crew, and the national colours were displayed from the masts. Next day the swell returned. For three days the sea, heaving under a strong breeze, beat violently against the ship, while the wind whistled fiercely through the rigging. The

'Audacieuse' rolled and pitched more unaccount-
ably than ever. It was impossible to write or sleep,
and barely possible to read and eat by holding fast
to the table. Days spent so cannot be said to belong
to one's existence. Under such circumstances a man
does not live, he vegetates. Happily every event in
this life has its good side; and during these three
days we sped onwards, thanks to an ill wind, at the
rate of 74 leagues on an average, and in the right
direction, which carried us far from the entrance to
the channel of Mozambique and the stormy meridian
of Madagascar.

Saturday, August 22.

Yesterday at noon we had left a fourth part of our
route behind us. We are now within a few hundred
miles of the island of Amsterdam. These seas, in
winter, are decidedly uninviting and of difficult navigation. We passed suddenly from a dead calm into
the heart of a gale. The breeze would freshen, the
sea would heave, and then down would come a blast
which swept all before it. All our sails were now
reefed. The jib, foresail, and main-topsail only were
hoisted; each of the latter being taken in by a double
reef. Notwithstanding all this we made ten knots
an hour. At last a rain came in torrents. With it
the wind fell and a calm succeeded. But the calm

did not yet reach our length. The ship, no longer
lying-to under the wind, was at the mercy of the
swell, which continued to roll long after it had ceased
to blow. We were tossed about from wave to wave,
and everything was again turned topsy turvy on
board. We amused ourselves in calculating the
number of times the vessel rolled. We counted 16
oscillations in a minute, or 15,600 oscillations in 20
hours. The process is trying both to ship and
passengers. On the 29th of August, in the evening,
after a day worse than any which had preceded it, we
were alarmed by a noise which startled every one on
board. It seemed as if the frigate had burst in two,
or had struck when at full speed against a rock. The
commander called for lanterns, and looked over the
whole ship. He found nothing wrong. Two huge
waves had broken at once upon the frigate as she lay
over under the swell to her larboard side. Some
days before we had sprung a leak, but it was of little
moment. One of our sailors, who had been suffering
from a chest complaint, died yesterday in the sick-
room. This is the first death on board since we left
France. He had been consoled with the hope of
recruiting when we got into a warmer climate, and
death had just anticipated the change of air. This
morning, after the burial-service had been read by
the chaplain, and his old messmates had taken their

E

last farewell, the corpse, wound in a sheet of sail-cloth, with a cannon-ball at the feet, was lowered into the sea. There is a sadness in the ceremony which all the consolations of religion cannot remove.

'Exitio est avidum mare nautis.'

The hungry sea receives the mariner at last.

Tuesday, September 1.

We passed yesterday within a hundred leagues to the north of the island of Amsterdam. Since we left the Aiguilhas bank, we have been buffeted by the blasts from every point of the compass, north, south, east and west. The word tempest is not used at sea. But for the last three weeks entries such as the following appear in every page of the log-book— Foul weather, high sea, fresh breeze, squalls, very heavy swell, rain in torrents, a heavy gale of wind! and so on; now all these expressions, in nautical parlance, mean what we landsmen, in a somewhat homely and inexperienced way, would call a tempest. We were left in darkness, everything was wet. Both rain water and salt water trickled and ran everywhere. The lower deck, where the crew slept and messed, was converted into a lake. We spent the day drearily, closely fastened to our chairs, and yet condemned to a perpetual see-saw. From time to time a great wave would break over the deck and shake every beam and spar of the vessel. A strong swell setting in from the south impeded our progress. The wind is excessively cold. We are anxious to get into the monsoons, which will waft us from the Indian Ocean to the Straits of Sunda.

Wednesday, September 16,

Yesterday at noon we crossed the tropic of Capricorn in the 127th deg. 27 min. of French longitude. We are more than two hundred and forty leagues from the Straits of Sunda. We are within two hundred leagues of New Holland. The hot weather which we had left behind us at Ascension is returning. The rough weather and its tiresome accompaniments with which we started on our passage has given place to a clear sky and calm seas. We have now been thirty-nine days at sea without seeing the smallest island, without catching so much as a glimpse of the land, and time begins to fall rather heavily on our hands. For five days back a merchant ship has been in sight. She is a quick sailer, and it awakens a little interest in our monotonous life to see if we have gained upon her or been gained upon by her during the night. We have entered the monsoons and all our canvas is spread.

On Monday the 21st day of September, after a passage of fifty-five days, we came in sight of Java, and entered the Straits of Sunda under all our canvas and steam power. At sunset we dropped anchor near the Isle of Gulls, and we scanned with delight the long denied spectacle of mother earth, and the rocky coasts of Java. The shore is covered to the water's edge with a luxuriant network of lianes and gigantic trees. A dense cloud of smoke ascending from the interior of the forest, was all that betokened the presence of man. With a favourable wind blowing, eight ships, all bearing different flags, and some of them war vessels, passed near us. Among these was the 'Assistance,' which had left Simon's Bay a week before us. She had encountered a heavy gale, and had a part of her rigging carried away. We sent the English officers the newspapers we had brought from the Cape, full of heart-rending details of the Indian insurrection. They had not yet heard the bad news. The soldiers in their red coats clustered on the gunwales and crowded the deck. The band welcomed us with its liveliest tunes, and the gloomy recesses of the primeval woods rang till night came, with the latest European waltzes and polkas. Next day we set out again by dawn, anchoring as before, in the evening, and this process we repeated from day to day. Great precaution was necessary, owing to the size of the vessel, in its passage through narrow channels, in which for miles we had only a few feet of water under the keel. We kept sounding cautiously as we went. The sight of the dismantled hull of the 'Transit,' a large English transport ship, laden with troops for China, which had been shipwrecked a few weeks before on a coral reef close by which we passed, justified the prudence and confirmed us in our good opinion of our worthy commander's seamanship. We never lost sight of land. On one side was the coast of Java, its wild luxuriance subdued by advancing civilization, and replaced by cultivated fields, in which were grown the sugar cane, the coffee shrub, and the pepper plant, while on the other side lay Sumatra in all its untamed beauty of a virgin forest sweeping to the water's edge. We passed Anjer, a small port or calling place on the way to Batavia. We then came to Banca, which is celebrated for its tin mines, afterwards to Lucepara, and the Two Brothers, which are situated midway in the strait, their rocks hid under a dense tangle of tropical vegetation. The sea is smooth and transparent, resembling in its colour and unruffled surface, a vast sheet of oil or some yellow liquid harder to stir than water. We continued for several hours to pass through immense shoals of spawn destined to people the ocean with its finny tribes. As far as the eye could reach, this sea had a bright yellow hue. It was in fact saffron coloured. The Malay proas, with their curiously shaped sails, were to be seen in every creek along the coast.

Several of these vessels hailed the frigate and brought us cocoa-nuts, chickens, bananas, and sweet potatoes. There is something wild and stern in the look of these natives. They have quite the appearance we should expect to meet in a race of hardy and relentless pirates. The heat continued to increase as we approached the equator. From eight o'clock in the morning the thermometer stood at 88° Fahrenheit in the shade; but at daybreak when we opened our port-holes, the breeze was deliciously fresh and cool. Gradually we passed beyond Java, then Sumatra and Banda, the three richest possessions of the Dutch, and re-entered the open sea. Java is after Cuba the finest colony within the tropics. The revenue of this island fills half the budget of the mother country. On the Malay archipelago, the prosperity of the Netherlands depends. Having allowed the Dutch to take possession of the Straits of Sunda, the English took good care to retain in their own hands the key to the Straits of Malacca. To strengthen their position, they have founded Paulo-Penang, and Singapore. We arrived at the last named town on Monday, the 28th of September, at six o'clock in the evening. We had scarcely time to drop anchor, when the frigate was surrounded by sampans or Malay boats, laden with eggs, vegetables, and fruits. There were live birds too on board for sale, and in such numbers, that one might have thought that the whole feathered population of parrots, paroquets, and cockatoos all over the globe had made our ship their rendezvous for the day. The white parrots with a tuft on their heads obtained the preference among us in respect of their plumage, for with regard to their voices, they all chattered alike noisily. We had not much time to look at them. Under some pretext or other, the whole noisy mob of Malays, Hindoos, and Chinese, clambered over the side of the ship and jumped upon deck. One would wash our clothes, another had articles to sell, a third was a ship chandler, and so on. The commander called the master to the rescue, and it was with the greatest difficulty that the latter could clear our decks of the invaders, who were however compelled at last to retreat into their boats. A person named Salomon, our *daubachi*, a good-looking fellow, a mussulman, who wore a turban and a long white muslin dress, and who looked wonderfully demure, serious, self-possessed, and unconcerned, remained on deck alone of all the crowd, as our only recognised purveyor. Letters from home, which had been addressed to Singapore, were brought us, with the first direct intelligence we had received from Europe for four months. We soon afterwards landed, and saw the town. In walking through the streets one cannot fail to be impressed

with the magnificent results of English colonial enterprise.   In this place there are a hundred thousand
persons, consisting of Chinese, Hindoos, and Malays,
all emigrants who have come from neighbouring
countries, in the hope of making their fortunes, and
with the purpose of exchanging Asiatic tyranny for commercial and religious freedom, and who live together
in harmony under the restraint imposed upon them by
a few Sepoy troops, who are as black and as little
akin to their European masters as the rest of the
population.   Six hundred Europeans, chiefly English
officials of the government, merchants, and capitalists,
move about in the motley crowd, apparently quite
unconscious of the fact, that if these immense multitudes were to combine for an instant, the ruling caste
might be exterminated without an effort.   Happily
for the Europeans, all these races mutually detest each
other.   The Chinese despise the Hindoos, and by
their persevering industry destroy all their chances
in the labour market. The Hindoos accordingly have
an instinctive hatred of the Chinese.   The Malays,
again, live with both races without coming in any
way into collision with either.   There are eighty
thousand inhabitants of the Celestial Empire at
Singapore, nearly all of whom have come from the
southern provinces of China.   They could of themselves, if they thought fit, overpower the other races,

massacre the Europeans, and take possession of the island. But, although there has been an occasional outbreak on a small scale, their own interest, which they perfectly understand, has always sufficed to keep them within the bounds of duty. They are overawed by the dread that the English government would take signal vengeance of a temporary success. They fear that it might resort to the expedient employed by Sir James Brooke, the Rajah of Sarawak, in the neighbouring island of Borneo. The reader may recollect that this enterprising Englishman, attacked by the Chinese working at his mines, escaped with his life only by swimming, while his niece was taken prisoner by the insurgents, and subjected to the most detestable outrages. The Rajah then invited the Malays to join in a foray against the Chinese, and this invitation was so well responded to, that six thousand of the insurgents perished in one day.

The residence of the governor is built upon an eminence which overlooks the roadstead. This official only lives there for nine months in the year; during the remaining three months he resides at Penang and Malacca. The European town of Singapore, separated from the Chinese and Hindoo towns by a small river, is composed of elegant mansions and villas. Each house is surrounded by a garden, and no precaution is neglected to catch as much fresh air as possible. A large verandah surrounds the lower story, and a punka kept constantly in motion by a Hindoo servant, keeps up a constant current of air through the large apartments, while overhead bread-fruit trees, bananas, and palms serve further to protect the inmates under their cool shade. The Chinese and Hindoo town is neither so spacious nor so open to the fresh air, and it has the entire monopoly of the noise and tumult of business. Broad macadamised streets, straight as an arrow, enable the police to see from end to end and keep order in the crowd, while they enable, at the same time, the small dealers to expose their wares along the footpaths. With regard to the Malay population, wherever there is a bit of coast midway between sea and land left dry at ebb tide, wherever there is a bank of mud along the beach uncovered at low water with its pools and streamlets of brine, thither the race of the islands rush enthusiastically to build their huts, which are stuck down upon the top of piles driven into the ground. These abodes are generally sheltered by the spreading top of a cocoa-palm. The owner has his highly-prized sampan drawn up under the shelter of his elevated dwelling, while his little family puddle about contented and happy in the surrounding mud.

The utmost religious and commercial liberty prevails at Singapore. Pagodas and mosques are seen in immediate proximity to Christian churches and chapels. Protestants and Catholics, Budhists and Mahometans, meet with the same protection in the celebration of their religious observances. Thanks in a great measure to the zeal of Père Beurel of the French foreign mission, who has lived in Singapore for twenty years, there are three thousand Catholic converts in the town. A fine church has been recently built in lieu of the original chapel, and nuns of the order of St. Maur and brethren of the Doctrine Chrétienne, educate the Chinese and Hindoo youth connected with the congregation, Accompanied by Père Beurel, we visited the church and schools, and were delighted to have France recalled so vividly in all respects, at such a distance from home. Trade is no less free than religion; cannons are to be seen for sale on the quay of Singapore; they are sold by weight like any other article of merchandize, and the Malay pirates daily purchase from English merchants gunpowder and ammunition, to be used in attacking British ships. No one has a right to prevent a trader from selling guns and gunpowder, if he finds a customer for them who will give him a remunerative price. It will be afterwards shown that the pirates of the Canton river purchase their fire-arms

at Hong-Kong, that is to say, are supplied by the
English themselves with the means of fighting
against their own troops.   Frenchmen are naturally,
at first, astonished at this process, considering it, of
course, from their own point of view.   What would
we think of one of our own countrymen who should
sell muskets to the highlanders of Algeria?   But it
seems we Frenchmen are, as yet, mere children in all
that concerns political economy!

There is another spectacle less warlike, but no less
worthy of interest, to attract the attention of the
inquiring traveller at Singapore.   We refer to Chinese
emigration.   Here is a young Chinaman now, who
came to the colony yesterday, blessed with no other
property than a few tchen or coppers.   He has taken
to the sale of slices of sugar-cane in the streets, and
moves about accosting the passers by, and in a per-
suasive voice asking them to buy a bit of cane.   To-
day he has made a hundred coppers, to-morrow he
will make two hundred more, and so on until he has
scraped together a good round sum, and is able to
return to the land of flowers.   It is seldom indeed
that the shrewdness and perseverance of a Chinaman
fail of success.   Perhaps like Whampou the celebrated banker, this same penniless boy may become
a capitalist and a power in the colony.   We visited
this successful financier.   He is from Canton, and

although still a young man has made an enormous
fortune. We found him dressed in the simplest
Chinese costume, busy counting money at a desk.
But for all this he has English clerks in his employment. He drives out in a handsome English carriage,
and gives grand balls to the European residents. His
eldest son has been sent to England for his education, and he purposes to go there himself in a few
years to bring the young man home, passing through
France on his way. The Chinese of the middle
empire are very successful as bankers and small
traders, but at Singapore their success in every
enterprise connected with the cultivation of the soil
is still more remarkable. They are hard working
labourers, and every day, thanks to their exertions,
cultivation is extending farther and farther into the
primeval forest round Singapore, and on the main-
land of Malacca. The beasts of the wilderness seem
to be their chief enemies. Every other day a Chinaman falls a prey to the tigers. These dangerous
animals cannot be destroyed on the island. They cross
when the tide is back from the continent where they
abound. The English at Singapore will have it, that
the tigers make it a rule to kill one Chinaman a-day,
that is to say of course 365 per annum. The brute
has such a predilection for Chinamen, that one European in company with two celestials, is perfectly

safe.   Whether it is that the sight of a naked body
whets its appetite, or that the pungent smell of the
Asiatic skin determines its choice ; certain it is, that
a tiger under such circumstances, without hesitation
and at a bound, will pounce upon his habitual prey,
without casting even one look at the European, who
stands by.   Strange as this statement is, the accident
has happened more than once, and in the colony
there is no doubt whatever about the universality of
the rule.

Without tempting fortune, by joining a tiger hunt
into the interior of the island, one may enjoy many
delightful walks in the neighbourhood of the town.
Everywhere there are fine macadamised roads
bordered with cocoa-nut palms, leading past a
delightful country, covered with pepper and gambier
plantations, cloves, nutmegs, and coffee shrubs.   The
road which led to the bungalow of the French Consul, M. Lagorce, was beautifully verdant and well
shaded, but that running along the sea-coast leading to New Harbourg, the recently founded establishment of the Peninsular and Oriental Steam Navigation Company, is still more picturesque.   Here in
the midst of a garden, laid out in the English style,
among beds of flowers and clumps of bananas, rises a
black mountain of coal, so nicely built and so symme-
trically shaped, that it might pass for a work of art.

Captain Marshall, who is the very perfection of a
thorough-bred English seaman, has the whole management of the Company's affairs here. He superin-
tends a whole army of Coolies, who are constantly
employed in preparing the supplies for the numerous
vessels belonging to the Company touching at this
place. At Singapore the visitor is less struck by the
bustle in the streets than by the novelty and variety
of the costumes. All Asia is represented here. The
three races placed in juxta-position, but never blend-
ing, exhibit at once before us the superstitions of
India, the wild habits of the Malay archipelago, and
the old rites of the Chinese worship. Sometimes
another figure enters the scene. This is the Parsee,
the descendant of the ancient Persians. He is a fire-
worshipper, of the creed of Zoroaster, and rejoices
most likely in the name of Artaxerxes. Here we
see the black Hindoo, in his jaunty turban and his
graceful garment of white muslin, bustling past a
heavy Chinaman, with his shaven head, trudging
along in his wide silk gown, with a big umbrella in
one hand, and an equally capacious fan in the other.
Then comes the European, rattling along in his
palanquin, drawn by a high-mettled Javanese pony.
The plaintive cries of the Indian dancing girls ring
through the streets, while the air smells of the
joss sticks which the Chinese burn assiduously

before the images of their ancestors, or the idol of the god Fo.

Having taken up our quarters on shore, we had been enjoying this change of scene for some days, when the ambassador, anxious to join his English colleague who had come out over land, gave us notice to return on board the frigate. The north-east monsoon had not yet set in, and it was desirable to catch the last breezes of the south-western winds in order to reach the coast of China. We left Singapore on the 3rd October, and fired a salute in passing at Pedra-Branca, and Paulo-Condore. We had some fear of encountering a typhoon, but we escaped this misfortune, and we arrived without accident in sight of the Chinese coast on the 13th October. We passed a whole fleet of junks drawn up in a row, and each pulling a broad net after it. The whole horizon, indeed, was covered by these vessels, we could count them in hundreds. Nothing on the coast of France can give the smallest idea of the sight which met our eyes. We passed through the midst of them, taking great care not to run them down. We sometimes saw a whole family stowed into one of these tiny vessels. It was their whole property; their work-shop by day, their sleeping-place by night. As there is a great population living on board these junks, the fisheries are one great nursery of hardy and excellent seamen. We dropped anchor at sunset at the mouth of the Canton river, near the island of Lema. Next day we ascended the river, which in this place is about fifty miles broad, and we sailed through the groups of islands which are situated at its mouth. We soon reached Castle Peak Bay ; and thus, after a voyage of four months and a half, the 'Audacieuse' at last dropped anchor in Chinese waters, in the midst of the French squadron.

Hong Kong, October 27.

'The frigate "Audacieuse," which conveys the special embassy from France to China, entered the Canton river on the 14th of this month. She cast anchor in Castle Peak Bay, a small harbour situated between Macao and Hong Kong, in the midst of Admiral Rigault de Genouilly's squadron. The arrival of the ambassador extraordinary of the Emperor was proclaimed by a salute of nineteen guns from the "Nemesis," the admiral's frigate. The sailors belonging to the other ships, in full dress, manning the yards, received him with five good cheers for the Emperor. Next day all the commanders, meeting on board the "Nemesis," were presented to the ambassador.

' Baron Gros, accompanied by the admiral, set out the same day to Macao to visit the French minister,

F

M. de Bourboulon. This visit has no official character. Nevertheless, the governor gave orders that a salute should be fired on the arrival of the special envoy of France within Portugese territory. In the evening M. de Bourboulon entertained to dinner the embassy, the commander of the "Audacieuse," and the members of the French legation.

'Next day, the 17th October, Baron Gros proceeded to Hong Kong, where he received a warm welcome from the English authorities. The "Audacieuse" had no sooner cast anchor than the ambassador received a salute of twenty-nine rounds from Admiral Seymour, as well as from an English frigate, an American and a Dutch sloop of war. Baron Gros repaired on board the "Ava," distinguished by the English ambassador's colours, and he remained for several hours in conference with his honourable colleague. During the day Lord Elgin and Admiral Sir Michael Seymour came on board to visit the ambassador, as well as all the commanders of vessels in the roads, and the foreign consuls residing at Hong Kong.

'When Baron Gros went on shore to visit the governor, he found Sir John Bowring already awaiting him in his carriage at the landing-place.

'All the troops of the garrison were under arms, both along the road by which he proceeded, and in the

courtyard of Government House. At the same time
a salute of nineteen guns was fired from the fort on
the arrival of the ambassador. Next day Sir John
Bowring and General Ashburnham came on board the
" Audacieuse " to return officially the visit they had
received the night before.

' Before leaving Hong Kong, Baron Gros was
present at a dinner given in his honour by the
governor of the colony. Among the guests was
the special commissioner of Her Britannic Majesty
in China and the whole of the English embassy,
the commander-in-chief of the English troops, the
lieutenant-governor, the French commanders, Mr.
Parkes, English vice-consul at Canton, and the leading men belonging to the city. Sir John Bowring
proposed the health of the Emperor, and Baron Gros
replied to the toast by drinking the health of the
Queen of England.

' After remaining five days in the roads at Hong
Kong, Baron Gros returned to Castle Peak Bay to
rejoin the French squadron.'

Such was the notice of our first movements in
China which appeared in the columns of the
' Moniteur.'

We went occasionally, either alone or in company
with the ambassador, to pass a few days at Hong
Kong, and made a descent into every part of this

admirable English arsenal. The island of Hong
Kong was ceded to Great Britain by the treaty of
Nankin. It was, till 1842, a bare rock inhabited by
a few fishermen ; now it is overspread with the houses
of a great city, and inhabited by a population of
seventy thousand inhabitants. On the very spot
where a few miserable junks used timidly to anchor,
in terror lest they should be set upon by pirates,
now there is a forest of ships of war and merchantmen belonging to every nation under the sun. Where
a few half-starved fishermen were glad to scrape
together a few coppers in the course of the year, the
incessant rattling of money-bags may now be heard.
In fifteen years the English, by dint of their wonderful faculty for colonization, have converted a place
before then quite unknown into the best frequented
port in these seas. Docks, hospitals, stores for the
army and navy have been erected, a fine Gothic
church has been built, and all the rich European
merchants in China have made it a point of honour
to fix their abode here, and build a palace on this
English island. Now there is a wide street, macadamised, planted with trees, and bordered by foot-
paths, which runs along the harbour for a distance of
three miles, with two uninterrupted lines of European
and Chinese houses ; a great amount of capital
is employed in new buildings, which are rapidly

going forward. All that part of the town which adjoins the quay is occupied by stores and warehouses, and visitors are obliged to ascend to the high ground to reach their quarters. Government House is situated above the town. From the promenade which surrounds it you look down on the roads, where at all times something is going forward; a steamer or two plying, a merchant ship casting anchor, or a man-of-war firing a salute, or something else to attract the notice of saunterers. A dinner, to which Sir John Bowring entertained us on the day after our arrival, was possessed of interest in many ways.

We left the ship at seven o'clock, and found eight palanquins waiting for us at the landing-place. Baron Gros, borne by five Chinamen, went first. Then came Commander Aboville and the other members of the mission. The Coolies of the French consul, holding Chinese lanterns, lighted up the way over the hill. Contades, who by bad luck had fallen into the hands of short-winded porters, was obliged to urge them to get on as he best could. Sir John received us with the utmost courtesy; introduced us to his family, to the colonial authorities, and to the leading English merchants. It is a custom at Hong Kong for any one who is invited out to take his 'boy' with him. Those who, like us, are not provided with this article in the shape of a young Chinese, with a fresh-shaven head, an elegantly-plaited tail, and a long white dress, run the risk of starving at a table groaning with good things. On this occasion we were not compelled by this dire necessity into a breach of good manners, as our neighbours were kind enough to accommodate us with their boys—a little amused doubtless at our embarrassment and inexperience in Anglo-Chinese etiquette. We stayed till twelve o'clock at night. On leaving we had some difficulty in finding our chairs and Coolies in the midst of sixty palanquins mixed at random, and 150 Chinamen calling at the top of their voices for the guest they were to convey home. While on our way back we talked over what seemed most remarkable in what we had witnessed, to wit, that the English live in the midst of Hindoo and Chinese servants, and employ no others, although they are at war with their countrymen. We had seen Sir John Bowring, with a price set on his head by the Chinese government, quite unconcerned and at his ease, although in the midst of Chinamen. Lord Elgin, too, with whom it lies to decide on the steps to be taken against the Chinese, had returned on board in the evening without an escort in a palanquin carried by four Coolies. Such things are certainly only to be seen in the far East, and they are of a kind to surprise persons newly arrived from France.

Lord Elgin did not come on shore. He has his quarters on board a charming steamer furnished him by the East India Company. On hearing of the insurrection he sent the Governor-General of India his frigate, the 'Shannon,' with its gunners and cannon, and the Company gave him in exchange the packet 'Ava,' which it hires out at 200*l.* a-day at Calcutta. This was certainly a good revenue from such a source, and, not to abuse the generosity of the Company, his Excellency means to remove immediately with his suite into the 'Furious,' a steam frigate which has recently arrived, and which is now undergoing preparations for his reception.

We now made the acquaintance of our colleagues of the English embassy, Messrs. Bruce, Cameron, Oliphant, Fitzroy, Locke, and Morrison, and a cordial intimacy soon sprung up between us. We visited together the shops kept by the dealers in curiosities, and the ateliers of the principal native painters. We were present at a sing-song or theatrical representation, given gratuitously to their fellow-citizens by some rich Chinese merchants, who had hired the company of comedians, and erected a great bamboo shed for their accommodation. From a reserved seat which was somewhat elevated we could see the

great mass of heads swaying to and fro. People
were coming and leaving constantly; for the play
commences at eight o'clock in the morning and
continues without interruption till six o'clock in the
evening, the stage never being altogether deserted by
the players during the whole of this period. Gods,
and heroes, and mythological personages of divers
sorts make their appearance in the pieces performed,
and do battle with each other after a fashion altogether preternatural. For pantomime the Chinese
actors are unequalled, and nothing can surpass the
richness of their costumes, which literally glitter in
silk and gold. Women never make their appearance
on the stage in the Middle Empire; they are prevented from doing so by religious precepts, and
consequently the female parts are taken by young
men. The tone of voice of the actors is so sharp
and grating, and the music is so deafening, that the
patience of a European spectator who understands
nothing of what he sees never outlasts half-an-hour,
when he is heartily glad to make his bow and retire.
There are four thousand Catholics at Hong Kong.
They have a fine church, in which the officiating
clergymen are Italians. Near the town is situated the
procure, or chief station of the Catholic missions in
China. We went there more than once, with both
pleasure and profit, to see Père Libois, the Procureur-

Général, who has lived in China for twenty-two years, and who for some years back has left Macao to take up his abode at Hong Kong; Père Rousseille, who came out more recently; Père Mermet, who is to go with us to Japan; Père Deluc, and many others, who have all been tried by long years of privation and suffering, and yet with unabated zeal are ready to throw themselves into undertakings from which good is likely to result. Their memories are stored with a thousand curious facts regarding China and the Chinese, and their conversation accordingly is not only most pleasant and agreeable, but gives us an insight into the singular habits and character of the natives of the Middle Empire.

We were present at the procure when three Chinese couriers took their departure for the northern provinces, and one to the frontier of Thibet. They will be three months on the journey; in the course of which, however, they seldom require to leave the rivers and canals. Not long after leaving Canton, there is an enormous mountain-chain to be crossed. All goods conveyed over it are carried on men's backs—there being a well-arranged system of halting houses for the accommodation both of porters and travellers. Some idea of the immense traffic lying along this route may be formed, when we consider that all the chief manufactures of Canton, destined for exportation to other parts of the empire, pass along it. Beyond the mountains lie the great rivers of China, flowing through wide and populous plains.

With the money which is to be taken to the missions, the couriers purchase cloth and other articles of merchandise likely to sell in the interior, in which they pack up carefully the European and devotional objects which they are to convey to the Christian settlements. After arriving at their destination they sell the goods they have bought at Canton, hand the money to the priests at the mission, and retain any balance left to themselves as their own legitimate profit. It is in this way that Père Libois sends once a-year money received from France to the missionary stations. The poor priests, shut up in the heart of Asia, have only once a-year tidings sent them of what is going on in Europe and the civilized world. What a frightful life of isolation it must be! With what anxiety they must long for the day when the merchant is to come with his bales. It must be recorded, to the credit of the Chinese, that there is scarcely any example of a courier disappearing with the money. Yet the sums sent in this way are not small; they amount occasionally to a thousand pounds and upwards at a time.

With Père Rousseille we one day took a Chinese boat, and went up the bay to visit the missionary college. We landed at the Jardine pier—Jardine being the name of a leading Hong Kong merchant. The same gentleman has built a charming villa on a height ; and beneath it the warehouses and counting-houses of the firm. They form a magnificent building of freestone, which might well be taken for some important public edifice. Mr. Jardine has a private guard for his protection, composed of Sepoys of his own, whom he is allowed to hire of the government, on paying for their services. He has cannons and a flag too—the flag of the great mercantile house of Jardine, Matheson, & Co. We saw one, gorgeously yet tastefully blazoned ; and were a good deal surprised to observe that it bore the sun and fleurs-de-lis of Louis XIV. What chance has thrown the device of the Grand Monarque in the way of this grand financier ? Mr. Jardine deals in everything ; and turns over millions of pounds annually. He has a dockyard of his own, where he repairs the fleet of vessels employed by him to barter opium for tea and silk in all parts of China. The fortune of this great firm, like that of all the other great mercantile houses at Hong Kong, has been made in the opium trade.

Clambering up the hill, we proceeded to the missionary college, which lies in a sequestered upland. The poverty of the priests protects them from the pirates who infest the coast. However, eight of these desperadoes once made their appearance at the college; but finding nothing to take, they went away, not, however, without threatening to stab one of the missionaries. The reverend fathers are now armed with pistols and guns, and protected by large dogs, which keep constant watch. We received an affectionate welcome from them. We met here with our old friends Père Leturdu and Père Fontaine, who had come on board the frigate. We drank tea with them. The biscuits we ate had been brought from Canton. After tea we went into the school-room, where we found a number of young Chinamen, in long blue gowns, busy learning Latin as well as their own language. These lads do not belong to Hong Kong, but are brought from all parts of the diocese of Canton, which includes the provinces of Kwangtong, of Kwang-si, and the island of Hainan. They will, after their education is completed, return to the missions as native priests and catechists. Monseigneur Guillemin, the Bishop of Canton, is now in Europe, about some matters connected with his diocese. We caused the pupils to write our names in Chinese; and went for a little into the class-room of the native master, in which all the pupils repeat their lesson at once. The noise is discordant, but the system is practised in conformity with the 'rites' or general directions of the ecclesiastical authority. On leaving

we came down the hill, making a circuit to see the
Happy Valley, where the English have staked off
a drive and race-course through a superb meadow.
The turf is rolled down regularly, as in the English
parks. The name of Happy Valley, given to this
place, comes from the cemeteries which surround it.
There are three of them. One belongs to the Church
of England; another is Roman Catholic; and a third
Parsee, or Zoroastrian. In the latter the bodies are
burned. On the opposite side, scattered over the
slope of the hill, in the midst of fir-trees and rocks,
there are a number of Chinese tombs, marked by an
upright block of granite, mentioning the name of the
deceased, and the year and day of his death. All
round is a circular bench, put up by the relations of
the departed, on which the spirit may rest when so
disposed. All along the road we found strewed bits
of silvered paper. These are intended to keep the
devil employed, and prevent him from devouring the
soul of the deceased, when a body is about to be
deposited in its last resting-place. The devil is deceived by these glittering slips of paper; he mistakes
them for coins, and keeps stooping to pick them up.
In this way the evil spirit has his attention diverted
until the body is fairly placed in the tomb. It
appears that the Chinese, not content with their success in hoodwinking the barbarians, venture on the

same game with the powers below; and really and truly I believe, that their cunning, their roguery, and their subtlety are such that they may not in all cases come off worst!

On our way home by water we stopped half-way to visit the sisters of St. Paul de Chartres, sent out to Hong Kong to do the good work of the Sainte Enfance. These poor nuns give themselves up to their duties with rare devotion and self-sacrifice; they have almost succeeded in putting an end to infanticide in the colony. Daily, infants are brought to them, whom they receive, and, in this way, preserve from certain and immediate death. Unhappily it is not possible to save them all; they are brought to them often in such a state from starvation and exposure that a large proportion die in spite of all the care taken of them. We were shown into the workshop, where we saw a number of little Chinese girls, who were decently clad, and who spoke to us in French, busily engaged in making flannel jackets for the sailors of the squadron.

Sir John Bowring is the third Governor of Hong Kong. Under him the colony has made an immense stride in advance; new streets have been opened, districts entirely new have been built, and the population of the island has more than doubled in numbers; there are now at Hong Kong six thousand

Europeans and sixty thousand Chinese. Unfortunately, Sir John places quantity above quality, and the English colony has, under this system, become a rendezvous for all the pirates of the Canton river; fearlessly they enter the port to provision their ships, and the Governor confessed to us that in the course of the year there had been sold to these pirates and owners of junks in the river no less than four thousand small cannons and swivels. The white and coloured police at Hong Kong night and day perambulate the streets with muskets over their shoulders; yet they have great difficulty in preventing thefts. An adventure, which last year befel the commander of the ' Catinat,' is characteristic; he had no faith in the honesty of the Hong Kong people, and never went on shore without putting a pair of pistols in his pocket. One day, when he had been to town and was returning in broad day at two o'clock in the afternoon, within a few paces of his small boat, four stout fellows sprung upon him and caught him by the arms from behind; then a mite of a Chinese boy came coolly up, took his purse quietly out of his waistcoat-pocket, and relieved him of his watch and watch-chain. This done, he was pitched violently to the ground, which completed the operation. The Chinese standing about stared, grinned, and smiled, not a soul of them came to the rescue, and the robbers disappeared in the crowd. What can the authorities do in the midst of a population such as this, which exhibits no sympathy with the cause of order and good government?

Midway between Europeans and Chinese we must place the Parsees, or fire-worshippers; who are numerous both at Hong Kong and Macao. They come from India, most of them from Bombay, and are rich opium-dealers. They are a distinct race, the descendants of an old Persian population who immigrated into Hindostan. In all respects they are superior to the Chinese and Hindoos; they are very fine-looking, and wear a long white flowing Eastern dress, with a black cap of a singular shape, which bears some resemblance to that of the modern Persians. They form the most pleasing feature in the crowds which throng the walks about Hong Kong and Macao; their liberality, and their good faith and honesty in business transactions, are highly spoken of.

Besides numerous frigates and gunboats carrying the English flag, there are at present in the roads at Hong Kong three English vessels of the line, the 'Calcutta,' the 'Belle-Isle,' and 'Sanspareil.' Their triple row of bristling cannon infused an element into the landscape not without its moral influence upon the spectators, but these huge floating towers are very ill adapted to the navigation of these seas,

Light ships, which can float in shallow waters, are
at all times more useful. The 'Primauguet' and
the 'Phlégéton,' two steam-sloops forming part of
our squadron, appear to our officers to be, in all
respects, just what is required. At Macao the
'Audacieuse' is obliged to ride at anchor five miles
from the shore, while the gunboats can come within
a mile of the water's edge; the immense superiority
of the latter is apparent where military operations
must constantly be performed in the shallow waters
of rivers. Among the ships which crowd in the road
of Hong Kong, we observe vessels of war which belong to the king of Siam. They are entirely of
European build, and hoist colours with a white
elephant as a device.

Baron Gros, after much serious deliberation, and
long and anxious conferences with the French and
English authorities in China, resolved on going to
war. The north-east monsoon and the ice on the
northern coasts prevented, in the mean time, the war
from being carried on in the Gulf of Pecheli, but the
winter months could be employed in an attack on
Canton, and in revenging the special grievances of
the French government upon the haughty and stubborn Commissioner Yeh, the governor of the two
Kwangs. In the spring the belligerents would proceed to the north, to compel the Chinese govern-

G

ment into some redress for those injuries inflicted upon the French, for which the government of Pekin was responsible. If the capture of Canton had the effect of bringing the Manchoo dynasty into a less hostile attitude towards Europeans, then the ambassadors might consent to enter into negociations; if not, more immediate pressure would be directed against the Court of Pekin, by ascending the waters of the Pei-ho towards the Chinese capital; where our vessels might float the banners of the allies, and by the pageantry of European warfare spread terror in the very heart of the enemy's country. This plan of the French ambassador was also that of his colleague the High Commissioner of England. The preparations for war were accordingly continued with renewed activity at Hong Kong and Castle Peak Bay; the two admirals endeavouring to make up for the smallness of the force at their disposal by using every means in their power to inspire with pluck and determination those under their command.

Hong Kong, November 14.

Five hundred of the Royal Marines who had come out from Portsmouth by the 'Imperador' arrived at Hong Kong in the commencement of this month. The 'Imperatrice' arrived a few days afterwards, with another five hundred men belonging to the

same body of troops. Another ship is expected
shortly with one thousand men. All these are
ordered, as they arrive, to proceed up the Canton
river, and to take up their quarters in the forts which
have been captured from the Chinese.

There is a talk of the departure of Admiral
Seymour for Whampoa. Forty-five English war
vessels are already employed in the blockade of the
river; and besides the ' Calcutta,' an 80-gun ship, on
board which he is himself, the admiral proposes to
take with him the remainder of the gunboats which
are lying at anchor in the roads at Hong Kong.
Two hundred English soldiers, a few companies of
Sepoys, and one war sloop, will then alone remain
at this place to protect the town, and overawe the
Chinese population.

This rapid concentration of the English forces in
the river, and the preparations making at Castle
Peak Bay, began to spread great alarm among the
inhabitants of Canton. It is said that they have
already begun to pad and put bags against their
principal buildings, to make them proof against shot;
several villages have been deserted by their inhabitants, and six hundred women and children
have sought refuge at Macao.

General Ashburnham, having no command corresponding to his rank in the service, in consequence of

the departure for India of the troops which were to
have been sent to China, was recalled to Calcutta.
He will leave with his staff by the next mail. General
Straubenzee, the officer next in rank, will take the
command of the land forces. During his stay at
Castle Peak Bay, Baron Gros received a visit from
Vice-Admiral Count Poutiatine, the aide-de-camp in
chief of the Russian emperor, and the special envoy
and minister plenipotentiary of Russia to China. He
had come from the river Amour in a small steam-
boat named the 'America.' While we had come
out by sea round the Cape and across the Indian
Ocean, the Count, who had been in Paris shortly
before our departure, joined us again in China, after
having made a journey overland through the whole
width of Northern Asia. We learned that the
interest of the journey bears no adequate proportion
to the fatigue it entails. The vast plain of Siberia
soon palls upon the traveller, with its boundless, un-
diversified snow-fields. The posting-houses on the
way are admirably managed *qua* posting-houses;
but the fare is miserable. There is literally nothing
to be had but tea and salt fish. By night and day
the traveller, driven on in his roomy carriage, lies
stretched at full length as in bed; for sitting upright
and looking out he could not undergo the fatigue of
the journey. After remaining more than a month

in Kiachta, partly to recruit, partly to see the town, which is the great mart between China and Russia, and partly to await the melting of the snow, the admiral descended the Amour in a small boat through the midst of the great forests bounding its course, and in this way reached the town of Nicolaief in the Gulf of Tartary. It was this same Count Poutiatine who throughout the whole Crimean war, moving from place to place and never seen, managed so cleverly to baffle all the skill of the Anglo-French squadrons in the Pacific.

His name is indissolubly connected with the Russian colonization in the basin of the Amour, that magnificent route for an extended commercial inter-course between Siberia, Mongolia, Manchuria, Japan, and China. The Amour takes its rise at a spot situated about one hundred miles from Kiachta. In summer it is an immense navigable river; in winter a long sheet of smooth ice, forming an admirable highway for sledges drawn by dogs. Wood, iron, and coal abound in this scarcely-explored territory. The appearance of the Russians as colonists in this region sufficed to alarm the colonial press of Hong Kong.

Attached to the mission of Count Poutiatine were two persons who belonged to the famous Russian College at Pekin, and who had lived there ten years to learn the language. One is the papa or

priest; the other the medical officer of the mission.
They liked their life at Pekin very well.   Dressed
as Chinese, they were allowed to extend their ex-
cursions as far as the mountains in the neighbourhood
of the capital.   In summer they had a pleasant life
in a large country house, situate close by the Great
Wall.   Every one to his taste.   The study of Chinese
literature may be a pleasant occupation enough, and
interesting it may be to have a close view of the
working of the Chinese government; nevertheless
ten years so spent seems neither more nor less than
a ten years' transportation and banishment from
European society.

Mr. Reed, the special envoy and minister plenipotentiary of the United States in China, arrived in the
roads at Hong Kong in the steam frigate 'Minnesota,'
which is propelled by engines of one thousand horse
power, and carries fifty guns.   It had taken 115 days
to make the voyage from New York to the Canton
river.   On the southern shores of the China Sea she
had encountered a violent typhoon, which obliged
her to put in at Anjer in Java.

Expressions of the most cordial sympathy have
passed between the French embassy and the American
minister.   Baron Gros could not have desired a
colleague who had his interests more sincerely at
heart, or who could have exhibited greater courtesy.

But this was all it amounted to. The government of the Union had instructed their envoy to remain a simple spectator of the struggle; to be present at the operations against the Chinese, but to take no part in them—in the mean time at least; indeed until the Americans could, without expense to themselves, reap a share of the advantages won by Anglo-French shot and shell. This position of the American squadron will explain why there was no good will lost between them and the allied fleets. Whilst the seamen of England and France were risking their lives in the cause of civilization, four American ships of war, manned to their full complement, and bristling with cannon, were riding tranquilly at anchor in the roads at Hong Kong.

We remained at Castle Peak Bay amid constant firing of cannon. The 'Audacieuse' has just been tested. She discharges 150 balls a day, and the admiral, who was present, has expressed his satisfaction with the proficiency of the gunners. The other vessels have since been put through their practice, and the little rock selected as the mark is cut up in all directions by the balls. Every one is busy on board in casting balls and making cartridges. Every day the disembarkation companies go on shore for exercise, and to get used again to the fatigue of long marches and the drill on land. At noon a gunboat puts on her steam to go and fetch them, and tug back the long file of small craft by which they are conveyed to and from the shore. In coming near the anchorage all these small boats let go their hold, and an amusing race takes place between them to get first on board. On high days and holidays there is a reception on board the ' Nemesis,' and the theatrical company of the ship treat the visitors to a performance. The stage, lit up with Chinese lanterns, is ornamented tastefully with reeds and branches. The verses are well conned, and trip readily from the players; they are delivered indeed with fire and spirit, and the spectator is shocked neither by the big hands nor the shaven chins of the female performers. The costumes are brilliant, although one can see at a glance that they are not the productions of a first-class dressmaker. The skirts of the female performers are stretched out to fashionable dimensions upon lef-toff crinolines picked up second-hand at Macao. The whole crew, perched upon the shrouds and rope ladders, look down upon the scene in a high state of glee and excitement, and give the performers all the encouragement of hearty laughter. We have had various plays, among others the ' Double-Bedded Room,' the ' Bear and the Bashaw,' the ' Corporal and his Country Cousin ' (' la Chambre à deux Lits,' 'l'Ours et le Pacha,'

' le Caporal et sa Payse'), and indeed the whole budget
of Levassor of the 'Nemesis.' The 'Audacieuse,' not
to be outdone, has resolved to start an opposition
company of theatricals. Our fair performers cannot
pretend to cope with those of the 'Nemesis' in the
matter of petticoats, but they bid fair to excel them
in emulating the sweet and gentle voice of woman.

We stand in need of a little amusement while
stationed at Castle Peak Bay, for there are few places
more likely to fill the mind with gloomy and melancholy impressions. On every side we see nothing
but bare crags, without one tree to throw a refreshing
shadow over the sun-scorched soil. Indeed, excepting
at the watering place, where there are the huts of a
few fishermen, all the islands about are quite uninhabited. For this reason they are well adapted to
rifle-shooting and gun practice : but no other attrac-
tions have they ; and the admiral, wisely considering
how important it is to keep up the spirits of the men,
and to allow the officers a little solacement before
entering on the serious work of the expedition, has
ordered the squadron to leave Castle Peak Bay for
the road of Macao.

CHAPTER IV.

The Portuguese Colony of Macao.—The Garden of Camoens.—The
Pagoda of the Rocks.—The Parsee Cemetery.—The Decline of
Macao.—The French and English Squadrons re-ascend the Canton river.—Bocca Tigris, or the Bogue.—The Anchorage at
Whampoa.—The last pacific attempt to negociate with Commissioner Yeh.—Delivery of Baron Gros' Ultimatum.—Absolute
refusal of Yeh to come to terms on any of the points.—The Ambassadors delegate their powers to the Admirals.—The commencement of military operations.

HONG KONG represents future and present commercial activity. Macao is a quiet town which belongs
to the past. The time was when the bold seamen of
Portugal were the masters of the China seas. Their
degenerate offspring are now reduced for bare sub-
sistence to seek employment from the great English
and American houses. The palmy state of Portugal
has passed away, and fickle fortune bestows her
favours on another race. The colony never prospers.
It had the good luck to be placed under the administration of Amaral, a man of genius, but he was assassinated by emissaries of the mandarins. Then the

court of Lisbon, with the view of revenging this out-
rage, armed, and at great expense sent out its finest,
it may be its only war frigate; but scarcely had
this vessel anchored in the road, when it was blown
to pieces by an infuriated gunner who had been punished for some fault by the commander, and who, to
wreak his vengeance on the man who had injured
him, did not hesitate to send to destruction three
hundred of his countrymen!

The neighbourhood of Hong Kong deprives Macao
of all the importance it at one time enjoyed as a free
port. Besides, its harbour is gradually being silted
up with mud, like all the right bank of the Canton
river. Large vessels are obliged to anchor three
miles from the shore, and small gunboats alone can
approach the quay of the Praya-Grande. Nevertheless
Macao is not altogether destitute of attraction. It
has the charm of interesting associations. This town
was for a long while the only spot on the coast through
which intercourse was permitted with the Chinese
empire. Saint Francis Xavier, Camoens, and other
distinguished men besides, have died within its pre-
cincts. Its noble churches, convents, and other public
buildings, discoloured by time, are silent witnesses to
a splendour which has long since fled. Macao has
another advantage over Hong Kong—the climate is
better. While the latter, lying under the lee of

Victoria Hill, scarcely benefits by the wholesome breath of the north-east monsoon, Macao, exposed to the sea, receives these fresh winds without obstruction. The consequence is, that the Hong Kong people frequent the Portuguese town for a change of air during the hottest weeks in summer. For the same reason the French government erected an hospital at Macao at the opening of the campaign.

At this moment the preparations for war give unwonted animation to the old Portuguese town. Every day a crowd of small boats come on shore with officers and sailors of the French squadron, glad to escape from the dust of Castle Peak Bay, and to see something else than a bare uninhabited rock. We have been very hospitably received by the French minister and Madame de Bourboulon. We spent an evening very pleasantly at the Legation. It is very amusing to walk out after dark into the streets, which are lit up with Chinese lanterns, and to wander about among the gambling-houses, opium-smoking saloons and sing-songs—this name being given to all those noisy concerts of which the Chinese are fond, and which are often patronised by wealthy native merchants. Macao in ordinary times only contains five thousand Europeans and thirty thousand Chinese. At this moment, in consequence of what is going forward at Canton, and the emigration which has taken place thence, the Chinese population is increased to seventy thousand.

When the sea is smooth the visitor may go by tanka to the pagoda of the Rocks, and come home on foot by the highway. This temple is badly kept; it had not the rich and imposing appearance of the great pagoda of Singapore, but its situation is very picturesque. Beneath it lies the inner harbour, with its fleet of junks and tankas; above it rise bare rocks of granite, and giant forest trees, which strike their roots firmly into fissures of the crags. Half way up are kiosks and chapels dedicated to the minor divinities, for the principal god receives the homage of the faithful at the threshold of the temple. He is, it appears, the patron of mariners, and accordingly there is above the entrance a large junk painted red, with a Chinese inscription on the rock at its side.

The garden of Camoens is now private property. It belongs to M. Marquès, a Portuguese, but it is thrown open to strangers. Here we sauntered about for a long time in the cool shade of its leafy bowers, a pleasure not often to be had in China. We saw the grotto of Camoens and the place to which this great man retired from the world to write the 'Lusiad.' We read several quotations from the poet, which were inlaid upon the marble, and also a few creditable French verses, which we perused with as much pleasure, composed by some one who admired the garden, as well as the man to whom it had belonged. We had a delightful view, from a low terrace, of the interior harbour, seen in the last rays of the setting sun. We heard the cries of the tanka boatwomen, the measured stroke of oars from boats crossing the water, and loud above all the horrible row the Chinese seamen made on board a junk about to set sail. They were invoking, we understood, the god of the pagoda, by the sound of gongs, to protect them from the evil spirits of the vasty deep.

The Parsee cemetery, which rises in terraces above the sea; the small Portuguese forts, built like eagles' nests among the crags; Green Island, and the narrow neck of land which connects Macao with the Celestial Empire, were each visited by us in turn. We spent a good deal of our time in lounging over the balcony of Duddel Hotel, watching what was going forward in the roadstead, and enjoying the delightful freshness of the north wind.

At length, on the 11th December, the whole French squadron left the road of Macao, to ascend the Canton river. We left at daybreak, towing the 'Nemesis' up after us, and about two o'clock we cast anchor at Bocca Tigris, in the very heart of the English squadron. As far up as the Bogue we met with no object of interest. The width of the estuary shows that it belongs to the sea up to this point; but here it becomes rapidly narrowed into a river, and we pass up between the two banks bristling with small Chinese forts. Some years ago these had a threatening appearance, but the English cannon have battered them into little more than heaps of rubbish. The Union Jack now floats over their ruins, and red coats mount guard on their dismantled ramparts. During the whole of this day the English have displayed French colours from their mast-head, while we in reply have hung out British colours.

Next day, taking advantage of high tide, we crossed without accident the first bar on the river. There was one critical moment when we had no more water than was absolutely necessary to float us, although we had wheeled the artillery into the fore part of the ship, and unloaded our coal into lorchas. We have cast anchor at the extremity of Danes Island, and within sight of French Island, where we will await the great tide of the 19th of December, to ascend to Whampoa.

We were surrounded by a crowd of old boats filled with wretched-looking people,—men, women, and children. The poor children, putting their hands to their stomachs and then to their mouths, made a sign to us that they were dying of hunger. By means of a net fastened to the end of a bamboo cane, like a naturalist's apparatus for catching butterflies, these poor creatures gathered the bits of bread, biscuits, and orange-skins which floated along the side of the vessel. They ate greedily what they got in this way. It is impossible to imagine greater wretchedness. Flocks of geese and wild ducks were every now and then flying past the vessel. The English soldiers amused themselves in firing upon them with small shot, and they never failed to bring down some of them; but Admiral Seymour soon put an end to this fun. The country is pleasing. Villages surrounded with trees make their appearance everywhere in the midst of extensive rice-fields. A great number of canals open into the river, and bear junks, only the sails of which are seen, in the midst of the country. Where the water of the canal is not visible, they have a very singular appearance. The English gunboats go and come constantly from Bocca Tigris to Fort Macao in front of Canton, to keep the course of the river clear. Our compradors, or purveyors, pass from one side of the river to the other, purchasing without any great difficulty provisions for us in the villages.

The captain of an English gunboat at anchor near Blenheim Reach resolved for a brag in a foolhardy way to capture the mandarin of a neighbouring village. He set out on the expedition. He did not

After M. de Trevise.

Day & Son Lith⁰ to The Queen.

THE CUSTOM HOUSE AT SHANGHAI.

find the dignitary himself at home, but he found his cap of office, which he carried away in triumph. On their march home, however, the captain and his men found their way intercepted by a strong party of Chinese soldiers; a struggle ensued, and it was with difficulty that they got to the small boat on the river. Five of the crew were killed, and six wounded. The captain himself received two gun-shot wounds, one in each leg. It was a Chinese who had put it into his head to catch the mandarin, telling him that the latter was generally detested by his countrymen. The English concluded that the whole affair had been got up to entrap the party. Two hundred men, therefore, from the 'Nankin,' a sloop of war at anchor in the same channel, disembarked and burned the village, after a brisk fire between them and the Chinese soldiery. It was observed that the Chinese had cut off the heads of the seamen who had been killed. The conduct of the commander of the English gun-boat was very severely censured by his superior officers, and he stands a chance of being punished for his temerity by the withdrawal of his commission as well as the loss of his limbs.

On the 19th of December we put on our steam in order to change our anchorage ground, the whole of the ships belonging to the squadron being attached, so as to tug each other. We crossed the second bar,

H

thanks to the Chinese pilot of Admiral Seymour, whom we had on board. To work such a heavy hulk as the 'Audacieuse' within such a narrow space, in the midst of a channel which changed in its character and direction continually, was no easy matter. The pilot acquitted himself admirably, and we soon exchanged the anchorage of Blenheim Reach for that of American Reach. We cast anchor at Jardine's Point, opposite Danes Island and French Island, close to Whampoa. In the foreground is a village built on piles, which is completely deserted by its inhabitants. Beyond are fields of sugar-cane and the two pagodas of Whampoa Island, whence are seen the forts of Canton. Bounding the horizon is a chain of hills which form the first spurs of the mountains of the White Cloud. Behind us stretches French River and its picturesque banks, which are so graceful in their outline that they seem the conception of a landscape painter, and a steep hill cut down into terraces, with a whole city of tombs built upon it. We are fifty miles from Macao and nine miles from Canton.

The population seem to be quite indifferent as to the results of the war, and manifest no hostility to us. We meet often with a hearty welcome when we go to the villages, where the inhabitants offer us tea and bananas. Curiosity and fear seem to be the two feelings with which our appearance is greeted. The children generally run away screaming when they see us, and the women slam the doors in our faces; but in Whampoa it is different; there, the whole population come into the streets to have a good stare at us. The town is surrounded by a deep canal, but all the bridges over it, excepting one, have been cut down to protect the inhabitants from the barbarians. The mandarins and soldiers have withdrawn to Canton; and a Chinaman has just told us that the people will not allow them to return, lest their presence should involve the town in a quarrel with the foreigners.

In spite of the pacific disposition of the population, the Admiral would only allow us to go on shore in large numbers at a time, and well armed. In front of each ship there was placed a large triangle of bamboo, to keep off fire-rafts. Ships' boats, armed to the teeth, are passing to and fro on the road from morning till night. Sentinels are placed on watch, in front, behind, and to the right and left of each ship. There is something solemn now in the watchman's call, heard in the silence of the night. We have laid in provisions for a month, and in the lower deck the men are busy preparing cartridges in thousands as rapidly as possible. Meanwhile, the ambassadors are making a last attempt to obtain satis-

faction, without declaring war against the haughty governor of the two Kwangs.

'It is my duty to acquaint your Excellency,' wrote Baron Gros, 'that the time for wavering is past. Nearly two years of patience and moderation should suffice to convince the Chinese nation that they may depend upon the good will and friendship of France. However, for the honour of this power, it is necessary that the present state of things should now immediately cease, and that just reparation for grievances should be granted. I earnestly beg that the noble governor of the two Kwangs will reflect maturely on the present situation of European affairs in China. They are about to enter upon a new phase, the importance of which will certainly not escape the penetrating mind of your Excellency.

' The government of the Emperor has a right to demand satisfaction for the grievances which French subjects have suffered in China. The government of Her Britannic Majesty is in a similar position. A reparation is then legitimately due to these two powers, which are at one as to the means to be employed in obtaining it.

' France and England ask nothing which is not equitable—nothing which is not founded on their rights; and when this is the case, a reparation frankly made, so far from humbling him who makes it, on the contrary should exalt and aggrandize his importance in the eyes of his countrymen.

'Let the noble governor yield to evidence; let him, with a good grace, grant to France and England what he will be obliged afterwards to concede to them, and peace and prosperity will soon reappear among the populations entrusted to his care. If, on the contrary, he neglects the course which a wise policy dictates to him, misfortune, perhaps irreparable, may arise from a violent situation which he had it in his power to prevent, and which he might bring to an end by a single word.'

Then the ambassador asked various concessions in the name of the French government: he insisted on the degradation and exile of the magistrate guilty of the murder of Père Chapdelaine; the insertion in the official Gazette of the punishment suffered by this magistrate, and the reason of its being so inflicted; and the insertion on the same day, and in the same journal, of an article intended to acquaint all public functionaries that they would incur a like risk if ill advised enough to follow the example of this mandarin. The ambassador farther asked an indemnity for Frenchmen and persons under French protection, equivalent to the losses sustained by them through the destruction of the factories by the disorderly mob of Canton. Lastly, he claimed the full and complete execution of Article Second of the treaty of Whampoa. Under it, Frenchmen were to be admitted to Canton, and protected by the local authorities, with the same good faith as in the other four ports opened to foreign commerce; although, hitherto, they had not been allowed to enter the gates of the town; while all their demands had been met by an unendurable system of delay and equivocation.

The delivery of the ultimatum of Baron Gros took place on the 12th of December, at noon; when the 'Dragonne,' with Lieutenant Ribourt, the aide-de-camp of the admiral, and an English gunboat, with Mr. Wade, the interpreter to the English mission, made their appearance before Canton. There was an immense crowd assembled, shouting and making signs to them to keep back. A mandarin's junk pushed off, and, with all sails spread, came up to the vessel. The delivery of the two Notes, French and English, took place on board the junk; and the delegate immediately returned to his master, glad, no doubt, to get back in safety from his interview with the barbarians. On both sides there was a certain display of force as a precaution against a surprise.

The reply of the Imperial Commissioner was not long in coming. It was addressed, on the 14th of December, to Baron Gros. It was equivocal, and betrayed bad faith. It was, besides, couched in a tone of levity quite unsuited to the occasion. Yeh replied, by a formal refusal of the demands made upon him by the French ambassador, in a playful way, as if there was no serious stake at issue, and without attempting to answer the arguments in the well-reasoned note of his opponent. The reply made to Lord Elgin was conceived in a still more original style, and was throughout characterized by contemptuous irony and persiflage. ' Peace is signed for ten thousand years, why then would you renew the treaty? You have not yet been able to erect warehouses in the island of Honan, close by Canton ; how then can you quarter troops there? Profit by the example of your predecessors. One of them, Sir John Davis, was insolent towards the Chinese. He went home disgraced and branded by his country- men. Another, Sir John Bonham, was peacefully disposed. Honours were heaped upon him by his Sovereign. He was raised to the rank of baronet, and received the most brilliant marks of distinction. You see then,' concluded the facetious Commissioner, ' that it is for your interest to imitate Bonham and not Davis.' This despatch of Yeh is composed throughout in a language quite new in diplomatic correspondence.

In reply to the communication he had received,

Baron Gros despatched the following note: 'The reply of the Governor-General, not being serious, and containing merely evasive words, without an attempt to do justice to the demands of France, must be held equivalent to a formal refusal; and therefore the duty of the undersigned is to inform the Governor-General of the two Kwangs, that henceforth the solution of the present question is placed in the hands of the Commanders-in-Chief of the allied forces of France and England, who are empowered, so soon as they think fit, to employ rigorous measures to obtain by force the just reparation which, in his blindness, the noble Governor-General has been unwilling to make to the Allied Powers, whilst they addressed him in conciliatory and amicable language.'

On Monday the 21st of September a council of war was held on board the 'Audacieuse.' Baron Gros, Lord Elgin, Admiral Rigault de Genouilly, Sir Michael Seymour, and General Straubenzee took part in it. The plenipotentiaries now formally declared that their attempts to negociate with Yeh had failed, and that they handed over their power to the admirals to obtain by force what they could not obtain by peaceful negociation. The business on hand now was to take Canton, and afterwards to retain it in our possession as a means of coercion

while endeavouring to treat with the Chinese government. Ten days now had been allowed to Yeh.
They were nearly up. The allies might commence
the attack on the morning of the 23rd December.
Out of mercy to the inhabitants, however, a new
delay of forty-eight hours was granted to the civil
and military authorities of Canton. The Tartar and
Chinese generals were summoned to evacuate the
town with their soldiers. If the authorities and
troops retire, our troops are to take possession of the
places which they desert, and fortify them, keeping
up close communication with the river, without
causing any injury to the town or its inhabitants. If
they do not retire, the allies will bombard Canton
and take by force the positions which they wish to
occupy.

The Chinese military authorities have replied by a
disdainful silence to the summons of the Commanders-
in-Chief. Thenceforward the bombardment is decided
upon. Admiral Rigault de Genouilly, in a stirring
order of the day, made known to the seamen that the
campaign had commenced. All the light ships ascended to Canton or its immediate neighbourhood.
The 'Audacieuse,' the 'Nemesis,' the 'Meurthe,' and
the 'Capricieuse' only remained in the anchorage at
Whampoa, but their disembarkation corps left them
immediately. When the 'Marceau' passed up, tug-

ging the small boats, they were loudly cheered from the vessels left behind. Our men, with their linen gaiters and their knapsacks strapped on their backs, and carrying five days' provisions with them, besides their arms, had a fine martial appearance. Captain Collier is at the head of the disembarkation corps. Commander d'Aboville has under his orders the six French vessels moored before Canton. The members of the embassy have now been separated into two parties, between the 'Primauguet' and the 'Durance,' lying before Barrier Fort, two miles from Canton, the 'Audacieuse' being too far from the scene of events.

CHAPTER V.

ON Monday, the 28th December, 1857, at half-past six o'clock in the morning, our preparations were completed, and the military mandarins not having replied to the summons to evacuate the town, the order to open the bombardment was given. Our four gunboats, the 'Dragonne,' the 'Avalanche,' the 'Mitraille,' the 'Fusée,' the corvette the 'Phlégéton,' and the advice-boat the 'Marceau,' with a whole fleet of English sloops and gunboats, opened fire upon the town. Each piece should discharge forty shots in twenty-four hours. The English battery erected on Dutch Folly acquitted itself admirably. A shower of balls, rockets, and shells kept thundering down on Canton during a whole day and night. The cone and sphere balls discharged by the gunboats were sent as far as Fort Gough, some miles from the river. Two great columns of smoke rose from the burning town. At intervals the roar of the cannonade would cease, but only to recommence again. The white smoke of the cannons mingled in the air with the black clouds rising from the burning houses.

Our fire was concentrated on the eastern side of the town, where the assault was to take place, with the double purpose of battering down the wall and clearing it of its defenders. A sailor perched upon the topmast of each ship gave information when a shot told, and noticed what effect was produced by the rockets. Two balls only discharged by the Chinese artillerymen found their way as far as our gunboats. One fell near the 'Fusée,' on board which was Commander d'Aboville, and made a splash of water over the ship.

During the whole morning of the 28th, as on the preceding days, a compact crowd of frightened citizens covered the banks of the river all along the line where the vessels were moored. Seeing an unwonted bustle, from some cause, on board the gunboats, several Chinamen clambered up on the roofs to see what was the cause. Our men hallooed and made signs to them to keep out of the way, but not one would stir. It was not till a cannon-ball had chopped off the head of one of them that the crowd dispersed.

In the mean time the disembarkation of the sailors and soldiers was taking place. Without any difficulties beyond those presented by the nature of the ground, it was effected at a distance of about a mile from the town, half way between Barrier Fort and French Folly. Overnight six hundred Englishmen had taken possession of this point. Our men advanced but slowly, on account of the rice-fields and the narrow footpaths. They soon met the Chinese army, or rather bodies of Chinese soldiers. Not an officer or leader was to be seen among them. Hid in the thickets and behind the tombs, these Chinamen surprised our troops with a quick discharge of musketry, after which came pouring in upon them a perfect shower of bullets and arrows. Several of our party were wounded, among others a young sailor belonging to the 'Audacieuse,' who was struck with a ball right in the chest. It was remarked that this was the first time that Chinese soldiers had ventured to cope with Europeans in the open country: the bombardment of the city, from which they were glad to escape, may account for it. The Chinese have a singular mode of fighting. They wave red or yellow flags, partly to defy the enemy and provoke him to an assault, and partly to stir up and keep up their own courage. They use matchlocks and enormous carabines or gin-galls of seven feet and a half long, which they place in a battery or work in pairs, one holding the barrel over his shoulder, and the other taking aim and applying the match to the touchhole. They besides discharge arrows and arrow-rockets, which, by the peculiar whistle they make in passing through the air, frightened our men a little at first.

The French troops met with annoyance in a village. The admiral ordered it to be set on fire. General Straubenzee, coming up, objected to this being done. An hour afterwards an aide-de-camp of this same general, Lieutenant Hackett, passing through the same village, accompanied by an orderly bearing a message to the river bank, was attacked by thirty Chinamen. He shot two of them with his revolver, but a blow from a bludgeon levelled him to the ground; immediately afterwards a Chinese severed his head from his body with a sword. His companion killed four of his assailants and escaped. The English soldiers were infuriated; they returned to the village and set fire to it. The murderer was recognised; he was dragged by the tail right in front of the Chinese army, and hanged from the bough of a tree. It was frightful to see the look of this man while he was pulled along to the place of execution by the soldiers.

The Imperial troops continued to retire. The allies arrived before Lin's Fort. The English and French gunners placed themselves in line. They saw from a distance heaps of moveables thrown out of the fort by the Chinese, who feared the fire of the shells might set them a-blaze. Some time afterwards, Martin des Pallières, a French serjeant of marines, who had been sent out with his men as sharpshooters, observed that there was no fire returned from the embrasures of the fort. He resolved to enter it. He did so. He found that the door was open, and the fort deserted. It was he who first planted the tricolor upon the wall. The 59th English regiment, which had just gained the position, came up cheering. The 'Durance' struck her colours by way of salute to the conquerors, and Lord Elgin, who was on board of the 'Furious' at the time, complimented Baron Gros on the achievement.

An English detachment was for a moment driven back by a great body of the Chinese troops, who kept pouring upon them a shower of arrows and arrowrockets. The English were not long repulsed. They charged with the bayonet this body of Chinese troops, which was repulsed and dispersed, and did not reappear in the struggle. There were fifteen thousand Chinese spectators of the combat standing on the surrounding hills, who remained neutral so long as the allies were in the ascendant, but who would certainly be ready to fall upon the Europeans in the event of their meeting with a check. The English discharged their muskets upon them, and dispersed them by a bayonet charge. Then a shower of arrow-rockets came plumping down from a thicket of bamboos. The admiral ordered a few shells to be dropped upon the spot from which they proceeded, and the demonstration was at once silenced. The day's work was over. The troops bivouacked on the position they had won at Lin's Fort. It was a moonlight night—cold, but clear. They were not disturbed.

All night the bombardment was continued on the side of the eastern gate. From daybreak the gunners of the disembarkation corps had been battering a breach in the wall. English riflemen, placed behind the enclosures of the rice-field, shot the enemy's artillerymen as soon as they appeared upon the ramparts. Captain Bates, of the 'Actæon,' while making a recognisance to place the scaling-ladders, received a ball in the chest. A young midshipman, about fourteen or fifteen years of age, belonging to the English ship the 'Sanspareil,' was mortally wounded by an arrow in the heart. M. Maduron, of the

'Durance,' was mortally wounded in the shoulder. He was the only one of our officers who was injured.

At length the breach was made, the rampart was battered down, and the order was given to bring the ladders. The assaulting column drew up in order of battle, behind the rampart of a small village; went on by a narrow passage between the houses; crossed a stream, and reached the wall. Unluckily, a French shell dropped just at this spot. It burst; and hiding the men in a cloud of smoke, it severely wounded a marine, who was carried into a thicket where he died. The scaling-ladders were then applied to the walls, and found to be too short; so bits of ladder had to be added to them. One of them broke down with an English officer, who was severely injured. A quartermaster of the 'Capricieuse' first gained the wall. The Chinese soldiers were chased all round the ramparts. The seamen belonging to both fleets pursued the Chinamen before them till they were quite out of breath; and then they passed the great red pagoda, which is five stories high, and overlooks Canton, and they did not stop till they reached the northern gate. The first French battalion, under Captain Collier, was placed at the northern gate; Commander Vrignaud, with the second battalion and the English, took possession of the pagoda. Accommodation for the camp-hospital and powder was found in a little pagoda situated half-way up. We found that the mandarin of the place had hanged himself above the door, as he had not desired to survive his defeat. The two admirals and General Straubenzee fixed their head-quarters on the top of the eminence called the City Hill by the English, in a Joss-house, or Buddhist temple, defended by a small fort. On each battlement of this fort are painted the heads of tigers, and other savage beasts, intended to strike terror into the enemy. The position, in a military point of view, was unassailable. The view from it was exceedingly beautiful and picturesque: from our head-quarters, which were in the midst of very fine old trees, you looked down upon the whole town, stretching as far as the river; you could see the long line of the French and English gunboats, the island of Honan with its celebrated pagoda, and all the bends and creeks of Pearl River. At the lower part of the encampment there was a small Bonze-house, a little damaged by balls, where a detachment of English marines were quartered. The English, besides, occupied the east gate, as well the north-east gate, with their artillery, sepoys, and marines. Vautré, who sat next me at mess on board the 'Audacieuse,' was sent with twenty-five men to reconnoitre, and plumped, at the turn of a street, right into the midst of a Tartar drill-court—full of soldiers. It was impossible to draw back. He charged with the bayonet; several of his men were killed; he stabbed a soldier through the body himself. Then the Tartars, of whom there were about a hundred, gave way and abandoned their position. This was one of the most glorious episodes of the day.

The English, meanwhile, followed the outer wall, and reached Gough's Fort, which crowns the ridge. They found it completely deserted. At two o'clock in the afternoon, Gough's Fort, Blue Jacket Fort, and the Fort of the Marines were blown up, and the Tricolor and Union Jack planted over the ruined walls. In all quarters were found great stores of gunpowder, which were blown up by the English. These explosions, seen from the ship, had a singular effect.

At two o'clock in the afternoon of the 29th the whole affair was at an end. The allies were in possession of all the positions commanding the town. There was no longer any body of Chinese soldiers to offer them resistance. From the summit of the battlements were seen, at a distance in the plain, the scattered remains of the Chinese army, composed of from ten to fifteen thousand men, encamped in scattered bodies along the rivers. They were beyond the range of the cannon, and too far off to be pursued. They were not meddled with. All that day their red flags could be descried fluttering in the wind. Next morning they had disappeared; and they were not seen again. They had either retired into the interior, or, being a mere militia, had abandoned the sword for the plough, and returned to their habitual occupations as husbandmen.

The famous braves of the ninety-six villages, who were so long the terror of Europeans and the hope of Chinese, were nowhere to be seen. The Tartar soldiers, amounting to six or eight thousand men, are Chinese by female descent; and, having been settled for six or seven generations at Canton, they have exchanged the courage and vigour of their ancestors, for that want of firmness, and promptness to turn and run, which characterizes the Imperial troops of China. Moreover, there is nothing to distinguish them from the Chinese soldiers; they carry the same arms, which belong to primitive times, and recall the period of Genghis Khan and Timour. They wear a round hat, a breastplate, a cartridge-box, after the Circassian fashion, at their belts, a long musket, arrows, and a flag, which they wave about to rouse their courage. Some trace, however, of their Tartar descent they do preserve. They are stronger, bigger, more broad-shouldered, and not so dark in the complexion as the ordinary Chinese.

The day following the capture of the town we went

to spend a couple of days at the camp. I stopped at the spot where the assault had taken place, and still saw the bamboo scaling ladders lying at the foot of the rampart. In various places fresh lime, and newly laid bricks, showed that the military authorities had carefully repaired the wall within a recent period. I was told that this had been done within the last three years, since the time indeed when the rebels had made their attack on the city. I passed the Hall of Examination, where I saw the cells of the literati. Wide avenues planted with trees, and elegant porticoes, give a very handsome and even noble appearance to this building. But this establishment, like everything else which we see, is only another proof of the present decline of China from its former prosperity and splendour. Literature is certainly not now held in high esteem, nor can it be considered to flourish if we are to judge by the nettles and parasitical plants which grow in unweeded luxuriance in this sanctuary of the muses. We counted the number of cells. There was accommodation for seven thousand students. If the great soul of Confucius could revisit this sublunary sphere, with what sadness would that spirit contemplate the manners of this degenerate age! The children of the Land of Flowers now worship mammon. They are absorbed in the race after material wealth. To the computation of filthy coppers, they have turned from the contemplative study of the sacred Book of Changes. In China there is a general break up of the old system; the great administrative machine is getting daily more and more out of gear. It is kept going merely in virtue of old habits and prejudices. All its wheels are worn down. It is gold now, and not knowledge, which obtains the diploma necessary to preferment. Why then should a man now shut himself up in a hole four feet square to write his thesis? It is more to the purpose to insinuate a handsome bribe into the pocket of a rapacious and powerful mandarin.

General Straubenzee turned these cells to account in accommodating the English military train, which was formed of Chinamen. The Hong-Kong Coolies commit depredations on their countrymen at Canton; but in other respects they do their work with the greatest regularity. We met constantly with long bands of them, between the river and the camp, carrying powder and shot, provisions and huge joints of beef over their shoulders. Our French military train not having come up, a hundred men belonging to the 'Nemesis,' and one hundred and thirty belonging to the 'Audacieuse,' under the command of Messrs. Mallet and Lespès, at first performed the duties of Coolies to the French troops. They were put up in sampans or boats, as well as the troops, under the command of

M. Martineau des Chenetz, who defended the shore.
The escorts were no longer disturbed, and passed
quietly by the wall. An earthen mound was constructed by which to ascend and descend, and the
rubbish of the fallen houses was pitched into the
river, in order that there might be a low-water quay
at which a landing might be effected at all times of
the tide, for the latter affects the stream as high up as
Canton.

The officers of the various ships received us at
the camp, and spared no pains to make us understand
what had taken place on the two preceding days.
While we sauntered over the northern rampart,
and along the grey old wall which had been erected
in the best days of China, treading upon the grass
which grows upon it, we could scarcely fail to be
deeply impressed by the fact that before our time
no barbarian had ever passed within this sacred
enclosure, had ever clambered over these battlements, or, from this eyrie polluted with his glance
the holy city of Canton. I saw a dozen corpses of
Tartars still lying about, who had been precipitated
at the point of the bayonet over the edge of the
rampart, or who had fallen from it in their flight.
Their arms were lying on the ground near them.
They had been tall, stout, dark-complexioned men.
They were frightfully mutilated; one was half-

consumed by a shell which had burst near him. We were accommodated separately in the different pagodas during the night, some sleeping on tables, others on the floor, rolled up in a blanket, and all surrounded, like saints in a picture, with a glory, formed in our case of mosquitoes, which effectually drove sleep away. There was the greatest stillness in the town. Although the terror was general, the authorities in their impenetrable pride would as yet give no acknowledgment of their defeat. We heard only from time to time the distant howling of the Tartar dogs, the sputtering of some smouldering fire which had gone a-blaze again, the call of the sentries, and the occasional discharge of musketry from the distant outposts. The appearance of the camp was very picturesque, and such only as an Asiatic war can exhibit. Long spears, arrows, red and yellow banners were lying about on every side. The wardrobe of the mandarins had been well ransacked by our seamen, and with what result was everywhere apparent. The altars had been converted into sleeping berths, while the cloaks of the Chinese ladies supplied night-gowns. Everywhere there were gilded Buddhas dragged from their niches, by one to be employed as a pillow, and by another to be used as a lampstand. The abdomens both of the human figures and the horses had been broken open, the English soldiers recollecting that in the first war large sums of money were found in this way. Every one eat and drank out of China ware, but, as the only dishes in use in the country were cups and saucers, soup, beef, and cheese were eaten off them. Propped against a fierce-looking dragon, or seated upon a moral maxim, we laid into the good cheer of the mandarins. In everything there was an indescribable mixture of the comic and grotesque.

Near the great five-story pagoda, which is said to be twelve centuries old, there is a small interior fort, the walls of which are whitewashed, and which appears to have been constructed in anticipation of the present attack in order to command the route by which the English descended upon Gough's Fort in 1841. The Chinese never for a moment doubted that the barbarians would enter the city precisely by the road they took on the former occasion: in point of fact they came in precisely at the opposite extremity of the town. The artillery along the walls is wretched. The carriages are not even moveable, so that the enemy to be shot must take up his position right in front of the mouth of the cannon ; and of course the barbarians are infamous enough to come in behind the forts, and make their attack before the Chinamen have time to turn round their clumsy machinery.

In China the military profession is not held in

honour. No one attempts to introduce improvements on the present system. A distinguished wit says, in speaking of gunpowder, that, if the Chinese discovered it, they have not yet discovered the use of it. As for the Minié rifle, that is out of the question. They seem to depend for success in war on various fantasia—to runs they make forward, and runs backward, and loud shouts of defiance. They flourish their double-handed swords, they wave their flags, they shoot their rockets and arrows into the ranks of the enemy, but never do they come to close quarters with cold steel. Two regiments of Chasseurs and two regiments of Zouaves would suffice to conquer China. There is not a corps in the empire who could stand fast under a bayonet charge. The sight of a body of men marching coolly and resolutely up to them is so alien to their nature, so utterly incomprehensible and terrible, that all courage deserts them, and it is ten to one if they do not immediately take to their heels. Formerly the Chinese, up to a certain point, were a warlike people. The business of a soldier was in no degree repugnant to their national manners. But the Tartars introduced a change. They found that their number after the conquest was very small when compared to that of the Chinese people; there were only a million of new comers to three hundred and sixty millions of the old inhabitants. As a means of self-protection, therefore, they set themselves with perseverance to the task of extinguishing in the people all taste for military display and love of warlike adventure. They converted China into an immense hive of labourers. The country became a great workshop, in which all the arts of peace flourished, and the whole national activity was concentrated upon the great struggle in which man is engaged with nature. What was to be feared of a man who would spend twelve or fifteen years of his life in polishing a bit of jadestone? But then again, what could be expected of him in the hour of danger, when the country required his services as a defender against a foreign foe? The result of the Mantchoo policy has been that six thousand energetic Europeans have taken possession in two days of a town of a million and a half of inhabitants, surrounded with lofty walls and defended by one of the most numerous garrisons in the empire.

The English, in the capture of Canton, had a hundred men killed and wounded. The French had thirty men wounded, of whom three died. In two days our men used sixty thousand cartridges. One hundred and thirty pieces of ordnance, without counting mortars, for four-and-twenty hours, continued to spread conflagration through the town.

In this way the conceit, the pride, and the blindness of the Cantonese and their imperious governor have met with their fitting punishment. On the evening before the attack the people of the city had stopped, in passing the proclamation of the allied forces, to take their laugh and sneer at what they considered the impudent threats of the barbarians to take possession of Canton, the impregnable city, which, never since the foundation of the Mantchoo dynasty, had opened its gates to an enemy. Two days afterwards, these same barbarians, having made themselves masters of its fortifications, gates, and walls, planted their victorious flag in the Hall of State, and made the hills about ring with their shouts of triumph.

January 1, 1858.

New-year's day on board the ' Durance,' opposite Barrier Fort and Kuper Island, was not kept with much gaiety. Indeed it almost passed unnoticed. What a difference was there from the mirth and bustle of Paris on the same day! We had the usual service on deck. A man wounded on board of the ' Audacieuse' had died, and was buried under the wall of the fort. Mass was said on deck; the service was conducted by a missionary and a Chinese Christian. In the country there were straggling parties of Chinese going towards the town or leaving it;

some carrying their valuable effects with them, others bearing off stolen goods. There were groups of men with their wives on their backs, the latter being unable to walk from the tenderness of their small feet; and women by themselves, helping each other to limp along painfully as they best could. In the ninety-six villages the braves were doubting what course to take, and whether or not they should buckle on their fighting gear and proceed to assist the Imperial army. On the river, gunboats were plying up and down the stream, carrying the wounded to a place of safety, and conveying ammunition and food to the troops.

At noon the two ambassadors, preceded by military bands, and followed by a numerous escort of officers and sailors, proceeded to the camp to hold a conference with the admirals. When they set foot on shore, all the ships in the road hoisted their colours and discharged a volley of twenty-one guns. The staff replied with a loud hurrah. The Chinamen thought a new bombardment was at hand, and scampered off in every direction. A tremendous explosion, shaking the very earth, took place at sunset, to celebrate the return of the ambassadors on board. The English had heaped together large quantities of Chinese gunpowder under the dismantled walls of Fort Gough; and by way of jubilant demonstration, had blown up what remained of that stronghold.

The 2nd of the month came, yet no mandarin made his appearance. No submission was tendered on behalf of the people. The town was sad and silent, but no admission was made by its inhabitants that they were conquered. The Tartar quarter remained hostile. Yeh continued his rule, and by way of publishing and proving that he did so, the report ran that he had beheaded four hundred persons in one day. The admirals recommended a second bombardment of twenty-four hours. Lord Elgin objected to this, on grounds of humanity. The two admirals and General Straubenzee, with two thousand men, made a reconnoissance all along the wall, from the northern gate as far as the river. They found the wall free and deserted, and returned without having fired a shot. The western gate was occupied by five hundred Frenchmen and gunners, and all communication between the town and suburbs was intercepted.

On the 3rd the leading men and principal merchants of the city came to head-quarters to make their submission, with Howqua, the millionnaire, at their head, the son of the celebrated Hong. Numerous petitions were presented to the ambassadors, begging them to establish some government which would put an end to plunder and keep order in the town. The inhabitants were in consternation, many of them had died of hunger, and there was now nobody who spoke of fighting any more, at least so said these petitioners.

On the 4th the ambassadors received a despatch from the Tartar general and the Governor of Canton, proposing to treat and to settle amicably the various questions in dispute. But this mission was still arrogant in its tone, and the style and forms of expression used were those of a superior towards functionaries of inferior rank, so ridiculously blinded by self-conceit and pride were these petty despots. The reply of the High Commissioners was soon made.

On the 5th of January, at daybreak, a column of three thousand men descended the heights of City Hill, and entered, with their cannon, the streets of the town. Not a single shot was fired; some of the people had run to hide themselves, the remainder offered no opposition. The palace of the mandarins was invested; they were all caught at once as in a trap. Commissioner Yeh, the Tartar general Muh, Pih-Kwe the Governor of Canton, and a host of petty mandarins and subaltern functionaries, were taken prisoners to the camp in their sedan-chairs, through the midst of the chapfallen population. The papers belonging to Yeh were removed immediately to head-quarters, as well as the exchequer strong-box, and the seals of the high dignitaries.

Yeh was in the midst of a group of mandarins when the doors of the yamoun where he had sought refuge were broken open. The captors were puzzled to know which was the right man; but Mr. Parkes, long the British Consul at Canton, recognised him by his corpulency, and pointed him out to the English soldiers. The latter put him into a sedan-chair, and when the door was shut upon him they made the Coolies trot with him to the camp, running after them, and giving them an occasional nudge with the butts of their muskets, to make them hurry along. When Yeh passed by the English military train, composed, as we have said, of Chinamen from Hong Kong, these patriots had a joke or two at his expense; they grinned and made signs to him that he was going to have his head chopped off. Yeh turned an angry scowl upon them: he must have felt this reverse of fortune keenly. What a trial for a man to have been only the night before at the very summit of power and fortune, the favourite minister of the court of Pekin, and now to be the scoff and jeer of a mob of miserable Coolies! With what relish would he have ordered them to the executioner, like some hundreds of rebels a few years before! The Commissioner was at first frightened and downcast, but he soon recovered his old perverse spirit, and even conducted himself with arrogance and hauteur towards the admirals, when he saw that he was in no danger of his life. On being asked what had become of some English merchants who had recently disappeared, he replied, with a contemptuous smile, that they might be quite at ease on that head, as he had given them decent burial. In spite of his expostulations he was sent as a prisoner on board the 'Inflexible,' which immediately put on her steam and left for Bocca Tigris ; and so the haughty Commissioner was removed, quivering with fresh fear, from the scene of his political importance.

The Tartar general, Muh, was arrested in a large apartment of his house by a French detachment, under the command of Captain Collier, of the navy. He is a magnificent fellow, nearly six feet high, and about sixty years old ; and so dreadfully corpulent that it is no easy task for him to stand upright. Quite taken aback, he allowed himself to be put into a chair without resistance, and was hurried off to head-quarters. He seemed to have been selected more on account of his stature than for any other quality. He is a most insignificant personage, and a perfect nonentity in all that relates to political arrangements. He had only been in Canton since February last. If the court of Pekin chose him in anticipation of the events, it must be admitted that Muh has quite come up to the expectations formed

K

of him by his sovereign.   What steps did he take to
resist the attack of the Europeans ?   What was he
about while the battle was going on under the walls
of Canton ?   There is not a doubt that, surrounded
by his boon companions, he was tranquilly smoking
opium and sipping tea, leaving it to the gods who
watch over China to defend their holy city against
the barbarians.   We took a good stare at him when
at head-quarters in the room assigned him.   He
seemed quite absorbed in some gloomy train of
thought; saying a few words now and then to the
literati who surrounded him, and twisting about
mechanically, with his long fingers, his elegant collar
of first-class mandarin.

As regards Pih-Kwe, he is a Mongol of the
yellow banner, brought up at Pekin; accustomed
to the polished manners and choice language of the
court.   He is a very intelligent man, with an energetic and unflinching look.   The admirals saw at
once how superior he was, in all respects, to the
military mandarin ; and, in the absence of any other
high dignitary, they resolved to make use of his services at Canton.   On the 7th of January, after a
long conference between the admirals on the one
hand and Pih-Kwe on the other, the latter was
continued in his functions as governor of Canton.
He undertook the administration of the Chinese

town, and the maintenance of proper order. It
would have been too heavy a task for the allies to
have governed the city by themselves, ignorant as
they necessarily were of Chinese habits and juris-
prudence. This arrangement relieved them of a
great difficulty. They declared that they would
continue the military occupation, and retain Canton
as a pledge, until the conclusion of peace with the
court of Pekin; but that they would allow and support Pih-Kwe in full power, so far as the management and administration of the city were concerned.
A commission was appointed to regulate the intercourse between Europeans and Chinese, and to
form the only competent tribunal in any dispute
or cause to which a European should be a party.
Colonel Holloway, Consul Parkes, and Commander
Martineau des Chenetz were named the members of
this commission; which two days afterwards commenced its sittings in one of the yamouns of the old
town, and opened proceedings under the protection
of four hundred men.

On the 9th of January Pih-Kwe was solemnly
installed as governor of Canton by the two High
Commissioners of the Allied Powers. At two o'clock
in the afternoon we left on board the 'Lily' steamer,
the gunboat of Lord Elgin preceding us. We were
in full dress; the ambassadors alone were in black,

with a ribbon merely. This *nuance* was highly appreciated by the English colony of Hong Kong. We found the troops of the escort drawn up at the landing-place. We got into sedan-chairs, which had been prepared for us, and set out, accompanied by a brilliant crowd of officers, and preceded by bands of music. The day was very fine. For a time we followed the line of the wall. At the eastern gate we entered the town. We proceeded down the street, between a line of French seamen and English soldiers. It was narrow and winding, obstructed everywhere with projecting doors and signboards. Our chairs occupied nearly its whole width. The Chinese crowd was silent and downcast. We arrived at the yamoun, where the admiral received us at the head of the four hundred men set apart as a guard for the European Commission. We penetrated as far as the hall of the governor, where the ceremony is to take place. After waiting for nearly an hour we were surprised that the two high dignitaries did not make their appearance. We learned that the English sentry had refused to allow Muh and Pih-Kwe to pass without a written order from General Straubenzee, such being his instructions. The necessary signature was at once obtained, and three guns were fired—this being the Chinese salute to announce that the cap-

tives had been restored to liberty, and were on their
way to be reinvested in their honours. M. de Bellecourt and Mr. Bruce, the two chief secretaries, went
to receive them at the door of the hall. They
entered, accompanied by a numerous escort of servants and petty mandarins, and saluted us with many
tchin-tchin and obeisances. The two ambassadors
placed themselves in the middle of the raised floor,
and the two high dignitaries at the extremities,—
Pih-Kwe at the side of Baron Gros, and Muh at the
side of Lord Elgin. His Lordship enumerated, with
a severe tone, all the grievances of the Europeans
against the Cantonese and their governors; and declared that such a state of things must thenceforth
cease. Baron Gros reminded Pih-Kwe of his engage-
ment to conduct the administration of the town with
good faith, and to do nothing, directly or indirectly,
which would interfere with the military operations of
the allies; adding, that if he so conducted himself, he
would do the highest service to his fellow-citizens.
Mr. Wade and M. Marquès translated alternately
these addresses, and the replies of the high Chinese
dignitaries. The two embassies were placed behind
their chiefs. It so happened that I was placed close
by Pih-Kwe. My eyes fell upon the swan which
ornamented his back, the peacock's feather and the
red button which surmounted his blue hat, and I could

note the amount of artistic care expended in eking out his scanty locks into the dimensions of a tail. These little things were all new to me. A salvo of one-and-twenty guns proclaimed the conclusion of the ceremony and the departure of the cortège. At six o'clock we returned on board of the 'Primaguet' and the 'Durance.'

On the next and the following days we perambulated the town, dropping into the few shops which were open, and endeavouring to ascertain what really were the feelings of the inhabitants towards us. Confidence is not yet restored. People are still moving out of the town. Opposite the Treasury there is a fine street filled with elegant shops ; not one of these was open. At intervals along this street there are triumphal arches in stone, ornamented with sculptures in good taste, and intended to perpetuate the memory of rich or distinguished citizens. We passed these monuments. Further on we came to a vast space which had been completely destroyed and burnt by our shot and shell. It was strewed with the rubbish of the fallen houses. I saw several corpses of Chinamen lying about, who had been killed by the exploding bombs lying on the ground. We then came in sight of Baron Gros, with an escort of officers, proceeding along the wall. We joined him, and went to visit Yeh's palace. *Fuit Ilium et ingens gloria Teu-*

crorum. Of the yamoun there is not one fragment
left. The mandarin poles have been smashed by
the shot; the porches are demolished and the trees
burned; the very shape of the building cannot now
be traced. There is nothing left but a great irregular
heap of bricks and rubbish. It was on the morning
of the 28th that the 'Mitraille' and the 'Fusée'
opened fire on that part of the town. From six
o'clock till eleven in the forenoon the torrent of
bombs and balls never ceased. By mid-day not one
brick or beam of the Commissioner's abode was left
standing upon another. Chinese insolence had been
taught a lesson. Yeh, at an earlier period in his
career, was less hostile to the Europeans. But his
father, a superstitious old Chinaman, who spent his
whole time in the society of priests, encouraged him
to resistance, because, forsooth, a number of good
omens had foretold that he would have good luck.
Yeh knows now what truth there was in these predictions. On board of the 'Inflexible' he may brood
at leisure over the folly of his faith in his father's
friends and their predictions.

We re-entered the old town by the south-west
gate, and returned by the eastern street. The streets
of the Chinese towns form such a labyrinth that one
cannot leave the one or two principal thorough-
fares without getting confused. Indeed it is neces-

sary in some parts of them to make use of a compass in crossing from one place to another.

We met at the corner of a street three young Chinese ladies, bedaubed with rouge, very elegant in their appearance, but having their feet so much compressed that they limped along with difficulty. When they saw us they screamed aloud, and rushed up against the wall, hiding their faces in their hands, and turning their backs towards us in the most contemptuous manner possible. The attitude was so ridiculous to us "foreign devils," that we could not help bursting into a hearty laugh.

We returned to dine on board, passing before Dutch Folly, the ruins of the factories, and Red Fort on the island of Honan. Red Fort belongs to the allies. The factories, as before stated, were burned a year ago by the people of the town. Dutch Folly is a pretty little island, or rather rock, planted with trees, and situated in the middle of the river opposite the town. Through the foliage gleams the wall of an English battery, which has taken the place of the old Chinese fortification. From it a sentry carefully watched during the bombardment the course taken by the shells, and the effect produced by the balls.

Every day we make it our first business to visit the camp. From the northern gate we went into the town one day with commanders Vrignaud, Ray-

naud, and Lévêque. We can go anywhere now in
perfect safety. The shops are not yet opened, many
streets are still deserted, and many houses shut up,
but in the great artery which, running from one end
of the town to the other, terminates at the western
gate, and which is now opened again, there is considerable traffic and bustle. The Chinese begin to
recover confidence, and collect in crowds to stare at
the foreigners. Now, however, instead of caning
them as they used to do, they make way for them,
and silently unroll their tails to the barbarians as
they pass—a mark of respect which is quite novel,
and which dates from the shells. None of the fine
shops are yet opened, but the stalls already display
their manifold nicknacks and grotesque ornaments.

We visited successively the palace of the Tartar
general, that of the governor of Canton, the pagoda
of the five hundred gods, the temple of Confucius, the
house of the criminal judge, the Treasury, and various
other public buildings and pagodas. All these edifices
are spacious and imposing. They each form an
immense assemblage of yards, avenues, porches, pas-
sages, waiting-rooms, court-rooms, and halls of justice.
Before each there is an open court-yard, in which
stand two lofty masts or poles painted red. This
distinguishes the residence of a mandarin. A gigantic dragon is represented in black or red upon the

wall, by way of scaring the multitude. On each fold
of the doors an enormous mandarin is painted, with
a swan upon his breast if he belong to the civil
service, or a lion if he belong to the military service.
Stretching away in front there is a paved avenue
planted with banyan-trees of ancient growth. At
the sides there are numerous porches and inner courts.
Behind there are open meadows, in which graze
Tartar horses, or fields planted with bamboos and
forest trees. Nowhere is there any trace of the watchful hand of a gardener; whatever grows is allowed
to grow, so the weeds flourish luxuriantly. There
are no flower-beds; a few pomegranate and orange
plants, bamboos, camelias, and even palms and
elms, all of the tiniest size, are displayed in vases or
flower-pots, and exhibit that stunted and microscopic
leafage which is held in so much esteem by the
Chinese. Gold fish spirt about in the basins, but
everything is in decay, neglected and uncared for.
A great part of the yamoun of the Tartar general
has been abandoned to the bats. They have mul-
tiplied in this retreat, and they flutter about and
squeak incessantly in the principal apartment, where
a thick coating of guano on the floor proclaims the
fact that there they have had their abode for years.
The bat and the toad are honoured in China.

The only placse which are truly elegant, well-furnished, and comfortable in these dwellings, are the female apartments, situated in the most distant part of the house, and the hall which adjoins them, where the magistrate receives his friends. Muh's house was sumptuously furnished. There were time-pieces and clocks innumerable, halberds, lances, and all those weapons for show and not for use which the Chinese are so fond of parading, as if they would thereby coax themselves into the belief that they are a warlike people.

Just as in Paris the whole life and activity of the town lies to the right of the Seine, so at Canton the heart of excitement and commercial bustle is the western suburb. It is this quarter of the city only which can give trouble to the allies. It is the centre of moral resistance. For this reason columns of troops are sent to march through the streets. The rattle of the heavy ordnance over the pavement produces a wholesome effect. The eastern suburb is neither so populous nor so extensive. The small-pox district, the hospitals, and the various charitable institutions are situated there. The Mantchoo or Tartar quarter, situated between the northern street and the wall, intersected by the eastern street, and exposed to the fire of the western gate, gives little cause for alarm. This is the case also with the whole of the old town, which, with its temples, yamouns, and numerous open spaces, is completely overlooked by the batteries at head-quarters. The new town contains a denser population, but it, too, is under the fire of our gunboats. The same may be said of the suburb along the river,—neither the gate of Eternal Joy, nor the gate of Eternal Purity, could protect it on the occasion of the insurrection. It was clear then that it was only the western suburb, with its swarming population and unwalled streets, which called for watchful attention on the part of the commanders-in-chief.

I have spent a couple of days more than once at the yamoun of the Tartar general with Commander Martineau des Chenetz. The European Commission conducts its proceedings with great order and regularity. Every day, from ten o'clock in the forenoon until one in the afternoon, it sits on the bench, hearing the complaints of the Chinese, and giving judgment upon them. It is now assiduously engaged in consolidating our occupation, and establishing a European and Chinese police. I saw a great many mandarins who came to pay their respects to the Commissioners. Seventeen Chinese junks of war, commanded by a naval mandarin, were placed at the disposal of Admiral Seymour, to assist him in putting down piracy on the river. The Tartar soldiers were disarmed, and came to surrender their arms at

the house of the lieutenant-general.   There were,
according to the admission of Muh, nearly eight
thousand Tartar soldiers in the town, or at least appearing in the official lists.   But as the Tartar general
draws the pay, and as his income is augmented in
proportion to the smallness of the number of men
really serving under his banners, it may be reason-
ably concluded that this number is purely fictitious.
Up to this time no European has had such a good
opportunity as we have had of closely studying the
manners and springs of action of the old Chinese
society.   It is laid bare to us.   It is curious to hear
in the streets, of an evening, the thundering din of
the military bands of the English and French troops.
The Chinese are surprised to see our soldiers keeping
step ; and seem to have no idea whatever of such regularity in military drill.   A body of Chinese troops is
a mere herd, thrown together pellmell, without regard
to order of any kind.   The easy familiarity and simplicity of our authorities, who walk about in the streets
and go into the shops, gives them unfeigned astonishment, they never having seen their mandarins except
when borne in stately palanquins, preceded by satellites, attendants, bands of music, and executioners,
and followed by a numerous suite.   Never once during
the last four thousand years has a Chinese mandarin
deigned to walk down a street like an ordinary citizen.

Yeh remains at Bocca-Tigris on board the 'Inflexible.' His pride and irritability have been wounded by the neglect with which he has been treated by Lord Elgin and Baron Gros, who have not yet visited him. There is a talk of sending him soon to Calcutta. His friends have been trying to bribe the English sailors to let him escape; besides his presence in the neighbourhood of Canton is a disadvantage. Several leading citizens and mandarins, dreading his vengeance, will not yet venture to come forward and countenance the new order of things. Various places, such as the Cape, Mauritius, and Singapore, have been spoken of as his future residence, but Calcutta has been at last selected in preference to any of these.

CHAPTER VI.

IT will be recollected that the allies, a few days
after the capture of Canton, had very fortunately
got possession of the correspondence and official documents belonging to Yeh, hid in a yamoun near his
own. These numerous documents were carefully
removed to a sampan anchored half way between
the 'Furious' and 'Primauguet,' nicknamed the
Foreign Office. There they were assiduously perused by Mr. Wade and M. Marquès, the interpreters

to the two missions. Few of these papers related to barbarian affairs, Yeh doubtless having had time to burn his correspondence on this subject. Most of the despatches related to the administration of the province; among them, however, were discovered the principal of the five treaties entered into between China and the Western Powers. M. Marquès brought us the ratification of the treaty concluded by M. de Legrené, under the reign of the Emperor Tao-Kouang. It bore the seal of Louis Philippe and the signature of M. Guizot. The title of king in China implying the idea of vassalage, the King of the French had, on this occasion, assumed the title of Emperor of the French. Several persons have concluded from this discovery that the treaty had never been made known at Pekin; but this is quite a mistake, and the fact is that our missionaries, when apprehended in the interior of the empire, are brought back to the nearest port with special attention, under the stipulations of the Legrené treaty. The management of barbarian affairs having been entirely delegated to Yeh, to whom authority had been given to centralize them, and all intercourse between foreigners and the court of Pekin having hitherto taken place through Canton, it was natural that the documents which regulated this intercourse should be found lying in this city. A curious document found among the diplomatic

papers is worthy of a place in this narrative. It pur-
ports to be a memorandum, addressed, in 1845, to
the Emperor Tao-Kouang by Ky-Ing, the governor
of Canton, who signed the five treaties. It is entitled 'Supplementary Memorial, detailing parti-
culars concerning the reception of the Envoys of
different Barbarian Nations.' It is authenticated
by the autograph of the Emperor in vermilion. It
runs as follows:—

'Your slave Ky-Ing, humbly kneeling, lays this
Supplementary Memorial at the feet of your Majesty.

'The details of the administration with which
your slave has been entrusted in treating with the
barbarians, and the intercourse which he has had with
their envoys when they have come to this country,
have already been the subject of several memorials
drawn up by your slave. Having also negotiated with
the barbarians several supplementary conditions respecting commerce, he has had the honour of placing
the articles containing them under the sacred eyes of
your Majesty; who has authorized the Committee of
Finance to examine those articles and report upon
them.

'He has the honour now of reminding your Majesty
that it was on the 27th moon of the 22nd year
(August 1842) that the English barbarians were
pacified. The Americans and the French arrived,

L

after each other, in the summer and autumn of the present year (1845), and during this period of three years our position towards the barbarians has undergone a great change; and to an extent corresponding to this change it has become necessary to modify our conduct towards them, as well as the means to be employed to preserve peace, and keep them in a respectful attitude towards us.

'Although it is no doubt useful to act towards them by employing fair and straightforward measures, it is much more prudent to lead them by wile. In some cases they must be made aware of the motives which dictate our conduct, but in others their susceptibility is such that it can only be soothed down by acts of a kind calculated to drive away their suspicions.

'It is sometimes a good plan to try to please them and make them grateful by treating them as equals; and in some cases, before aiming at the results which it is possible to attain, one must pretend not to see their roguery, and it is useful not to push too far the just appreciation of their acts.

'Born and brought up within the bounds of distant countries, there are many things in the manners and customs of the Celestial Empire which the barbarians cannot fully understand; and they are continually making observations on things, the full bearing of which it is impossible to explain to them. For instance, it is the duty of the members of the Great Council to prepare decrees; well, the barbarians treat these decrees as if they proceeded from the hand of the Emperor himself; and if they are told that these decrees are not the production of your Majesty, instead of respecting them they do not attach any importance to their terms.

'The repast which the barbarians take in common is called the ta-tsan, or dinner. They are very fond of meeting with each other at this time in large numbers, and eating and drinking together.

'When your slave did them the honour of asking them to dine with him at the Bogue or at Macao, ten, twenty, or even thirty of their chiefs and leading men accepted his invitation. When afterwards your slave has had occasion to go to their residences, or on board of their ships, the barbarians came and sat down round him and vied with each other in being the first to offer him food and wine. To get their good-will your slave could not do otherwise than make use of their glasses and spoons.

'Another thing: It is the custom with the barbarians to be proud of their wives. If the person who pays them a visit belongs to the upper classes, the wife of the barbarian to whom the visit is paid never fails to come out and meet the visitor. When the

American barbarian Parker and the French barbarian Lagrené were here, for instance, they brought out their wives in their ships with them; and accordingly, when your slave went to their houses on business, he had no sooner entered than these foreign women made their appearance and saluted him. Your slave was quite abashed by this custom, and felt very awkward; while the barbarian women, on the other hand, were quite delighted with the respect your slave paid them.

' All these facts go to prove that it is not possible to regulate the customs of western nations by those of China. If we attempt to force the barbarians to adopt our usages, we shall gain nothing by teaching them, but shall on the contrary stir up their suspicions and draw down upon us their ill will.

' At the time when there was friendly intercourse between foreigners and China, several barbarians were received by us on the footing of a certain equality; but now that these relations have ceased to exist, it is more than ever our duty to repel the barbarians and keep them at a distance. With this view, every time that your slave has had a treaty to negociate with a barbarian state, he has sent Kwang-Hang-Tung, the commissary of finance, to let the barbarian envoy know beforehand that a high dignitary of the empire, charged with the administration

of foreign affairs, was never free to give or receive on
his own account, and that if he was offered presents
he would be obliged peremptorily to refuse them;
that, if he accepted them secretly, the ordinances of
the celestial dynasty were very severe on the subject;
and that, besides loss of dignity to the functionary
who should so act, the guilty party would be unable
to escape from the penalties enforced by law.   The
barbarian envoys have had the good sense to conform
to this usage, but in their interviews with your slave
they have often offered him some of their foreign
wine, perfumery, and other things of the same kind
and of little value.   Whatever their intentions were,
whether good or bad, in so acting, your slave could
not openly reject their presents; and he gave them
in exchange snuff-boxes, scented purses, and those
other small objects which are carried about the
person, always putting in practice the Chinese principle which says, Give much but receive little.
Besides, with respect to the Italians (*Portuguese*),
English, Americans, and French, your slave offered
them a copy of his insignificant portrait.

'As regards their government, they have at their
head sometimes men, sometimes women, who retain
power either for life or for a stated time.   Among
the English barbarians, for instance, the sovereign is
a woman;   among the French and Americans the

sovereign is a man. Among the English and French the head ruler is appointed for life; while among the Americans he is elected by his fellow-citizens, and only for four years, at the expiry of which time he quits the throne, and becomes again a simple citizen, belonging to the non-official class. Each of these states has a different name for its head ruler. In general they adopt (*literally they steal*) Chinese names. They affect, pompously, a style of speech which they have no right to employ; and they all seem to desire to pass themselves off as having great power. When their purpose in doing so is to honour their rulers, it is not our business to take notice of this. But it is my belief that, if they were asked to submit to the rules adopted by the countries tributary to China, they would refuse to obey, for they have not even adopted our way of reckoning time; and they will not recognise the royal investiture which your Majesty has bestowed upon them, whereby they were placed in the same rank with Loo-Choo and Cochin China.

' With races so little civilized as they are, so stupid and unintelligent in their style and language, and so obstinately attached to forms of words in their official correspondence that they will persist in placing the superior last and the inferior first, it is the best course to disregard their customs, and not to take any notice of all this (*literally to slit the tongue and sear the lips*), for if we do otherwise, not only all personal intercourse, but all official communication must cease, to the great injury of the all-important question of peace. Instead, then, of entering into discussions about the use of terms, which really have no practical value, we have preferred to neglect insignificant details for a great and useful policy.

' Such are the expedients which, after a serious study of barbarian affairs, a mature examination of the exigencies of the moment, and the important character of the question now before us, it seems quite necessary to adopt ; whether the difficulties are merely to be staved off in the mean time or finally settled.

' Your slave has not thought it necessary to submit these details separately to the appreciation of your Majesty, because they have no importance in themselves, and because time does not permit him to do so. Our disputes with the barbarians being now completely terminated, your slave has thrown together all these statements into one long despatch, which he respectfully presents to your Majesty.'

To return to our narrative :—acts of piracy in a small way, for some days back, have become more frequent on the river ; junks commit depredations on sampans ; sampans pillage tankas ; and tankas waylay small fishing craft. This process indicates that the Chinese new year is approaching. The same thing occurs regularly at the same season. It is the time when every one puts his affairs in order, makes up his books, collects his accounts, and pays his debts. A man who finds on striking his balance, at the end of the commercial year, that his debts exceed his assets, makes no scruple to put his hand into his neighbour's pocket to obtain the wherewithal to pay what he owes. According to Chinese notions, he does not cease to be an honest man by stealing from his neighbour, but he ceases to be such if he fail to pay his debts. At Hong Kong several watch-dogs were recently poisoned to facilitate these thefts, while eight houses were broken into in one night. Without exaggeration it may then be said that, at this period in the year, Chinese society is divided into two classes, the robbers and the robbed.

On the morning of the 13th February squibs and crackers, sing-songs, and boats decorated with flowers, gave us due notice that the Chinese new year had come, and that the amusements of the season had begun. These were to last for more than fifteen days. It was the first day of the first moon of the eighth year of Hien-Foung. It rained, the weather was shockingly bad; the land of flowers was a land of mists. It thundered in the morning, which, in the eyes of superstitious Chinamen, is a bad augury, and presages no good for the empire. The shops were almost all shut or decked with garlands of artificial flowers. Numerous chairs belonging to mandarins passed through the crowd, for this is a great day for official visits. Every good Chinaman, at this time of year, indulges in the pleasures of sam-chou, opium, sing-song, and squib-firing.

While these rejoicings were going forward in the Chinese city, we had, in the French encampment, to lament the death of a good seaman and excellent man, Commander Collier, who fell a victim to dysentery, after a three months' illness. This is a great loss for the navy in general, and a greater loss still for that part of it now on service here. The Admiral decided that the ' Marceau' should convey his remains to Hong Kong, in order that they should be buried in that town. At one o'clock we assembled at the landing-place. We saw the cortège arrive, and we accompanied the body in ship's boats as far as the ' Marceau.' The ' Avalanche' fired six guns: all the small craft, English and French, ranged round the ' Marceau,' shipped their oars; then the body was hoisted on board, and the whole assemblage departed. All day the French ships had their colours hoisted and the sails slung on the yards. When the body passed at

Barrier Fort, the 'Capricieuse' which was the sloop of war which he had commanded in the campaigns of Siam, Cochin China, and China, discharged a farewell salute of seven guns.

Another event, which might have terminated fatally, caused about this time no small emotion among the members of the embassy. Trévise, Maubourg, and Flavigny, accompanied by their servant, left one afternoon in two tankas from Barrier Fort, for American Reach, in order to pass the evening on board the 'Audacieuse.' They had not laid their account with the strong current which was running, and were overtaken by night setting in. Where the stream passes the great pagoda of Whampoa, they saw three large boats leaving the shore, and pulling hard towards them. The tanka boatwomen dropped their oars and roared murder; Maubourg, whose tanka went first, sprung from under the gunwale, and fired upon the boats as they came alongside; Trévise and Flavigny were a good way behind and could only see what was going on indistinctly. They also fired upon the pirates. The latter, who thought they had attacked persons who were unarmed or asleep, took to their oars again on meeting with this warm reception, not, however, until their party numbered three less than it did when they made the attack. There might be five or six in each boat, so that there could not be less than from fifteen to eighteen pirates. The following day an English officer, proceeding in broad daylight from his ship to the camp, happened to fall asleep in his tanka, and woke out of a comfortable nap just in time to anticipate some fellows who were preparing to tie his hands and pitch him into the river. In consequence of these occurrences, an order of the day was expressly promulgated among the officers of both nations, forbidding them in future to make use of Chinese boats.

The English gunboats brought this week to Canton two regiments of Sepoys, who have recently come from India. They have been barracked in the temple of Confucius, which has given a deal of dissatisfaction in the town. We have already alluded to the antipathy of the black-skinned Hindoos to the yellow-skinned subjects of the Son of Heaven; the Sepoys abhor the Chinese, and *vice versâ*. The feeling is embittered in Canton by certain recollections of the war of 1841, in which the Sepoys committed many thefts and cruelties, but it is universal wherever the two races come in contact, as at Penang and Singapore,—its general and real cause being the certain fate which awaits the Hindoos of being done out of house and home, and utterly ruined, by the greater acuteness, perseverance, and greed of the Chinese.

A great difference in the character of the two races also serves to account for their mutual antipathy. The grave and dignified Hindoos cannot endure the loquacity and obsequiousness of the Chinamen. These regiments had shown symptoms of a mutinous spirit in Hindostan, and as a precaution had been disarmed. It was an act of wisdom to send them to China, where they could do no harm, and where they might, on the contrary, in venting their own wrath, do infinite service to the allies. Their dress and appearance when on duty are superb, and their accoutrements are all that could be desired. The remainder of their time they spend basking in the sun under a white cotton sheet, stretching out their long and lank limbs into the sun. They belong to various castes, and, for this reason, each one prepares his own meal. If by accident any of us happen to touch their food, they throw it away, and break the dish polluted by contact with us.

Our military occupation now appearing to be perfectly consolidated in Canton, and the new government being recognised by the population of the town and suburbs, the blockade of the river was raised. The junks began again to move about on the river, and European steamers made their appearance off the city. The question of the factories was settled; they are to stand, as before, in the suburb, on the banks of the river, but a little more to the east, opposite Dutch Folly. In order firmly to establish the right of inhabiting the town of Canton, and to break down ancient prejudices, the ambassadors were anxious that the Europeans should take up their abode within the town, but the foreign merchants objected to this themselves, and insisted, as a *sine quâ non*, that they should not be shut up in the town, but should have their establishments on the banks of the river, as near as possible to their ships. It was, of course, necessary to yield to the commercial interest. Within the space allotted for the French factory a consulate and a church are to be built, with a sum which it is proposed to set aside, in the first instance, from the expenses of the war, which the Chinese are to be compelled to pay, by way of indemnity.

M. de Trenqualye has been named Consul of France at Canton, and was solemnly installed in office on the 17th of February, at Whampoa, where he will in the mean time take up his abode, as well as the other agents of the foreign powers. The disembarkation corps now came on board again. Besides the English, there were left at Canton five hundred French seamen, under the command of M. d'Aboville, who was replaced on board of the 'Audacieuse' by Commander Vrignaud. The 'Capricieuse,' the 'Marceau,' and the 'Catinat,' also remained before

Canton; all the other ships taking their course down the stream towards the sea. Important political events, however, occurred about this time. After a visit paid by Mr. Reed and Count Poutiatine to Baron Gros and Lord Elgin, the four plenipotentiaries agreed to address a collective note to the court of Pekin, requesting that there should be sent to Shang-hai, on the 31st of March at latest, Imperial commissioners, duly authorized to treat with the ambassadors of the Allied Powers regarding all the pending difficulties. In default of this request being acceded to, it was arranged that the ambassadors should proceed to the north and approach the capital with all their forces, in order to bring a stronger pressure to bear on the authorities at Pekin. In order to demonstrate to the Chinese government the glaring bad faith of the high commissioner Yeh, and to give it an opportunity of throwing upon his obstinacy the whole blame of the war, a copy of the correspondence between him and the plenipotentiaries was also transmitted to the capital. M. de Contades and Mr. Oliphant left immediately for Shang-hai, in the packet, as the bearers of these diplomatic documents to the tao-tai of that town. Duplicates were entrusted to Pih-Kwe, who undertook to get them transmitted overland to Pekin. The Chinese question had again entered a pacific phasis.

Baron Gros left the ' Primauguet,' and took up his quarters again, on the 20th February, on board the ' Audacieuse.' On returning on board we were grieved by a very sad piece of news. A frightful accident had happened during the day. A number of our shells, which had not exploded, had been picked up in the streets of Canton. The admiral had ordered them to be emptied that they might be made use of again. This is a very delicate operation, and must be conducted with great caution. The men had been supplied with copper tools, to ensure them as much as possible against accident. The work went on at Jardine's Point, within sight of the ship. A hundred shells had been cleared out by one o'clock in the afternoon ; when after dinner the crew went back singing to their work. All at once a frightful explosion was heard. On contact with the air merely, a shell had burst while one of the sailors had it between his legs. Of nine persons who were at work, all of whom were picked men, seven were severely wounded. The tent also took fire, and there was a risk that the other shells would explode. The commander, the chaplain, and the surgeon, M. Combe, proceeded immediately to the spot. The shells remaining were thrown into the water. The poor man who had the ball on his knees was literally torn to pieces. The person who had been sitting at work immediately opposite to him had lost his hands and feet, and had his face horribly disfigured. He expired before he could be conveyed on board. The five others were wounded and burned frightfully, and their hands and other parts of the person were lying in the mud. This accident had cost us more men than the capture of Canton. Two days have been appointed for. the funerals of these unfortunate sufferers. All the commanders of ships of war at anchor in American Reach have been invited to attend, with a few of the officers belonging to each, and a long procession of boats will pay a last tribute to these unfortunate men who perished so miserably in the performance of their duty.

The vessels began to move down the stream. We left the neighbourhood of Whampoa, and proceeded to Bocca Tigris, followed by the 'Phlégéton,' the 'Nemesis,' and the 'Meurthe.' We crossed the two bars without accident, thanks to the Chinese boats placed as buoys the evening before to point out the passes. This time we crossed the Bogue alone; overnight the 'Audacieuse' cast anchor in the road of Hong Kong.

On board the 'Audacieuse,' March 12, 1858.

Our short stay at Hong Kong is over. We have exchanged the splendours of the club-house for our little cabins on board ship. We have had a good

deal of rain, wind, and a high sea, for some days, the
equinoctial gales blowing at present. Baron Gros
has, however, given intimation that we are to start for
the North,—the three other plenipotentiaries having
already left the Canton river a week ago. Our
delay is of little importance, as Mr. Reed has to go
in the first instance to Manilla, and Lord Elgin has
to call at the intermediate ports of Amoy, Ningpo,
and Fou-tchou-fou, whilst we are to proceed directly
to Shang-hai. We towed after us the ' Fusée' gunboat, which had been placed at the disposal of the
ambassador. We left in the hope that the differences
between China and the Western Powers would now
be terminated without farther difficulty, and in a
pacific manner. Recent facts all went to prove that
the court of Pekin was assuming a more conciliatory and peaceful attitude. The first of these was
the formal degradation of Yeh, and the continuance
of Pih-Kwe in his office until the arrival of the new
governor Houang-tzung-han ; then there was the ap-
pointment and despatch of old Ky-Ing, who had been
long disgraced, as plenipotentiary to Shang-hai, or at
least the rumour that he had been appointed among
the Chinese population ; and, lastly, there was the
favourable reception which M. de Contades and Mr.
Oliphant had met with among the great mandarins
of Sou-tchou-fou.

M

Here are the two Imperial edicts, brought in twenty - nine days to Canton by a courier from Pekin.

FIRST IMPERIAL EDICT.

‘ The despatch annexed, which has been addressed to us by Muh-Kih-Tih-Na and Pih-Kwe, informs us of the capture of the provincial city of Canton by the barbarians.

‘ Yeh-Ming-Ching, as Imperial Commissioner intrusted with the management of foreign affairs, evidently should have found some means of eluding the demands of the barbarians, if they were so unreasonable that he could not comply with them ; he should at the same time have arranged with the Tartar general, the governor, and the other officers, to take those steps necessary for the preservation of peace.

‘ The barbarians have twice transmitted communications to the Tartar general, to the governor-general, and the lieutenant-general. Yeh has not informed his colleagues of the contents of these communications. He refused to come to an explanation with them about the matters in dispute, and postponed their solution from day to day ; and the result has been that he exasperated the barbarians, till at last they made a sudden attack upon the provincial city and took possession of it.

' By this stubbornness and bad administration Yeh has shown himself to be altogether unworthy of the high functions with which he was entrusted, consequently we ordain that he shall be immediately deprived of his office.

' Muh-Kih-Tih-Na, the Tartar general; Pih-Kwe, the governor; the lieutenants-generals Shwang-Hi and Shwang-Ling; Hang-Ke, the commissioner of customs; Kiang-Kwo-Lin, the commissioner of finance; and Chow-Ya-Ping, the provincial judge, are all culpable of negligence and want of spirit in defending the town. However, as the governor-general had not admitted them to his councils, there is some excuse for them. Taking then into consideration their request to be severely punished, we have seen fit to show them indulgence, and to instruct the Office of Punishments to pass lightly over their offences. Respect this!'

SECOND IMPERIAL EDICT.

' We appoint Houang-Tsing-Han to be governor-general of the two Kwangs, and order him to proceed forthwith to his post. We have conferred upon him the seal of the Imperial Commission and the management of the foreign affairs of the empire.

' While awaiting his arrival, Pih-Kwe will be provisionally entrusted with the functions of Imperial

Commissioner and governor-general of the two Kwangs. Respect this!'

In the official part of the 'Pekin Gazette' it is stated, moreover, that the Emperor Hien-Foung is so much enraged against Yeh, that he has given orders to get new seals prepared for the governor of the two Kwangs, this being the greatest indignity which can be put upon any functionary.

Commissioner Yeh had been, up till now, the person third in importance in China. He added the title of guardian of the heir presumptive to the throne, to those of governor-general of the two Kwangs and Imperial commissioner entrusted with the management of the foreign affairs of the empire. His iron yoke weighed upon forty-six millions of Chinese (twenty-five millions of whom were in Kwang Toung and twenty-one in Kwang-Si); and it was with no small pride that he owned he had in the course of his administration caused to be beheaded no less than seventy thousand persons. Now in disgrace with his sovereign, deprived of his honours, and a prisoner of these same barbarians whom he had so cordially hated, he is under weigh for Calcutta, on board an English ship.

There is a report, which is something more than a mere passing rumour, in circulation among the Chinese at Hong Kong, which is very significant if true. It is, as we have already said, to the effect that Ky-Ing has been nominated plenipotentiary to Shang-hai. We know that this personage, who was governor of Canton at the time of the war on the opium question and the mission of M. de Lagrené, signed the treaties then concluded by the emperor Tao-Kouang with England, France, and the United States, and, after having occupied the highest position of imperial favour, was all at once thrown into disgrace, when the governing class and people of China lapsed once more into the old policy of opposition to the Western Powers. Since then he had acted as a mere clerk in an office at Pekin, being reduced to this humble position for having been guilty of the crime of allowing the barbarians to enter the Celestial Empire. His name, however, had served for the last fifteen years as a watchword to the party who, without having any liking for the Europeans (and who in China entertains any such feeling?), think that intercourse with them should be encouraged. Commissioner Lin, on the contrary, and his partisans, would hear of nothing but war to the knife, and the total extermination of the barbarians. Lin and Ky-Ing are, then, the chiefs of the two great parties. China must surely be sadly deficient in statesmen, for the same persons are constantly making their appearance in all negociations with the Western Powers.   We may be excused, since the discovery of the curious document found in the archives of Yeh, if we place a very limited confidence in the good faith even of Ky-Ing himself.

What serves, however, to confirm us more in our hopes of a pacific settlement is the successful result of the mission entrusted to M. de Contades, and the officious and friendly reception given him by the fou-tai of Sou-tchou-fou, in which it was easy to detect the influence of fear.   The reader may recollect that this gentleman had been entrusted, along with Mr. Oliphant and two Russian and American officers, to convey to the governor of Shang-hai the communications of the four plenipotentiaries to the prime minister Yeh, with the request that they should be transmitted with the least possible delay to Pekin. These communications related to the immediate despatch of the Chinese plenipotentiaries to Shang-hai.   M. de Contades and his colleagues, not finding the governor of Shang-hai at home, determined to take their despatches to the chief town of the province, and put them into the hands of the governor himself.   This was a courageous act. Nothing of the kind had ever been ventured on previously, China having hitherto been jealously closed against the barbarians.   The little squadron, consisting of eighteen junks, set out from Shang-hai on the 24th February, and in three days proceeded by the rivers and lakes to Sou-tchou-fou, a city alike celebrated, according to Chinese writers, for its places of amusement, wealth, and elegance. There was one boat set apart to carry the provisions, another served as a saloon, a third as a dining-room.   Each evening the party assembled to dinner at the sound of the gong; and the whole twenty-eight junks anchored close by each other as a precaution against pirates. A careful watch was kept up during the night.

M. de Montigny, the French consul at Shang-hai, whose experience in China and with Chinese officials was very great, undertook to answer for the success of the enterprise.   On the 26th the party arrived, without any accident, under the walls of Sou-tchou-fou, and they entered the town by one of the water-gates of the rampart opening upon the canal, and without any other difficulty than a few hot words with the boatmen and the men who kept watch over vessels entering the canal.

'The news of our arrival,' says M. de Contades, in his report of this expedition, 'had rapidly spread in the city, and it was through the midst of an enormous crowd, drawn up on both sides of the canal, that we made our entrance into Sou-tchou-fou. From all this multitude there did not proceed one cry, there was none of that noise which is customary among the Chinese. There was the deepest silence, as if the people made an effort not to stir, which with them is the sign of respect and fear. Such was the stillness that we could catch the sound of a few timid whispers. It was easy to perceive, in every upturned face of the dense crowd which pressed and was packed as close as it could stand around us, the expression of feelings anything but hostile to us; but more easy still to read astonishment and stupefaction in every countenance.

' A salute of six cannons was fired on our arrival at the yamoun, at the door of which the fou-tai received us surrounded by his officers. When we had gone into the court-room, where we were received by the governor with graceful courtesy, we were placed on two chairs on the estrade at the bottom of the audience-hall, so that the governor, seated in one of the arm-chairs at the side, was able, in compliance with Chinese etiquette, to have both of us on his left. The consuls and their interpreters had seats ranged along the sides. After the customary compliments were over, I spoke a few words to the fou-tai, which the interpreter to the French consulate interpreted as I proceeded. I said that I was about to have the honour of placing officially in his hands a despatch which was directed to him, as well as to his Excellency the Governor of the two Kwangs, by the High

Commissioner of His Majesty the Emperor of the French ; that this despatch contained another to His Excellency the principal Secretary-of-State at Pekin, which was of great importance, and which I begged the fou-tai to transmit by the most rapid means of conveyance, and to see that it reached its destination without the occurrence of any delay whereby he might incur responsibility.

' The governor replied that he would willingly undertake the commission ; whereupon I handed him the despatches. The fou-tai then opened the outer envelope, which bore his address, and read what it contained, while all the officers and secretaries, stooping behind him, perused it over his shoulder. It is asserted that there were present high dignitaries and emissaries of the governor of the two Kiangs among these personages.

' Mr. Oliphant then said a few words to the same purport with mine, after which the fou-tai offered us a slight repast, during which a rather animated conversation sprung up between us. The governor asked me if order had been restored at Canton, and if trade was now going on again as usual. I replied that the ambassadors had done all that lay in their power to attain this end, and that they were glad to think they had been successful. " What are you going to do with Yeh?" then inquired the fou-tai. A gentleman present replied that he had left for Calcutta. "Will you put him to death?" asked Tchao, with some indifference. I replied that his Excellency was ill-informed respecting the generosity of the ambassadors and their governments if he supposed them capable of inflicting such a punishment on a conquered enemy. He then asked us when the ambassadors were coming to Shang-hai. Without stating any definite time, we thought it best to reply that they would be there shortly. During the whole of this interview the fou-tai conducted himself with a politeness and well-bred reserve which delighted us. His physiognomy, which is almost European as far as features go, is delicate and intelligent. His manners are those of a man accustomed to the best society. In short, it was impossible to receive a more polite or more friendly reception than that he gave us.

'The fou-tai reconducted us to our chairs with the ceremonial observed on our arrival, and after many compliments and much shaking of hands he told us that on the following morning he would return our visit to the communal palace, called Kon-Kouan, situated without the town, where the highest Chinese authorities are habitually received on their arrival at Sou-tchou-fou. It was in this yamoun that we, in fact, received, on the 27th of February at midday, the visit of the fou-tai.'

Thursday, March 18.

I must | now return to my own narrative. We intended to have proceeded directly to Shang-hai, but we had not taken into account the gusty weather we were destined to encounter. Three times already we were obliged to stop after leaving. On one occasion the mist prevented us from distinguishing the coast and breakers. On another, the 'Fusée' shipped a heavy sea, and, while labouring hard, snapped her moorings. On a third occasion we were retarded by an English steamer, which fired a couple of guns just as we passed her. Thinking she had run aground, and taking this cannon for a signal of distress, we altered our course to come to her assistance. It turned out to be an opium smuggler, which had fired the guns as a signal for the junks engaged in the same contraband trade to come off to her. In spite of our six hundred horse power we could no longer make way against wind and current; we therefore sought an anchorage to leeward of the Ree islands, where we determined to await a change of weather. M. de Carpégna, commander of the 'Fusée,' was making an attempt to come on board the 'Audacieuse.' He missed his hold of us, and was

drifted by the current about three miles to seaward. We immediately lowered a whaling-boat
with all the rope we had on board. It could give
no assistance, however, and was drawn by the men
on board of her by the rope back to the ship.
Happily the current ceased to run so hard, and M. de
Carpégna got on shore. A small boat with sixteen
men was lowered to tow him out and take provisions
to him. It reached him, but the wind was so strong
that it was found impossible to pull against it and
draw along the vessel at the same time. We sent
another ship's boat to see what could be done, with
arms, clothes, water, and food. It was equally un-
successful in its attempt to make way against the
terrible current which was running. The three small
vessels then sought refuge in a little creek, which
prevented us from seeing them any longer even with
our spy-glasses. The evening, night, and morning
passed without a sign from them. The commander,
fearing that something had happened, discharged
one shot, then a second, and a third, as a signal to
them to make an attempt to get back, the current
being favourable and the wind lower. All eyes were
fixed in the direction in which they were expected,
but no sail made its appearance for a long while.
At last, however, they emerged from behind the
rock, breasting the broad-crested waves as they made

towards us. An hour afterwards our thirty men came on board, benumbed, famishing with hunger, wet to the skin, but very well content to have escaped the danger they had been in. They told us what had befallen them. They found three hundred Chinamen collected upon the coast, armed with bows, arrows, lances, and matchlocks. They were obliged to cast anchor, their boats all the while shipping water, plunging under the waves, threatening to capsize, dragging their anchors, and kept from getting among the breakers only by hard work at the oars. They had attempted to come out of the creek to sea again, but the violence of the squall had forced them to get back as quickly as possible.

Our signal let them know that they should again attempt to pull out to sea, and had rescued them from their frightful position. It was in the midst of exciting incidents such as these that our time passed. It was bitterly cold and wet; a hurricane swept fiercely down upon us, straining our anchors, making every timber creak, and pitching us about unmercifully under the darkness of closed portholes. Pleasant truly is it to navigate the China seas during the wrong monsoon!

March 23.

Our coal having nearly run down, and the wind having fallen a little, we made for Amoy, the best sheltered spot in the Straits of Formosa. This bay, surrounded by bare mountains, is completely closed against the open sea, and the largest ships can anchor in it close upon the land. The town is dirty and irregularly built, its crooked streets being narrower than even those of Canton. Neither sunshine nor fresh air can enter them, and accordingly small-pox and fever break out every year with great virulence. However, it was very pleasant to walk about among the shops decked out with Chinese lanterns, and the sing-songs, which we have already described. The latter were very interesting. Large junks, crowded with people, were employed as omnibuses between the two sides of the roadstead.

The scene around us has, however, an impress of its own. We are now in the capital of Fo-Kien, a mountainous and maritime province, which differs in many of its most important characteristics from the rest of China. The Fo-Kinese have all over the empire a great reputation for boldness, independence, and pride, and the court of Pekin always treats them with deference and attention as a community who should not be irritated. They wear roomy garments and head-dresses in the form of a turban, which gives them something of the look of Turks. They have a more masculine, and at the same time a handsomer appearance than the Cantonese.

To look at them one would say they belonged to a different race. The dialect of Fo-Kien, too, which is very different from the mandarin language and the idiom of the Canton river, is altogether unintelligible to the inhabitants of the other provinces of China. M. Marquès, our interpreter, could neither understand nor make himself understood by the Fo-Kinese pilot who came on board; he was obliged to write out what he wanted to say on paper, the written Chinese language being the same all over the empire. This circumstance of a different dialect in Fo-Kien is often turned to account by our young missionaries when they have pushed far into the interior of China. When they have exhausted their little stock of Chinese, and run the risk of being discovered to be foreigners by their ignorance of the language, they pass themselves off as inhabitants of Fo-Kien, in this way accounting for their bad pronunciation.

At Shang-hai, at Canton, everywhere else in China, the only European language spoken by the natives is English. But at Amoy, Spanish is to some extent understood among the inhabitants. There is frequent intercourse between the Philippine Islands and this port; and the greater number of the Chinese emigrants who are now settled in Cuba are natives of the coast of Fo-Kien. The European colony is composed of about sixty persons, nearly all of whom are

English. There is not one Frenchman among them; and there are few Americans. Each merchant has a room set apart in his house as an armoury; and small cannons placed at his door, to be used in time of danger. They live on very good terms with the inhabitants of the country, and are permitted, without annoyance, to leave the town and visit the environs. Amoy is the only place in China where the English ladies visit the Chinese ladies, and receive calls from them in return.

We loaded some Formosa coal to complete our stores. It is said to be better than that of Borneo, which we tried at Singapore. But it certainly had one great fault; it threw off so many sparks that the commander was afraid for some time that it would set the ship on fire. We found, on leaving Amoy, that the fine weather had returned ; and we passed in safety through the Straits of Formosa, or Fo-Kien Channel. At the Saddle Islands we left the 'Audacieuse,' and went on board the 'Fusée.' Our luggage covered the deck. We passed through the midst of numerous islands, which we could scarcely see through a dense fog. A Chinese pilot directed our course to the mouth the Yang-tse-Kiang, occasionally known in Europe as the Blue River, which is the greatest stream on the surface of the globe, after the Amazon. It is the great artery towards which the Chinese rivers flow, and, indeed, the chief thoroughfare of central China. The entrance to this stream is difficult, more especially for ships without steam. There are numerous sand-banks at its mouth; and the shores are so low that no good chart can be made, as land-marks are almost wanting on both sides. Fortunately for the inhabitants, however, the Blue River is not subject to inundations, like the neighbouring Yellow River, which is constantly bursting its dikes and sweeping all before it.

At Woo-sung we left the Yang-tse-Kiang, and entered the Whampou, the river of Shang-hai. The bed of the river was encumbered with a great fleet of junks, laden with provisions and rice, which were awaiting a favourable wind to proceed to the north, as far as Tien-tsin. We had considerable difficulty in threading our way through the crowd of large junks lying at anchor in the still waters of the river, or floating gently down stream. In spite of all the care we took, we ran against one, smashing its helm and masts. At last we got clear of this labyrinth; and after receiving a salute from the English, American, and Russian ships, we cast anchor alongside of the quay at Shang-hai.

N

CHAPTER VII.

Shang-hai : the European Town, the Chinese Town.—The Tea-
garden.—M. de Montigny and the French Concession.—The
Dinner given by the Tao-tai.—The Tigers of the Tartar Colonel.
—The Chinese Campaign.—The Mission of Kiang-nan.—The
College of Zi-ka-wei.—The Cathedral of Tong-ka-tou.—The
Sainte Enfance in Kiang-nan.— Commercial activity of Shang-hai.
—Reply of the Court of Pekin to the Joint Note of the Ambassa-
dors.

WE had scarcely cast anchor when we received a
visit from Contades, whom we had not seen since his
expedition to Sou-tchou-fou ; and a visit also from M.
Montigny, accompanied by the gentlemen belonging to the French consulate.   M. de Montigny asked
the ambassador to take up his quarters at his house·
The members of the embassy put up at the Commercial Hotel, which is kept by M. Barraud, the old
steward of the ' Constantine.' We crossed the French
grant, which, although less built upon than the others,
is the best situated of the three.   It was startling to
meet, in a distant country like this, with policemen
carrying the *bâton tricolore* ; and to read the names of

the streets in French at the corners.   The junks are drawn up together opposite to the Chinese town. More than one hundred merchantmen are at anchor before the European quarter, where an imposing line of fine houses runs along the bend of the river.   We were struck with the custom-house, which is a choice bit of Chinese architecture.   It was amusing to watch the perfect regularity with which the thousands of Coolies employed on the quays carried the bales of tea and silk on board.   All over the harbour our ears rung with their sharp, sing-song cry, which is given out by one, and taken up and repeated by the others. This noise, of course, stops at night ; but it begins again next morning by daybreak.   We dined with M. de Montigny, who introduced us to his family. His conversation abounded with most interesting information regarding China, where he has been settled for fifteen years.   Shang-hai holds no higher rank than a town of the third order in the province of Kiang-nan.   It holds a very unimportant place in the hierarchy of the Chinese towns, and owes its recent importance entirely to the opening of its port to foreign commerce.   The inhabitants of Kiang-nan are gentle, and well-disposed in their dealings with foreigners.   At Canton, Europeans dare not pass the walls without running the risk of being murdered ; but it is not so at Shang-hai, where the

merchants are in perfect safety within a radius of
several miles all round the town. They are great
sportsmen—hares, snipes, and pheasants being plenti-
ful in this part of the country. During the warmest
days in summer it is the custom to go 'to the hills,'
which are situated about thirty miles from Shang-hai,
where the air is more bracing and the country is
sheltered by trees. Each family has its junk, and
lives on the river. Great lakes spread out beyond
this place. It is here that the cormorant is employed
in fishing. The sight is a strange one for a European. Each fisherman has several of these birds in
his boat; they dive under water to catch their
prey: but a ring is put round their necks, which
prevents them from swallowing the fish so caught.
Finding that they can do no better, they bring their
spoil to the fishermen. The soil round Shang-hai
is extremely fertile; two or three crops are reaped
every year on the same surface. But for all this,
the country is very monotonous. On all sides extends
to the horizon a vast expanse of rice and cotton
fields, without one clump of trees to rest the eyes
upon. Small canals, tributaries of the river, cross
the country in all directions, by means of which the
rice, straw, and cotton are gathered and housed.
Over the whole of this part of China, that is to say,
over a great part of the empire, there are no cross-

roads. Everything is moved from place to place in vessels and along canals. Buffaloes are the only animals employed in agriculture, and in working the plough in the rice-fields. In the towns open to Europeans, the natives employ the female buffalo in lieu of the common milch cow, of which there are none. The Chinese do not drink milk; they say that it is white blood, and the only use they make of it is as a cure for dysentery. They never put it in tea, which they take without either cream or sugar. The people of these great plains, which form the most populous and most important part of the empire, are peaceful in their character, and entirely devoted to agriculture and commerce. Among them the inhabitants of Canton are noted for their arrogant and quarrelsome disposition. Throughout all the north they have a bad reputation; and whenever a murder or a theft is committed, it is almost invariably discovered that the perpetrator is from Canton. While we were staying at Shang-hai, an English brig, manned by Chinamen, going to Bankok with a large sum in ingots on board, to make purchases at that place, was robbed and found deserted at the entrance of the Yang-tse-Kiang. The seamen belonged to Canton, and had concerted to murder the captain and his two mates. After doing so, they took possession of the ingots, and let the vessel go adrift.

Coming as we did from the Canton river, we observed the great difference between the populations of the north and south, which was all to the advantage of the north.

At Hong Kong, and at Macao, Europeans live in China without ever seeing a Chinese dignitary. At Shang-hai, on the contrary, the consuls have frequent intercourse with the mandarins. Every now and then you hear the sound of a gong in the European town; this is a functionary proceeding with a numerous escort to see a consul or an admiral. The governor and other authorities of Shang-hai, having expressed a wish to visit the ambassador, the rendezvous was fixed at one o'clock. As soon as we saw these distinguished persons coming, we put our hats on as a mark of respect, and went forward to the flight of steps at the door to receive them. There was a great deal of compliment and a tremendous shaking of hands, and then each one sat down according to his rank. Baron Gros insisted on the tao-tai, or governor, taking his seat on the left side of the sofa, which, according to Chinese etiquette, is the place of honour. Tea was brought, the mandarins took a few puffs of their pipes, and conversation began. The subjects were the lofty stature of Baron Gros, the shape of his ear, which boded good luck and prosperity, the superiority of European weapons

to Chinese weapons, and the wonderful distance
which separates Europe and China.   The party
afterwards walked in ceremonious order into the
dining-room, where luncheon had been spread.   The
ambassador placed at his left the tao-tai, and the
Tartar colonel at his right.   M. de Bellecourt placed
the two other mandarins near him.   Each person
heaped sugar-plums, cakes, and almond-biscuits into
his neighbour's plate.   We drank champagne, drain-
ing our glasses and interchanging enthusiastically
good wishes for health and prosperity.   The conversation maundered on much in the same foolish and
insignificant way as before.   Coffee was brought, and
tea of course—indispensable tea—and then our guests
rose, which was the signal for departure.   Before
going, however, the Tartar colonel, with the tact of
true courtesy, proposed to Baron Gros to put his
tigers through their drill or manœuvres, his tigers
being the soldiers who accompanied him, and who
are picked men from the Imperial army.   The proposal was enthusiastically received on both sides.
Each warrior, thereupon, insinuated himself into a
yellow coat, on which were represented the black
stroke which runs down a tiger's back, as well as the
eyes and the ears of the brute after which they are
named.   Then commenced the drill.   For the best
part of an hour they kept flinging themselves into

the most fantastic positions. They kept jumping and stamping, and calling to each other to come on, threatening every moment to plunge into a deadly struggle, which never came however, and in this way they spent an amount of breath and muscular activity which perfectly bewildered us. The military mandarin, seeing that the desired effect had been produced, ordered his tigers to withdraw and return to their places in his suite, and we then took leave of our visitors, promising shortly to go and see them at their yamouns.

In point of fact, a few days afterwards we accepted of an invitation to dinner from the tao-tai, and we proceeded in chairs to his house, which is situated in the heart of the Chinese town. We were welcomed with a salute of three guns, the governor, surrounded by his functionaries and subalterns, receiving us at the entrance to the court-room. He treated us to a very choice and delicate dinner, at least so said the consul and chancellor, who were of course better judges than any of our party on such a point. To us it seemed altogether frightful. There were swallows' nests, sharks' fins, sea-worms, lapwings' eggs, lukewarm Chinese wine, and rice-brandy. It is the custom to eat fruit towards the middle of the meal, and to wind up with soup. The want of water and bread also makes a difference, and perhaps helped to mar our full appreciation of that infinite variety of fish and fowl thrust upon us with such hospitality. The tao-tai is excellent company, and he did the honours of his yamoun to perfection.

The climate of Shang-hai, like that of the whole of China, is unwholesome. It is subject to miasma, arising from the marshes, and to very sudden changes of temperature. During the south-west monsoon the heat is excessive. During the north-east monsoon, on the contrary, it is as cold as it is in winter in the north of France, and the river frequently freezes in spite of the rapidity of its course. From the 1st November to the 1st April the Europeans put on fires in their houses. I do not speak of the Chinese with regard to their custom in this respect, for they do not use fires for mere purposes of comfort. When the cold increases they put on dresses with thicker wadding and more fur. There has been no frost this year, and the foreign residents at Shang-hai have freighted a ship to bring ice from Kamtschatka.

In spite of the confusion and crowded state of the streets, we go occasionally for a saunter into the Chinese town. We dropped into the shops and purchased a few of those trifles, infinite in variety, which in all parts of the Celestial Empire are exhibited to attract the attention of foreigners. We walked all round the battlements of the city wall.

We visited the well into which the young children are thrown who are doomed to perish under the unnatural custom of infanticide. More than once we stepped into the tea-gardens, whither the Chinese repair to drink tea, to smoke opium, and to hear musical performances. There they enjoy their favourite amusements; and it is in these places that we may observe what is most peculiar in the appearance and habits of the people. An artificial mountain with rocks heaped one above the other, a small river with little bridges in zigzag, upturned eaves, and flags flying from them, form the principal ornaments of this garden, in which the fortune-tellers, jugglers, and dramatic performers have their head-quarters. However, the Chinese do not bestow much of their time on amusement; they are completely absorbed in business, and at Shang-hai their commercial activity is still farther promoted by the presence of foreigners. The Chinese merchants of Shang-hai are generally brokers or middlemen between the great European and American houses and the provinces of the interior. They travel into the agricultural and manufacturing districts to make their purchases of tea and silk.

I must quote here a few figures to give an idea of the immense business done at Shang-hai. They are taken from an official source, viz. the Custom-house reports; and they exhibit the extraordinary increase in the commerce of this place, which was only opened to foreign vessels about fifteen years ago.

During the year from June 1855 to June 1856, the total importation amounted in value to 8,325,772*l.*, which may be divided between the following heads, viz. :—

	£.
Piastres or silver ingots . . .	2,298,817
Opium	3,889,907
Miscellaneous articles of merchandise .	2,137,048
The value of the exports was . .	7,711,458

The total value, then, of the exports and imports was—16,037,230*l.*

From June 1856 to June 1857, the exports amounted to 10,857,554*l.*, divided as follows :—

	£.
Piastres or silver ingots . . .	2,435,204
Opium	4,390,691
Miscellaneous articles of merchandise .	4,031,659
The exports amounted to . .	11,467,456

The total value of exports and imports was—22,325,010*l.*

If it had not been for the great Anglo-American commercial crisis of last year, the commercial activity of Shang-hai would have reached a height still more remarkable, as we may see from the following figures :—

From the 1st July 1857, to the 31st December

1857, that is to say, during the first half of the year 1857–58, the imports amounted to 8,768,642*l.*, which may be divided as follows, viz. :—

	£.
Piastres	2,789,692
Tchin or copper money . . .	342,784
Opium	2,872,084
General merchandise	2,764,082
The exportation amounted to . .	7,277,625

The total value of exports and imports was —16,046,267*l.*

The amount of business, it appears, then has doubled in less than two years, and there are now few commercial towns in the world, not to speak of China, which can vie in importance with Shang-hai. Canton has now sunk to the third rank, Fou-tchou-fou is ahead of it as a tea exporting town ; but as regards Amoy and Ning-po, these two ports are quite ruined by their proximity to this city. During our stay at Shang-hai we counted as many as one hundred and seven merchantmen lying at anchor at one time in the waters of the Whampou, and there was scarcely room for a ship's boat over the whole length of the beach fronting the European territory, from the entrance of the Chinese town to the extremity of the American factory. The surface of the grant is sold by the square yard, like building ground in the business or fashionable quarters of a European city. A small house, with the accommodation barely necessary for one family, and a bit of garden ground, has been known to fetch the enormous rent of 400*l.* a year.

From the 1st of July 1855, to the 1st of January 1858, there was brought to China, not again to leave it, by Shang-hai alone, 7,521,193*l.*, in piastres and ingots of silver, and this process is going on increasing : each year the amount advances in more rapid progression. The first year the importation amounted to 2,280,000*l.*, the next to 2,400,000*l*, and the third to 2,760,000*l.* There is in all this a subject for the serious study of European economists. It is long since silver set in this way from the West to Asia, but it is only in recent times that the phenomenon has assumed gigantic proportions, of which the effects are felt even in the most distant villages of France.

One of the most pleasant rides one can take in the neighbourhood of Shang-hai is to the College of Zi-ka-wei, situate about five miles from the town. This college is under the direction of the Jesuits. Is it not a remarkable proof of the peaceful disposition of the inhabitants that such an establishment as this can exist in the midst of the country far from all European protection? In approaching it we saw the gilded vane of a church steeple glittering in the sun, and instead of the sound of gongs, to which our ears had become accustomed, we heard the ringing of church bells. The College of Zi-ka-wei has been in existence only for seven years, and it already numbers a hundred pupils. It is placed under the care of Père Zottoli, the principal, and under the distinguished surveillance of Père Lemaître, the superior of the mission. There are nine Chinese professors, who undertake literary instruction only, for without literature nothing can be done in the Middle Empire, and the missionaries have it in view to turn out pupils who shall become, in China, the leading men of villages, respectable merchants, and influential citizens. They are educated not with a view to Europe, but to China. There is only one hour of recreation a day, and thirteen hours of work. This is quite in keeping with Chinese custom, a whole life barely sufficing to acquire a knowledge of the language and literature of the country. At the Chinese new year the pupils have a fortnight of vacation, and holidays for a month in August. They study French for half an hour every week, this lesson being considered as a reward. We saw the different classes at work, the schoolrooms, sleeping apartments, and refectories, and were delighted with the order and excellent condition in which everything is kept. The little Chinamen are not allowed at first to write upon the walls and tables; it is not till they advance in their studies that they are allowed to make use of the brush or pencil,

and then slowly they cover every bench and seat
with a coating of varnish, which makes them
quite resplendent. The children of Kiang-nan
succeed in everything they attempt. They are sin-
gularly apt pupils. In spite of the short time
devoted to the accessory studies, such as singing,
drawing, and music, and in spite of the limited
resources at their disposal for obtaining instruction,
they attain to wonderful proficiency. Mandarins
have visited the college frequently, and have asked
permission to examine the pupils. They appear to
have been very well satisfied with the answers they
received. A blue-button mandarin even took with
him a few of the compositions of some of the farthest
advanced pupils, and sent them to Pekin to a mem-
ber of the Imperial Academy, who sent them back
with corrections and very encouraging remarks. The
College of Zi-ka-wei, as an example of what can be
effected by the Chinese race when influenced by
Christian precept and directed by Europeans, should
attract the deepest interest.

The mission of Kiang-nan, or diocese of Nankin, is
one of the most flourishing in China. It numbers
forty missionaries and nearly forty thousand Christians, fifteen thousand more than there were at the
time of M. de Legrené's mission. In 1857 the
seminary of Tong-Ka-tou contained twenty-eight

young Chinese who were studying theology. There were three hundred and sixty-four schools in full operation, and five thousand children were educated in them by Christian teachers. The girls had separate schools; eighty-nine female teachers gave instruction to twelve hundred and sixty young women, some of whom were preparing to become teachers themselves.

The Sainte-Enfance has been established for some time back in the neighbourhood of Shang-hai, and has already met with remarkable success, thanks to funds supplied from France. Four thousand seven hundred and sixty-seven children were saved from infanticide in 1857. There remained two thousand of these adopted in 1856. They are put out in the country into Christian families, who undertake to bring them up for a very small allowance, and who afterwards send them to school with their own children.

On the 1st of January 1858 there were in the Orphan Hospitals and in the houses of the Christians together nearly three thousand of these unfortunate little creatures, all of whom were expected to live. At the Orphan Hospital of Tsa-ka-wei, situated in the environs of Shang-hai, there were 190 boys, who were taught the various trades of tailors, shoemakers, stonecutters, printers, carpenters, and labourers. There were, besides, two hospitals for the little girls, where they were taught sewing, spinning, and embroidery. The blessed work of the Sainte-Enfance, it appears then, has been attended with the greatest success in this part of China, and even begins to extend a beneficent action over a vast area.

Can a Christian become a mandarin? This is the question which is suggested on seeing the efforts made by the missionaries to educate the Chinese youth. In principle there is nothing to stand in the way, but it is a very difficult matter in practice. For instance, a Christian could not conscientiously transmit a valuable present with his composition to the examiner. In the next place, there are certain pagan superstitions connected with the Emperor which he could not consent to recognise as consistent with his convictions. There is, however, in the Imperial camp before Nankin, a military mandarin who openly professes Christianity. After a good deal of recrimination, he has been allowed to pray for the Emperor at church instead of the ancestral temple. But I do not believe that it is possible to mention another case.

The cathedral of Tong-ka-tou, where the Roman Catholic service is conducted by Jesuit priests, stands in the middle of the Chinese town, between the wall and the river. We went there on Easter Day to hear the music at high mass, and found the service

o

as solemn and impressive as anywhere in Europe; there is, of course a difference. The organ, is of bamboo, the sermon is in Chinese, the young choristers have tails and upturned shoes, and the officiating clergymen wear a hat borrowed from the ancient dynasties, it being indispensable to remain covered while showing reverence or respect in China.

The Lazarists have, for some years back, removed their procure from Macao to Shang-hai. Their establishment covers a large space within the French grant. Their mission extends over the neighbouring provinces of Tche-kiang, Honan, Kiang-si, and Tcheli. Pekin lies within their jurisdiction. They are besides entrusted with the charge of all missionary undertakings in Mongolia. The great wall presents a serious difficulty to missionaries proceeding into this region of Central Asia from the Chinese coast, or returning from it. The gates are watched, and persons entering or leaving the empire are carefully searched. In the capital, where the police is too active to permit of European missionaries remaining undetected, there are only native priests. If Europeans were to intrude they would soon be brought under the notice of the mandarins. Monseigneur Mouly, the Vicar Apostolic of Tcheli, has fixed his abode at a place some miles from Pekin. Monseigneur Daguin, the Bishop of Mongolia, lives a

hundred miles away from the great wall. The Lazarists have founded a college or seminary at Ning-
po, and the Sisters of Charity have an establishment
there for the education of young women. Thus has
been realized the wish of Saint Vincent de Paul, who
foresaw that his order would one day extend as far as
China. In the distant regions of the far East the
Lazarists exhibit that self-denial, that spirit of self-
sacrifice and humility inculcated by their founder, of
which they have long given proof in the old towns
of the Levant and Asia Minor, more especially entrusted to their care.

In consequence of proximity to Hong Kong, France
plays a very subordinate part on the Canton river.
It is otherwise at Shang-hai; there, thanks to the
energy and activity of the French consul, ably
assisted by M. Edan, the chancellor, and by M.
Lemaire, the interpreter to the consulate, we are
quite able to maintain a position of perfect equality
with England and the United States. The number
of our vessels no doubt cannot be compared to that
of those two great maritime powers, but the French
flag floats over an equal extent of ceded territory, and
the French nation has an equal importance in the
estimation of the Chinese authorities. This important result is due to M. de Montigny. This gentleman
understands China and Chinese affairs better than

any one with whom we have ever come in contact.
He knows exactly what may be ventured, and he
makes the venture accordingly. If a missionary is
persecuted in the interior of Kiang-nan, he orders
his junk or his sedan-chair, and travels night and
day until he descends upon the double-dealing
magistrate. Sometimes by sheer force of argument,
sometimes by intimidation, he obtains satisfaction for
what has been done, and extorts a promise from the
authorities not to give annoyance in future to the
Christians of the district. He goes every year by
land from Shang-hai to Ningpo, giving notice beforehand to the authorities along his route that he will
hold them responsible for whatever may befall him.
He heard some time ago that a French whaler had
been lost upon the coast of Corea, and that the crew,
numbering fifteen hands, had been reduced to slavery.
He had no French ships of war at his command
(our squadron being occupied elsewhere); he took a
Portuguese lorcha, and set off with his interpreter.
He encountered severe weather, and was nearly
shipwrecked; but nothing could deter him. He
landed, in spite of the authorities, in Corea, and
proceeded into the interior without having any precise information to guide him. He at last found
where the prisoners were, and overtook them just as
they were about to be marched off to the mines. He

rescued them from the miserable fate in store for them, and brought them all back to Shang-hai—a success due exclusively to his energy and courage.

It was M. de Montigny who introduced the yak or long-haired ox from Thibet, and sorgum, or Indian millet, into France, the latter having now become so completely acclimatised that the seed employed all over North America is exported from Paris.

We hoped to find Chinese plenipotentiaries at Shang-hai; but we had been too sanguine. The grudge against the Western Powers still subsisted at Pekin. Yu, without deigning to reply to the ambassadors, appealed to the customs of the empire as freeing him from this duty, and deputed it to the governor of Sou-tchou-fou, whom he requested to make known the purposes of the Chinese government. The Russians are requested to proceed to the mouth of the Black Dragon, on the Amour, and a great Tartar mandarin is to be sent there to negociate with them. With regard to the representatives of the three other powers, their only course now is to return to Canton, where Houang, the new governor, will soon arrive with full powers to treat with them. Such is the answer of the court of Pekin to the joint note of the ambassadors. Our departure for the North was, on the receipt of this reply, immediately determined upon.

CHAPTER VIII.

Departure of the 'Audacieuse' for the Gulf of Pecheli.—Cape
Chantoung.—The Forts of Takou and the mouth of the Peiho.—
Conferences with three Imperial Commissioners sent by the Court
of Pekin.—The Son of Heaven refuses to open his Capital to the
foreign Ministers.—The Bombardment and Capture of the Forts
of Ta-kou.—The Admirals ascend the Pei-ho to the city of Tien-
tsin.—The four Embassies take up their quarters in this Town.
—Arrival of Kouei-Liang and of Houa-Cha-Na, the new Imperial
Commissioners.—Their Interview with the French Ambassador.—
Opening of the Conferences.—M. de Contades is appointed by
Baron Gros to take part in them.—Signature of the Treaty of
Tien-tsin.—Evacuation of the town by the Allied Fleets.—Ex-
cursion to the Great Wall of China.—Return to Shang-hai.—The
'Audacieuse' springs a leak.—Six Weeks spent at Shang-hai
during the Dog-days.

ON Wednesday the 15th of April, at seven o'clock in
the morning, Commander Vrignaud gave orders to
make ready; and, in the midst of foggy and wet
weather, we set sail for the Gulf of Pecheli.   A dense
mist completely hid the land; and the yellow waves
of the Yang-tse-Kiang even disappeared under the
fog.   In leaving the stream we encountered a stormy
sea and a fresh breeze.   We thought that the bad
luck of our *début* in the Atlantic had returned again.

But next day the sea fell, the good weather returned, and we made, without difficulty, nine or ten knots an hour under steam. We passed close to the place where, in 1847, the frigate 'La Gloire' and the war-sloop 'La Victorieuse' were lost at the same time. Admiral Lapierre commanded the 'Gloire;' and M. Rignault de Genouilly, who is now the admiral, the 'Victorieuse.' The crews were saved by the energy of the commander of the 'Victorieuse' and the intrepidity of Lieutenant Poidloue and Lieutenant Lapelin, who made a voyage of five hundred miles in a long-boat to get assistance from Shang-hai. We have very imperfect information about the geography of these waters; the soundings and reefs are not known, and the charts are defective. At all events, a very limited confidence can be placed in them. After a four-days' passage, under a brilliant sun, but a bitterly-cold air, we doubled Cape Chan-toung, or Cape Macartney, and entered the Gulf of Pecheli. On the 20th of April, at three o'clock in the afternoon, we came in sight of the 'Minnesota,' the 'Furious,' and the 'America;' and we cast anchor as near them as the size of the ship permitted. Baron Gros immediately entered into communication with his colleagues. Three Imperial Commissioners, entrusted with a verbal mission from the Emperor to treat with the Western Nations, have given notice of their arrival.

One of them is Tan, the president of the War-office, and governor-general of the province of Tcheli and its dependencies. The two others are Tsoung, the superintendent general of the public granaries and salt-pans of the empire; and Ou, minister of the council of the interior. The selection of a superintendent of public granaries and salt-pans, as a diplomatist, at first produced a little astonishment among the European envoys. It had been intimated to Yu, the prime-minister of the emperor Hien-Foung, that full powers, by written document, would be expected from the mandarins appointed to treat with us. Now Tan, Tsoung, and Ou produced none. They were therefore informed that they must comply with what was expected in this respect before the foreign ambassadors could consent to receive them. The governor of Tcheli, in the name of his colleagues and in his own name, protested that the court of Pekin was in perfect good faith, and asserted that it is not in conformity with Chinese custom to confer such powers. Ky-Ing and I-Li-Pou no doubt had, on the occasion of the first treaties, produced such deputations; but they had fabricated them themselves, and were degraded for this very reason. With regard to their own case, they had been instructed by the Celestial Emperor to go and meet the envoys of the Western Nations, and had proceeded immediately to the mouth of the Pei-ho to receive their communications and transmit them to the court of Pekin. A slight difference of opinion now occurred between the four plenipotentiaries. Count Poutiatine and Mr. Reed declared that they were quite satisfied, and ready to enter into a conference. Lord Elgin and Baron Gros persisted in their first resolution, and refused to receive the Imperial Commissioners. Tan requested to be informed what were the concessions demanded by the foreign envoys, in order that he might be able to explain to the court of Pekin what they were, in compliance with the instructions he had received from his government. The establishment of European legations at Pekin, or at least the privilege to the representatives of foreign powers of going, at certain periods in the year, to the capital, at once provoked a warm protest and a positive refusal from Tan. He also rejected the proposal to open the great rivers and markets of the interior of China. These points were quite inadmissible, and will not even be discussed. They would concede to the foreign ministers the right of corresponding directly, and on a footing of equality, with one of the Councils. The laws against Christianity would be revised. Four or five new ports, of small importance, would be opened, including Swatow and Chapoo. The indemnity for the burning of

the factories, and for the expenses of the war, would
be one of the articles discussed; but it was probable
that nothing would be obtained. Such, in short, was
the situation. The taking of Canton, it was evident,
had produced little effect; and the Cabinet of Pekin
still maintained its haughty and arrogant tone. The
two High Commissioners of France and England,
not finding the Mantchoo Tartar dynasty ready to
treat, resolved, after a council of war had been
held on board the 'Audacieuse,' to proceed into the
country and strike another severe blow in the immediate neighbourhood of the capital. But in the
absence of the gunboats, which were kept back by
currents and contrary winds, all along the China Sea
from Cape Chantoung to Hong-Kong, they sought
to temporize; and entering into a correspondence
with the Imperial Commissioners, they endeavoured,
but in vain, to persuade these personages by reasoning
to accede to their demands. The result was a more
firm conviction that force alone has any weight
with them.

May 1, 1858.

There is no sweet breath of returning summer for
us. There is nothing to prompt us, with Rémi
Belleau, to chant the praises of spring, and celebrate—

'Avril, l'honneur et des bois
Et des mois.'

For us, alas! there are neither leaves, flowers, buds, nor singing-birds. There is a rough sea, a high wind, and a fog, with minute, blinding dust floating about in it. When the horizon is clear, which happens once in eight days, we can see, far in the distance, five black spots on a level with the water, which are said to be the forts at the mouth of the Pei-ho. There is no great scope for amusement. Trévise sketches; Maubourg and Contades shoot gulls; the disembarkation corps go through their exercises on deck; the gunners handle their pieces, and the seamen hoist and lower alternately the topmasts of the ships. We are anchored at nine miles from the coast; and the shores are so low that we cannot even see them through a glass. We have no compradors, nor any communication with the Chinese villages. We live entirely on the ship's stores, as if we were at sea; and we begin to feel the want of fruit and vegetables. From time to time we perceived the large sail of a junk, bearing down upon us, hoisting a flag of truce. Then two or three white and blue button mandarins would come on board. We received them at the stern of the ship; and took them to M. Marquès, our interpreter. Then we entertained them to lunch. The leader on these occasions was Tchen, the Mantchoo colonel, who brought with him a communication from the governor of Tcheli. M. Marquès examined carefully the external form and title of the despatch; for there is always reason to fear some ruse on the part of the Chinese authorities, who attach so much importance to mere form, and who are always desirous of exalting themselves in the eyes of their own followers. The first day, the enumeration of the titles of the high Chinese functionary occupied more than half of the address; while those of Baron Gros were passed over in silence—the letters used in all that referred to him implying inferiority on the part of the representative of France. The ambassador refused to receive the despatch, and sent it back without opening it. Next day the communication was returned; this time as reverential in its terms as it had been haughty before. The letters employed were unexceptionable. The whole blame was thrown upon the shoulders of an inexperienced clerk, who knew nothing of diplomatic forms, and who had, of course, been disgraced for his blunder.

The weather, which for some days had been cold, dark, and foggy, gradually became more serene, the sun broke through the mists, and the waves fell, so that the plenipotentiaries had it in their power to communicate with each other several times a-day.

It was pleasant to see the ships' boats skimming along, now darting off from the 'Furious' to the 'Audacieuse,' now from the 'Minnesota' to the 'America.' It often happened that a thought came into the mind of the two High Commissioners at the same time; the whaling-boat of Lord Elgin and the long-boat of Baron Gros would put off from both the boats and meet half-way. Then a contest *de politesse* followed as to which was to proceed. The two boats, on these occasions, shipped their oars, and slowly sank and rose with the swell till an explanation was come to. The swarthy Russians, the ruddy English, and the sallow Yankees, often met on the deck of the 'Audacieuse.'

In spite of the intercourse maintained with the mandarins, everything is assuming a more warlike appearance. The 'Fusée' went to anchor near the land, in order to show the French flag. Besplas, with small boats belonging to the 'Audacieuse,' received orders to set buoys over the bar and to examine the passes at the opening of the Pei-ho. This bar is nearly a mile long; at full tide it is from nine to ten feet deep, and two feet at low water. Hence even long-boats are sometimes stranded on it. When Besplas, with his men, approached a little closer to the forts, they could see the cannons pointed upon them and wheeled about as they moved from place to place. The very matches were lighted. Yet the Chinese went no farther; they continued on the defensive. Mandarins called out at the top of their voices, and made signs to them to keep farther off. The admirals made several reconnoissances in order to select a proper place of disembarkation. A country more parched, desolate, and miserable, it is impossible to imagine. Nothing is to be seen but mud, slime, salt-pans, and a few sand-hills. Not a trace of vegetation meets the eye. As the vessels successively arrived they cast anchor alongside of the 'Fusée.' The four gunboats, under the command of Besplas, succeeded the same day in crossing the bar without accident. Fifteen English gunboats joined them next day. A gilt-button mandarin thereupon came off to inform the commanders that they must retire, threatening them, if they disobeyed, with the wrath of the grand mandarin and the Emperor. They replied that they were grieved to vex the Celestial Emperor, but that they would not quit the anchorage. The decisive moment seemed at hand.

The Chinese made a great many preparations; they constructed batteries, placed sand-bags, and diminished the size of their embrasures, and connected different parts of their batteries. Cannons were sent them from Tien-tsin and Pekin. Troops of picked men arrived daily, as well as bodies of

horsemen with banners, who pitched their tents upon
the banks. Heaps of powder and ball were collected
on the ramparts. Before resorting to force, the High
Commissioners of the allies made a last attempt at
conciliation by addressing an ultimatum to the court
of Pekin. The Son of Heaven sent a reply in the
shape of a distinct refusal to open his capital to the
foreign ministers. The permanent or temporary
residence of representatives of the Western Powers at
Pekin was a *sine quâ non* of the treaty, so all chances
of a pacific arrangement again fell to the ground and
left no course open but war. The 20th of May was
fixed for the attack.

Palladius, the Archimandrite or Superior of the
Russian College of Pekin, had obtained permission
to visit Count Poutiatine with one of his pupils. He
had only taken forty-eight hours to come from Pekin
and get on board the 'America,' and he gave us very
interesting information regarding the capital. The
Emperor, who had been long sick, was better, but
more irritable than ever. No mandarin would dare
to speak to him about foreign affairs, far less advise
him to treat with the barbarians. There was considerable excitement in the town; provisions were
very dear, and the arrival of the junks laden with
rice was anxiously expected. The Son of Heaven
was occupied, in the great gardens or pleasure-grounds

which surround the palace, in riding about with his wives for the benefit of their health. He had some thoughts, perhaps, of a flight into Tartary! Palladius had seen nothing in the course of his journey but what it was intended that he should see, having been shut up in a closed conveyance. He calculates that there are about ten thousand men forming the various bodies of troops between Pekin and Tien-tsin, and he counted seventy-two villages. The river is obstructed in several places by junks and chains, but these impediments are not of any great moment. After having remained for a short time on board ship, the Archimandrite set out on his return to Pekin, Count Poutiatine desiring that he should be at the head of his community in the event of any outbreak in the capital.

Admiral Poutiatine and Mr. Reed had several interviews on the shore with the Imperial Commissioners. One day the admiral urged them to give a fair hearing, at least, to the just complaint of the foreign powers; insisting on the bootless spilling of blood that would follow an ill-advised and stubborn course. He referred to the approaching bombardment of the forts. 'Oh!' said Tsoung, who is probably a Mantchoo, 'it is of no great moment, they are merely Chinese!' This is the first time that we had heard any allusion made to the two races who people China—to the conquering and the conquered race—or detected any evidence of the separate existence of the two peoples. Is the fusion of the two races less complete than is generally supposed, or was this a mere blustering talk of the envoy of the noble Mantchoo dynasty?

On Thursday the 20th May, at eight minutes past ten, the bombardment of the forts and batteries which protect the mouth of the Pei-ho began. As soon as the ebb permitted the gunboats to keep their position in the middle of the stream, the order to advance was given. Scarcely had the first English gunboat, the 'Cormorant,' made all ready, than the Chinese, contrary to their usual custom, opened fire upon her. Captain Saumarez, without answering, continued, amid a shower of balls, to push about until he had attained his position, and then he gave them a broadside. The 'Fusée' followed, and then the 'Mitraille.' The latter, having got her screw entangled in a fishing-net, remained for a quarter of an hour exposed to the fire of the enemy. She was completely riddled with bullets. Eleven men were killed on board. M. Bideau, a young ensign of twenty, had his head swept off by a ball. The commissary fell stunned by a ball, which, passing right through the ship just above his head, whipped off his cap without injuring him. The 'Avalanche' was uninjured. On board the 'Dragonne' a midshipman,

P

M. Baratier, was cut right in two and knocked over into the sea, his sword falling upon the deck. The mate of the 'Fusée,' M. Porquet, was also killed. M. Regnault, who from the yards commanded the riflemen, was wounded by a ball in the cheek. In all we had four officers killed and thirty sailors wounded. In about an hour the fire of the Chinamen slackened. Almost all their pieces were dismounted. The admiral then ordered the disembarkation corps to jump into the mud. They found the forts evacuated, and those who had defended them in flight. Although the Chinese, who are in this respect similar to the Turks, show a considerable amount of courage behind stone walls, they rush in terror and confusion from the point of the bayonet. It was estimated that about a hundred of the enemy had been killed. The sailors, as usual, displayed great pluck and vigour. The fire of the Chinese surprised every one by its obstinacy and precision. The force was composed undoubtedly of picked men, for all the soldiers who were killed wore the otter's tail and crow's feather. The Chinese thought they would be attacked at full tide, accordingly they had pointed all their guns too high ; the balls passed, in fact, above the rigging. This explains the great loss of officers, and, relatively, the small number of sailors wounded. Their pieces were of enormous calibre. Several of them had been cast in Europe. One bore the mark of the seventh year of the French Republic; it was one of those which did most mischief. Others were of bronze and of great value. In all there were a hundred and fifty pieces on the battery.

Higher up the river than the forts, a wide estacade of junks supporting cannon prevented the gunboats from proceeding farther. It was necessary to destroy them by battering them with cannon-ball to make way for a reconnoissance. During the action about fifty fire-boats or burning junks were pushed off towards the ships. Luckily, a contrary wind stranded them on the mud at the bend in the river. Besides the cannon there was also a gingall battery.

A frightful accident marred our pleasure at the success of the attack. Just as the disembarkation corps and the pioneers entered into one of the forts, a Chinese powder magazine exploded, blowing into the air fifty of our men, among whom were several officers. Some were killed on the spot; most of them were horribly burned. I saw them carried on board the 'Durance;' it was dreadful to see so many burned hands and faces. Nine in all had been killed. After a short prayer from the chaplain, they were dropped into the sea, deep into the mud of the Gulf of Pecheli. We had the misfortune to lose in this way M. de Gardanne, the grandson of the celebrated Persian ambassador, who was one of our midshipmen on board the 'Audacieuse.' Brought on board, he was affectionately tended by his messmates, but he died after much suffering in a few hours.

The two detachments of the allies took possession of the deserted fortifications, and placed howitzers at each extremity of the encampment, as a precaution against a sudden attack. A slight resistance was attempted in the large village of Ta-kou, where batteries and earthworks had been hastily thrown up. But the grapeshot of the gunboats and the Minié rifles, which brought down the Chinamen a thousand yards off, soon drove them from this defence, and the English and French gunboats, meeting with no farther obstacle, proceeded onwards to Tien-tsin, under the command of the admirals.

I took advantage of an invitation from Lieutenant Bailly, of the 'Phlégéton,' and M. Besplas, to share their tent with them for a day or two. Four great mats, firmly fixed to bamboos, protected us alternately from the heat of the sun and the chill of the night air. A sailor did our cooking, and we intercepted Chinamen on the way, who, on payment, readily supplied us with provisions. All our copper money went in this way, and then we had recourse to barter. We exchanged a bottle for a hen, a well-

worn pocket-handkerchief for a bunch of white ra-
dishes. With a little dexterity it is possible to secure
a dozen of eggs for a bit of ship biscuit, and a very
good salad for an empty bullyflask. The water we
are using is brought from the ships. That of the
Pei-ho, mixed with mud and animal and vegetable
substances in a state of decomposition, it would be
certain death to drink. A long line of sentries belonging to the allies were placed on watch over the
entrances to the camp, and kept a sharp look-out
over the plain. At four o'clock in the morning the
bugle was sounded; every one, stiff with a hard bed
on the hard ground, was glad to be up and to return
to duty. There was a certain amount of poetry in the
scene at daybreak. The rising sun, the tall waving
reeds, the noisy flight of the gulls and sea-fowl, produced an impression altogether new. We explored
all parts of the camp. There were lying about frag-
ments of broken bows, arrows, gunpowder soaked in
water, gingalls, matchlocks, cannons, banners, tents,
heaps of balls, case-shot, and arms of every kind. It
was evident that the commander of the fort had
spared no precautions. Poor man! he lay himself
stark and stiff among the ruins. When he saw that
his men had ceased to fire, and that the foreign seamen were clambering over the ramparts, he could not
survive his defeat. He threw himself on his knees at

the brink of the ditch, and, with his long sword, cut
a fatal gash right across his throat, before our sailors
had the presence of mind to rush in and prevent him.
He died immediately. This was Tchen, the Mantchoo colonel, whom we had received on board, and
to whom we would have been delighted to have given
a warm and friendly reception. We took a walk
several times towards the village of Ta-kou. The
space which separates the town from the camp was
literally covered with conical hats, which the Chinese
warriors had dropped in the hurry of their flight.
We saw the corpses of two or three Chinese soldiers
with their heads cut open and their hands tied behind their backs, whom the mandarins had caused to
be executed while they remained themselves at their
posts, for having run off a little sooner than their
commanders. The most of the streets are deserted,
and the appearance of the village is miserable in
the extreme. All the houses are built of mud. A
pagoda rises in the midst. Flocks of pigeons have
built their nests in the lofty trees which surround it.
When a gun is fired they fly off in a great cloud, but
they soon return. The English and French officers
come here to have a little pigeon-shooting of a novel
kind, and also to add, to a small extent at least, to
our limited supply of fresh food. The view was
dreary. In one direction, as far as the eye could

reach, there extended a vast plain, covered with salt
marshes. Small earthen tumuli, said to be burial-
places, alone broke the monotony of the landscape.
In another direction was the sea. On the horizon
we could discern the long line of the European ships,
lit up faintly in the setting sun, and anchored so far
from land that the mandarins and their soldiers must
have thought themselves perfectly safe from attack.

Meantime the admirals continued their progress to
Tien-tsin, and reached that place without having met
with any resistance. The inhabitants, who were
still under the influence of the terror produced by
the cannon of Ta-kou, tendered their submission in
every direction. The mandarins kept out of the
way. The leading inhabitants brought provisions in
abundance to the gunboats. The ambassadors, informed of all this, hastened on to Tien-tsin, in order
to judge for themselves of the influence produced
upon the Chinese authorities by this new defeat.
Baron Gros had no sooner arrived than he sent us
instructions to join him.

On the 1st of June, at six o'clock in the evening,
we left the camp of Ta-kou, and went on board the
English gunboat, ' No. 84,' which carried stores to
the ships. Flavigny, suffering at the time from
fever, remained at the mouth of the Pei-ho. With
our backs resting upon a cannon, we spent the night

under the starlit sky, on the crowded deck of the little steamer. The bands of the 'Nemesis' and 'Calcutta' were on board. One hundred English foot soldiers were also on deck, on their way to act as a guard to Lord Elgin. Our voyage was easily accomplished. Just as day broke we came in sight of an old tower with battlements, which had at one time been fortified, although now in ruins. It stands at the entrance to Tien-tsin. Two incidents only occurred to break the monotony of the passage. At the place where the current is strongest we cut right through a Chinese vessel, those on board, having no conception of the speed with which we advanced, not clearing away in time from before us. The twelve seamen were sent sprawling into the mud, where they roared lustily, and puddled round the gunboat, which drew up with a 'stop her,' to pick them up. The river, however, was not wide at this part, and they all managed to gain the bank in some way or other without our assistance. The other incident might have supplied Shakspeare with a picture. At a bend in the Pei-ho, on the bank left bare by the receding tide, the corpse of a Chinaman lay in the mud. Two large bull-dogs, with their forepaws upon the chest of the dead body, tearing at each other unmercifully, disputed which should have the prey. It made one shudder to look at the heads of the ferocious brutes, and the mutilated remains of the man, as they stood out in the morning sun.

It is twenty-five miles from Ta-kou to Tien-tsin by land, but more than twice as far by the river. The Pei-ho has many windings, and some of its turns are so rapid that the gunboats had the greatest difficulty in getting over them. The ' Fusée' ran aground forty-two times, the ' Cormorant' thirty-two times. When the English and French gunboats stuck in the mud, they threw a rope to the Chinamen on shore, who followed our progress in crowds, wonder-stricken at the sight of the strange monsters which were snorting and puffing up their rivers. They willingly lent a hand to pull us up. These poor creatures would take no money from us, being afraid of the mandarins, but they were highly satisfied with the ship's biscuits which the seamen gave them. They seemed to be a great delicacy for them. Steam navigation was something quite new to the people of these parts, and completely over-turned all their ideas in navigation. They seemed lost in astonishment when they saw these vessels going on against wind and tide, and never stopping. The junks which go up to Tien-tsin only ascend with the tide, and cast anchor at ebb. In this way they lose twelve hours out of the twenty-four, and spend four days over a journey which European ships can ac-

complish in one. The country is verdant and admirably cultivated, but its flatness and monotony
make it pall terribly upon one. The farm-houses
and villages are built of baked earth, like stables and
cow-houses in Normandy. The horses are small and
ugly, the asses and mules are superb. In the villages
there are troops of dogs running about nearly in a wild
state, which snarl and show their teeth at foreigners.
All along the banks of the river the inhabitants, who
were collected in long crowds to see us pass, betrayed
in their looks an odd mixture of curiosity and fear.
Our gunboats are the first European vessels which
have crossed the bar of the Pei-ho, and broken in
upon the old barriers of China. Lord Macartney in
1793, and Lord Amherst in 1816, went up to Pekin
in the character of tributaries, and in mandarin
junks. About nine o'clock in the morning we arrived
before Tien-tsin. Immense stores of salt, rice, and
grain, covered with mats, were heaped upon the left
bank of the stream. The suburbs extend along the
right bank, and at the termination of each street
a crowd was collected to see our gunboats pass. The
roofs were covered with spectators. Junks moored to
the shore, and bridges of boats, frequently interrupted
our course. At last, however, we dropped anchor at
a spot pointed out to us by Admiral Seymour, where
the Grand Canal abuts into the Pei-ho.

Here was the yamoun which the two ambassadors had fixed upon as their residence. Lord Elgin occupied the left side of the building, and Baron Gros the right side. This yamoun, which has somewhat fallen from its high estate, was built by the Emperor Kien-Loung, one of the ancestors of the present monarch, its founder having made it his summer residence, as is proved by various inscriptions which are still legible. It has been selected as the head-quarters of the ambassadors, in consequence of its proximity to the gunboats. Behind there is an extensive cemetery, from which fetid exhalations arise; then there is a small village, and beyond it is the open plain stretching away till lost in the distance. The Pei-ho makes a great bend in this place before proceeding again towards Pekin. Two English and French detachments were entrusted with the defence of the yamoun, and by night the call of the European sentries woke the echoes of the old abode of the Chinese monarchs. During the first days of the occupation there were only 594 Frenchmen and 2000 Englishmen in this town of many hundred thousand souls. The two forces made but a small army. But gradually reinforcements arrived from Pecheli and Canton, and our small army was increased to five thousand men, a number which enabled us to bid defiance to all the attacks of our enemies. We had no sooner disembarked than we took possession of the tent which had been set aside for our accommodation. We found nothing but the bare walls. We had hard-wood tables brought into it, on which we placed our beds. Then Sin, the intendant of the yamoun, brought us a collection of benches, chairs, and Chinese tables. We spread mats upon the floor, and covered the walls with painted papers representing gods and heroes. We were surrounded on all sides with bloodthirsty dragons and fantastic monsters of every shape, but they did not in the least interfere with sleep in our new quarters, which were very comfortable when contrasted with the accommodation to which for some time we had been accustomed. Two grey-bearded Tartar veterans were appointed to wait upon us. But the duties of old Ming-Tian-Na and his colleague were light. They had to keep our cups constantly full of tea, to drive away the flies, and to bring us from time to time great lumps of ice, which in the veriest excess and extravagance of luxury we made them set down in the middle of the tent to melt, thereby to cool the sultry air. When not so engaged, these worthies were always to be found smoking their pipes unconcernedly, sipping tea out of small teacups, and chewing melon-seeds, or else lying sound asleep across the threshold.

Admiral Poutiatine and Mr. Reed took up their

quarters on the other side of the stream. The Chinaman whose property they had selected as their abode, not caring much to accommodate barbarians, and fearing the animosity of the mandarins, offered them six thousand piastres, or nearly 1500*l.*, if they would agree to go somewhere else. There is something very Chinese in the idea of a landlord proposing to pay a person 1500*l.* not to become his tenant!

The Great Council has written officially to the ambassadors to inform them that two high Imperial Commissioners have been chosen to confer with them, from among the highest personages of the empire. While awaiting their arrival, we employed our leisure in visiting the town and its environs. In the morning, before daybreak, we rode out along the Pekin road, a sort of wide causeway, which is raised to some height above the level of the plain. We stopped at the marble bridge which has been built upon the Pei-ho, and which is nearly two miles from our flag-staff. To venture farther would have been imprudent, for there were Chinese soldiers and small encampments of Tartar horsemen scattered over the country. We explored the town in every direction, but could find nothing in it worth looking at. Like all the Chinese towns, it is surrounded by high walls. It differed however from Shang-hai and Canton, in having wider streets, greater width being necessary to permit of the passage of the heavy waggons of the country, which are drawn by mules and oxen. In the south of China all the traffic is carried on by men, who act as beasts of burden, the goods being strapped on their backs. In the north of China, on the other hand, there are roads and carriages. The whole commercial activity of the town of Tien-tsin seems to be confined to the suburbs, and chiefly to that which adjoins the Great Canal. In this extensive quarter are the shops in which the furs, paper-hangings, fans, and antiquities are displayed. We observed several European products among the wares exhibited for sale, including light bright-coloured Russian woollen cloths, Manchester cottons, and lucifer matches of German manufacture. We saw several caricatures at our expense, which the Chinamen, when they saw us coming, picked up hurriedly and pushed out of the way. At least they did so at first, but, when they found that we were quite amused with them, they showed them to us, and allowed us to take them away. One represented a European accoutred after the most outrageous fashion, buying a hedgehog, working himself into a state of excitement to drive a hard bargain, but at last making the purchase with a big bag of money. Another represented an English officer on horseback, holding his white umbrella in one hand, and the reins in the other, with a cigar projecting from his mouth, and a hat stuck on after a fashion as impossible as the attitude of the rider. We gave them some European drawings, which they showed great anxiety to obtain, and next day we saw copies of them, which however had already acquired a grotesque appearance, for the Chinese have no idea of art free from exaggeration or caricature. The beau ideal, the beautiful of the ancient sculptors, has no existence for the Chinese mind. Among us an expansive forehead is generally looked upon as an indication of intellectual power; but in China this is not the case. The Chinese are of opinion that the stomach is the seat of the mind, and the consequence is that the extent of a man's mental capacity is measured by the amplitude of his abdomen. Now, I would ask, what chances the fine arts have among a people entertaining such an opinion? They will never, of course, produce anything akin to the Apollo Belvidere, but will manufacture no end of Poussahs and Bouddhas, and other monstrosities of a like kind. Their productions by their quaintness may amuse or provoke a laugh from those who examine them, but can never waken any of those higher faculties in human nature, which it is the true object of art to gratify and foster.

Long-boats, well armed, were sent to take soundings in the Great Imperial Canal at a distance of several miles from the ships. The canal is not navigable in consequence of the locks, certain parts of it being often left dry. The junks are drawn over the mud in these places, but this could not be done with the gunboats, in consequence of the screw. The Chinese are delighted with the American flag, which they call the banner of flowers. It displays, as is well known, stars and stripes. There are thirteen stripes, in commemoration of the thirteen States of the confederation, and as many stars as there are States at the time. The number of stars varies in consequence of this. Several of us went to see the Hotel of the Four Felicities, which is the Hôtel du Louvre, the great hotel of the place. A shabby affair it certainly is. Lord Elgin was quite struck with the absence of all luxurious habits, and even of ordinary comforts, which was apparent everywhere in China. In India, diamonds, jewels, precious stones, rich embroidered stuffs in gold and silver, are displayed with Oriental magnificence in the great towns, but here there is nothing of the kind. It is not possible to conceive human abodes more comfortless than the yamouns where we are quartered; the occupants must freeze in them during the winter. From what we have seen we are inclined to think that Canton is the finest and most interesting town in

China. The population of Tien-tsin is a mere population of Coolies, and it possesses no industry. The town owes its importance entirely to its position at the junction of the Great Imperial Canal, of the Pei-ho, and the road to Pekin, which makes it the entrepôt of the capital. If this port is opened in future to the commerce of the West, Tien-tsin will become a great mart for the manufactures of Great Britain, which are destined, no doubt, ultimately to clothe the hordes of Tartary. There will spring up at this place an immense traffic in European products. The province of Pecheli is poor, and produces nothing. Its inhabitants are almost naked. It could only give furs in exchange, but these furs are good, cheap, and abundant. But, as we have said, it is its position which gives importance to Tien-tsin.

On going on board the 'Avalanche' we made the acquaintance of a countryman whom we had not seen before. This was young Bernard Pei-ho, a little Chinaman of five years of age, who had been found alive among the ruins of the forts, and whom the admiral had adopted, christening him in the fashion above set forth. His tail had been docked; he had been equipped as a cabin-boy; and now M. Bernard Pei-ho, made much of by the sailors, talked French, and indignantly pushed away every Chinaman who came on board lest he should be taken home again.

Q

When the disembarkation corps of the 'Avalanche' mounted guard at the yamoun, young Pei-ho came on shore with them and joined in the military salute.

A few days after hearing from the Great Council the two Imperial Commissioners arrived at Tien-tsin. The attachés of the English embassy were riding in the country as they came up, and the latter were terribly scandalized when they saw these barbarians treading with impunity on the domain of the Son of Heaven. They could not help showing their indignation. The suite seemed equally surprised. That evening the two noble Commissioners sent, according to Chinese custom, their red visiting cards to the Ambassadors. The following day, having been ascertained to be a lucky day, was fixed upon for the first interview with Lord. Elgin. It was arranged that the parties should meet in a pagoda situated without the town, at some distance from the wall. Bellecourt, Trévise, and I went, out of curiosity, to the spot, and on our way home had to pass through a dense crowd of Chinamen for nearly an hour, without any weapon of defence saving our silk umbrellas, and without any other escort than two seamen. There was not one trace of ill-will to be observed on any one of the faces turned upon us, but a very great amount of wonder and curiosity. Some of them were clad in long white or blue dresses, others in nankeen—a stuff

better known of old than now in France. All along
the road there were small shops and stalls, where
they were selling apples and apricots and drinking
iced tea. Ice is much used at Tien-tsin, and is preserved in large ·pieces with great skill and care.

Next day we proceeded in turn, with all due
pomp, to our interview with the Imperial Commissioners. I will quote the account of it which was
given in the official journal.

' Tien-tsin, June 7.

' Yesterday afternoon the official interview took
place between the plenipotentiaries of France and
the two high Chinese dignitaries who have recently
arrived from Pekin. At three o'clock the cortège
left the yamoun where the two ambassadors of France
and England have fixed their residence, and drew
out on the banks of the river. The seamen of the
disembarkation corps of the "Dragonne," in full dress,
went first, followed by the band of the " Nemesis "
and a compact body of soldiers and marines. The
ambassador followed in his palanquin, carried by
eight Coolies in gray silk dresses fringed with red,
the national colours being trimmed round their hats.
The chairs of the secretaries and attachés of the
mission, and those of the officers of the gunboats,
were carried behind that of his Excellency. The

commander of the "Audacieuse," on horseback, commanded the escort.   A body of foot-soldiers and
marines belonging to the "Avalanche," closed the
procession.   The cortège crossed the Grand Imperial
Canal over a bridge of boats, and proceeded along
the suburb which adjoins the city wall.   The high
Chinese functionaries, on the other hand, proceeded
to the interview with the customary attendance of
satellites, heralds, and servants.   From the starting-
point to the place of meeting, that is to say, for a
distance of two miles and upwards, the French ambassador passed through a double line of Chinamen,
crowding on each side of the way, quiet, amazed,
staring in wonder, or pushing about keenly past each
other to have a glance into the palanquins.   The
number of the spectators, without exaggeration,
might be estimated at more than a hundred thousand.   The procession afterwards entered a small
plain, in the midst of which, upon a hillock, stood a
Buddhist pagoda or temple, where the interview was
to take place.   This temple is only two hundred
years old, and is therefore, in China, without any
prestige from its antiquity; but it forms a rather
complete specimen of Chinese architecture, displaying, as it does, that assemblage of courts, porticoes, and
gardens, which give this style of architecture a very
striking and lively appearance.   The plain all round

is parched and treeless, giving one a very poor idea
of the vegetation of the country. To the right rises
the wall of the town, with its battlements. It still
bears traces of the attack of the rebels three years
ago. It is fortified, and still shows a few cannons,
although the best had been removed to Ta-kou, and
are now on board our vessels. Here and there a
heavy waggon, which might have dated from the
days of Attila, is seen crossing the plain, with huge
wheels painted red, drawn along by oxen or mules.
Far away in the distance a small Chinese camp,
with tents and banners, stands out against the
horizon.

' The farther they advanced the more compact
became the crowd. The Chinese police had the
greatest difficulty in keeping it back from the entrance to the pagoda. The ambassador approached
while the Chinese band was playing. Its feeble
strains were soon drowned in the din of our military
music. He entered, and was received by the two
dignitaries, who stood in the midst of a crowd of
mandarins of all the buttons. After the usual compliments were over, and the various members of the
embassy and officers of the squadron had been
presented to the great men, every one sat down, and
tea was introduced and passed round. Baron Gros
took his seat between the two Chinese Commissioners.

One of them, Kouei-Liang, is allied to the Imperial
family. He is, besides, minister of the Eastern Palace
and director-general of the affairs of the Council of
Justice. The other, Houa-Cha-Na, is president of the
Council of Finance, general of the Chinese Tartar
army and of the blue-bordered banner. The full
powers were exchanged. Those which expressed the
will of the august Emperor and Son of Heaven were
folded in a fine tissue of yellow silk,—yellow being the
colour and badge of the Imperial family. Those of our
ambassador, although not expressing all his honours
after the pompous Oriental style, are no less precise
in essential matters of detail. The representatives
of the court of Pekin examined long, and with much
attention, the signature of the sovereign of the great
empire of France; and having done so they protested
that it was their anxious wish to re-establish peace
and harmony between our country and China. After
some firm and energetic words from Baron Gros on
this subject the conference broke up, and each party
quitted the place of meeting in opposite directions,
the French sailors openly shouldering their bayonets,
the Chinese soldiers doing their best to hide their
long swords from the strangers.'

Such was the account of the interview given in the
'Moniteur.'

The full powers of the Chinese plenipotentiaries

having now been admitted to be complete, the conference for peace immediately opened. Mr. Bruce, a brother of Lord Elgin, assisted by Mr. Wade, the interpreter, appeared on behalf of England. Contades, accompanied by M. Marquès, represented France in the absence of M. de Bellecourt, the premier secretary, who was suffering from a violent attack of dysentery. It is the custom for the High Imperial Commissioners of China not to enter into discussion themselves, but to negociate through their subordinates. On this occasion they said that they desired to meet with the noble ambassadors on occasions of ceremony merely. They would be grieved, they said, to appear before them when in anger or heated by the fire of discussion. Contades, followed by M. Marquès, passed through the town daily, in his sedan-chair, on his way to the conferences. In the morning he received the instructions of Baron Gros concerning the part of the treaty which was to be discussed. In the evening he gave him an account of what had been attained, and of the squabbles that had taken place before each point was conceded. The duplicity, bad faith, and subtlety of the Chinese diplomatists are proverbial; but they were met by the ability and self-possession of our young colleague, who, although inexperienced in such a trust, acquitted himself, throughout this delicate mission, to the entire satis-

faction of Baron Gros ; and indeed so efficiently as
to receive the congratulations of the English ambassador.   The four powers having combined in a
joint application to the Chinese government, every
concession obtained by one was of course for the
benefit of all the others.   After a discussion more
animated than any which had preceded it, Contades
it was who secured the opening of Nankin to
European commerce. 'A man might be asked,' said
the Imperial Commissioners in talking of opening the
Yang-tse-Kiang, 'to cut off his arm or his leg, but
he could not possibly be asked to cut open his body.'
The Chinese commissioners, however, changed their
minds, and consented to this process of suicide for the
advantage of the Western Nations.   A third Chinese
plenipotentiary joined the others during the conferences. This was old Ky-Ing, who, after being so long
disgraced by the court of Pekin, had been dragged
from his obscurity and raised to the honourable
position indicated by the title of Imperial Commissioner.   There was some mystery connected with
his arrival.   There could be no doubt that he was
making mischief underhand.   He had scarcely set
foot in the town of Tien-tsin when the feelings of the
inhabitants underwent a change towards us.   Sir
Michael Seymour was insulted in the suburbs, several
English officers were stoned, and there was every

appearance of an impending row. The English thought they could detect, in these demonstrations of the mob, a return to the old policy of China which had been largely turned to account at Canton. 'You must see,' the mandarins of the south were wont to say, 'that we are most anxious to throw open our cities, but how can we control the people? You see what they are! Just look at them,—they won't allow you to enter!' The English felt so thoroughly convinced that the old Cantonese game had been repeated, that they resolved to use strong measures to put an end to all annoyance from this quarter. Accordingly Ky-Ing was sent for. The report found at Canton was shown him; about its meaning and purport there could be no mistake; there was no room for doubt this time. The poor old man was frightened, and quite lost his presence of mind. Feeling that the barbarians could have no more confidence in him, he hurriedly left Tien-tsin to return to the capital. As had been expected, the population of the town showed no farther symptoms of hostility. A few days afterwards we learned from the Pekin Gazette the painful news that Ky-Ing had been condemned to death for having left his post without permission. He had not been successful, and, according to Chinese custom, suffered for his failure irrespective of merit or demerit on his part. As the irresolution of old age was dreaded in Ky-Ing, four Mongol princes were sent to him by the Emperor to advise him to strangle himself in prison. They perhaps may have assisted him in the deed, which was at all events accomplished. Thus perished a man whose name was long familiar to Europeans in the negociations between them and the Celestial Empire, and who, after having held a position of the very highest distinction, had at the close of his life been reduced to the lowest depth of human misery and degradation.

The conferences threatened to be continued longer than was at first expected, in consequence of the stubbornness of the delegates of the Chinese Commissioners, who were only forced step by step to yield their ground, and who were constantly attempting to come back upon concessions already granted. The open and impetuous character of the French was matched against Chinese cunning and subtlety. There was, however, one thing in our favour, viz. the high price of provisions, which was beginning to irritate the population and to cause alarm to the Chinese government. There are no more junks arriving at Tien-tsin. The measure of rice, which sold at forty coppers before the recent events, now sells at one hundred and forty. Accordingly, at each fresh demand made by the Europeans, the reply of the

Chinese authorities invariably was, 'If we admit it, will you go away?' and we were obliged to disappoint them by adding, 'There is one item more.' At last the day for signing the treaty came, and of the ceremony attending it the description follows:—

'Tien-tsin, June 28.

'The 27th of June, 1858, will hereafter be accounted one of the most solemn and memorable days in the history of the relations between France and the Celestial Empire. After a discussion which lasted for fifteen days with the two high dignitaries sent from Pekin, the negociations were at last brought to a close, and the French nation having obtained all the satisfaction to which they were legitimately entitled, the treaty of peace, commerce, and navigation was signed last night. At half-past five o'clock Baron Gros left his yamoun to proceed to the pagoda of Hai Kouang, where the Imperial Commissioners awaited him. When he appeared upon the quay the ships anchored in the Grand Canal and in the Pei-ho slung up their colours; while the sailors manning the yards gave five good cheers for the Emperor, to which the English added an enthusiastic hurrah. An immense crowd covered the river banks. Admiral Rigault de Genouilly, on horseback and in full dress, followed by all the commanders of the

French ships of war, also on horseback and in full dress, headed the procession. The escort followed. It was composed of detachments of the disembarkation corps, of the artillery, engineers, and marines of the French section of that little army which, by the vigour of its blows, the ability of its leaders, and the boldness of its enterprises, in six months' time had forced to submit to the·will of France and England an empire which has four hundred millions of inhabitants, and boasts of possessing an army of eight hundred thousand men. The national flag was carried by a non-commissioned officer of marines in front of the ambassador. Two officers on horseback, Messrs. Besplas and d'Ozouville, escorted Baron Gros. His chair was followed by those of Messrs. Du Chesne de Bellecourt, de Contades, de Moges, de La Tour Maubourg, de Trévise, and de Flavigny, the secretaries and attachés to the mission. The interpreter, M. Marquès, preceded the ambassador, and twenty chairs with the officers of the squadron, who had come up from the Gulf of Pecheli to be present at the ceremony, followed the representative of France. On his arrival in the interior court of the pagoda Baron Gros was received by the two High Commissioners, who stood in the midst of a crowd of mandarins with buttons of all the colours. They then sat down and drank tea, and congratulated each other on the peace and mutual good understanding so happily re-established. The ambassador requested the Imperial Commissioners to sign first under the Chinese text, reserving the right for himself to sign first under the French text. Kouei-Liang and Houa-Cha-Na, accordingly took their brushes and drew or wrote, one after the other, the letters of their names upon the different copies of the treaty. Py-Hen, their secretary, who had made himself very busy during the conference, stamped the treaty with a great seal which had recently arrived from Pekin. When Baron Gros had attached his name to the French treaty, the troops mustered in the courts of the pagoda presented arms and gave three cheers for the Emperor. His Excellency then requested Kouei-Liang to fix upon the copy which was to be sent to Pekin; when he had made his selection he handed it to him, after having folded it in a rich cover of blue silk, bound with gold, which had been brought from Paris. Then turning towards the Commissioners, Baron Gros expressed the anxious interest he took in the welfare and prosperity of China, and, on concluding his short speech, drank to the health of the emperor Hien-Foung. The two high dignitaries replied in a few words of courtesy to the ambassador, and filling their porcelain cups with Chinese wine, heated and sweetened after the custom of the country, they drank to the health of the sovereign of the great French empire, turning them upside down to show that they had left nothing at the bottom. Then tea and fruit, and all the delicacies of a Chinese dinner, were brought, great preparation having been made for the occasion. After the repast Baron Gros took leave of the two High Commissioners, and the cortège set out in the order in which it had come. When darkness came, torches were lighted, the glare of which fell upon the long lines of spectators who crowded the streets, and sparkled upon the waters of the canal and Pei-ho. The effect was magnificent. The men on board the English gunboats, and the English troops ranged along the quay, kept cheering every now and then. The French gunboats discharged fireworks, which lit up their masts and rigging, while Bengal fires, set ablaze at the arrival of the ambassador in the court of the yamoun, brought into strong relief the quaint gables of the Chinese houses. Their upturned eaves and fantastic images in the torchlight lost all traces of the decay to which they fast were hastening, and they seemed to acquire new life from their contact with western civilization.

' I forgot to say that after the signature of the treaty the ambassador of France asked Kouei-Liang to give him the identical brush which he had used in writing his name, and that Kouei-Liang, handing it to him, had requested to obtain in return the pen with which the ambassador had signed the treaty of Tien-tsin.

'From this day a new era will begin for China. The great and difficult problem of opening the Chinese empire has been solved. Stepping forth from an isolation which has lasted for four thousand years, she is about to enter into the general life of the world, and to be brought in contact with the activity, intelligence, science, and commercial enterprise of the Western nations. The first act of the French ambassador, after the signature of the treaty, was to ask the two High Commissioners for the immediate liberation of the Christians who had been detained for a long series of years in the interior of the empire. He mentioned the names of some of them, and obtained a promise that an order would be despatched from Pekin ordering their immediate release.'

Such was the account given in the official paper of what took place on the occasion of the signature of the treaty at Tien-tsin. Although the treaties had been signed, the plenipotentiaries resolved not to leave the town until they were ratified, unconditionally and in toto, by the Emperor Hien-Foung. This step was adopted under the advice of those who had the most profound acquaintance with Chinese policy. It was in vain for the Commissioners to protest that what was asked was quite contrary to Chinese custom; that the very proposal would expose them—the Chinese Commissioners—to have their heads cut off by order of the Emperor. The ambassadors insisted. on accomplishing their object; and Kouei-Liang and Houa-Cha-Na, very much against their will, were obliged at last to transmit to Pekin this fresh demand of the barbarians.

In the mean time we were obliged to remain pretty close in our quarters at the yamoun, having various duties connected with the mission to attend to. We breakfasted of a morning in our rooms, with some of our friends from the squadron. In the evening we dined with Baron Gros; and then, taking a seat under the kiosk of the yamoun, we would listen to the lively notes of the English and French bands, which roused the sleeping echoes of Tien-tsin. The subjects of the Middle Empire did not appear to be at all taken with European music. Neither 'God save the Queen,' nor 'Partant pour la Syrie' elicited the faintest spark of approbation. One tune only seemed to please them, and that was 'La Casquette du Père Bugeaud.' When it was played, they kept time with their feet, and laughed and grinned to each other. Every Sunday military mass was said in a pagoda situated behind our yamoun. An aged banyan-tree sheltered the congregation from the rays of a scorching sun; while in the midst of the court an altar was constructed, tastefully decked with branches and banners, by Captain Labbe, of the Engineers. The heat was overpowering, and accompanied almost daily with a north wind, in which floated a thick brown dust, which filled the air, and found its way, in spite of all precautions, into the apartments. Violent typhoons and storms of dust occurred. In a terrific tempest of this kind, during which the sky was completely hid, the gunboats were blown from their moorings, and nearly stranded; while the temperature suddenly fell from 101° Fahrenheit to 65° or 68°. From this occurring in one afternoon, it may be concluded that the climate of Tien-tsin, although infinitely preferable to that of Shang-hai, is still very unhealthy for Europeans.

The bed of the Pei-ho is the great drain and sewer of northern China. The waters of the river are so very offensive, that the sailors were not allowed free permission to bathe in them. The little Chinese children seemed to be under no similar prohibition; they were constantly puddling about in the stream, going and coming from the shore to the boats; wading out with eggs in one hand and apricots in the other, and trudging back through the mud in triumphant

R

glee when they got a copper or two in exchange for their eatables. Nothing could be more amusing than to see this crowd of youngsters in full chace after a bottle floating down the stream, and to witness the dexterity they displayed in getting hold of an article which could possess no great value for them. Empty bottles were thrown overboard to amuse the men on watch, and to the infinite delight of the little China-men. It was amusing to watch the scramble. To punish a man who had thrown stones at the soldiers, we put him into the cangue, or Chinese stocks, a sort of heavy collar fastened round the neck, and made him squat, under his burden, at the door of our yamoun; but the punishment was too light, for the rascal smoked his pipe and drank his tea as uncon-cernedly as if he had been sitting by his own doorpost. Trévise one day plumped, horse and all, into the Great Canal; but he managed to get out again without serious injury. We have heard a good deal of thunder in the direction of Pekin—as if the tempest raging in the heart of the Emperor had been taken up and repeated by the heavens.

At length we received the unconditional ratifica-tion of the four treaties, signed by the Emperor; and, after a short visit to the Imperial Commissioners, we prepared to leave. The gunboats with the troops began to redescend the stream; and the long-boats

followed laden with provisions, and manned by
sailors, who made the banks ring with their oars. M.
Bellecourt and Mr. Bruce, who were appointed to
take to Paris and London the French and English
treaties, immediately left for Shang-hai. Count Poutiatine, preferring the route by land, despatched a
courier, who, crossing China and Mongolia on horseback, was to join the Russian mail from Irkoutsk
to Saint Petersburg. On Wednesday, the 7th of
July, at eight o'clock in the evening, Baron Gros
left the yamoun, to sleep on board the 'Dragonne,'
and leave next morning by daybreak. I took up my
quarters with M. Marquès in a small junk, to be
towed by a gunboat. An enormous crowd covered
the quays. The yamoun was packed with leading
citizens, in their long white dresses, who had come
out of curiosity to see the residence which the barbarians had just left.

At our departure the weather was moist and
rainy. During the first part of the voyage, the gunboat, being carried along by a strong current, and not
being sufficiently under command, ran aground twice
in the course of an hour. The first time we thrust our
bowsprit right into a dwelling-house, the next time
we plumped against a bank, upon which we might
have jumped from the deck. Each time that the tug
went aground our junk came thundering up against

her, and was nearly shaken to pieces by the collision. We were obliged, of course, to shift our quarters to the poop of the 'Dragonne.' We observed that all along the route the junks had hung out white flags as a sign of peace and neutrality. We passed near the junk of M. Delorisse, the naval officer, who, having charge of the transport service between Tien-tsin and Pecheli, had been for some time living with a few European sailors in the midst of the enemy's country. We learned to our surprise that he had hanged two Chinamen the night before. Two of his sailors had gone on shore in the usual way to buy provisions, and had been attacked at the corner of a street. One of them had received six deadly wounds from a spear. M. Delorisse armed his twelve Europeans, gave his junk in charge to the Chinese crew, and set out in pursuit of the mandarins of the village. He told them that, if they did not deliver up the perpetrators, their own heads would suffer for it. They brought the guilty parties without delay. One was already dead from wounds he had received. The two others were alive. They were hanged from the mast of the junk. A very curious incident, illustrative of Chinese manners, imparted a touch of the ridiculous to this fatal occurrence. Three old men came on board. They had been sent by the relations to offer themselves as substitutes for the prisoners.

They were willing, they said, to be hanged in lieu of those who had committed the offence.   They were very much surprised when their offer was refused by the commander, and indeed, on leaving, any one seeing them would have said that they had been badly used by him.   Had their proposal been accepted, they would have obtained a large sum in return for their lives, which would have enriched their relations for years.   They had missed a good bargain in consequence of the childish scruples of the French officer.   These extraordinary transactions are not uncommon in the history of the Chinese empire, and indeed they are closely interwoven with Chinese manners.   The English have often been deceived in this way on the Canton river when they have endeavoured to obtain justice from the mandarins for attacks upon their countrymen. In such cases, poor creatures, who had voluntarily taken the place of the murderers, and who were perfectly innocent of the crime, have been executed with great solemnity in presence of the persons appointed by the European authorities to see that the punishment was actually inflicted.

We arrived at Ta-kou at five o'clock in the afternoon, too late to pass the bar.   It was necessary to anchor opposite to the dismantled forts to await next day's tide.   On the 9th of July, at mid-day, we crossed the mouth of the Pei-ho without accident, and, after an absence of six weeks, we once more took up our old quarters on board the 'Audacieuse.'

We have been blamed by various organs of public opinion in Europe, and blamed pretty strongly too, for not having gone to Pekin to conduct negociations there, when we were so close upon it. A slight consideration of the obstacles we should have had to encounter will suffice to justify the conduct of the ambassadors. In the first place, if we had proceeded to Pekin as peaceful visitors, we must needs have gone through the ignominious ceremony of Ko-teo, which is too Asiatic by half to be submitted to by European ambassadors, consisting as it does in three prostrations and nine genuflexions, not only before the Emperor himself, but before the emblems of Imperial power,—as, for instance, the throne. Lord Elgin and Baron Gros learned from a reliable source that, rather than make an exception in our favour by exempting us from this formality, the Son of Heaven was prepared to leave his capital, and proceed into the wastes of Tartary with his whole court. It was on account of Lord Amherst's refusal to submit to the ko-teo that, in 1816, he left Pekin without having obtained an audience with the Emperor. In the second place, if the ambassadors had resolved to proceed to Pekin as enemies, undeterred by the uncertain and hazardous character of the enterprise, they would have exposed themselves to very great difficulties and perils. Let us see what would have happened. Out of our five thousand men, it would have been necessary to leave a thousand at Tien-tsin, which it will be recollected is an important town, of many hundred thousands of inhabitants, in order to protect it as the base of operations. Then it would have been necessary to establish another thousand in detachments on the way, between the army and Tien-tsin, to protect the escorts bringing up provisions and ammunition, and removing the sick and wounded, the Pei-ho not being navigable above Tien-tsin even for gunboats. Three thousand men would have remained. With them it would have been necessary to attack the Mongol prince Sang-Ko-Lin-Sin,who, ensconced in a fortified camp, intercepted our route to Pekin with thirty thousand men. After scattering this army we might have thundered down no doubt upon the capital. There is nothing, I verily believe, impossible to the soldiers and seamen of France and England under leaders of such experience and energy as Admiral Rigault de Genouilly and Sir Michael Seymour. But let us suppose that all this had been effected. What could we have done on reaching our destination, with the court in flight, the mandarins away, the authorities dispersed, and with no native party to back us? How could we have restrained, punished, and governed two millions of men wrapped in pride and prejudice ? In a few days we should have found ourselves alone and helpless under a systematic isolation, and have been under the necessity of retiring in the dread of an insurrection of immense multitudes, without advantages to compensate for the cost in human life of its suppression. For these reasons our ambassadors and admirals, who will not, I suppose, be reproached with timidity, did not provoke a gigantic struggle altogether out of proportion with the means at their command, and holding out no higher consummation or results than those so ably and pacifically obtained by the treaty of Tien-tsin.

Not having had the gratification of seeing Pekin, we resolved, at all events, to visit the Great Wall separating China, properly so called, from Mantchooria and Mongolia, which at one time was an important defence, but which now is a mere historical monument—a Mantchoo Tartar dynasty having reigned for two centuries over the Middle Empire.

Shang-hai, August 2, 1858.

'The treaties of Tien-tsin having been ratified by the Emperor Hien-Foung, on the 3rd day of July, 1858, the four plenipotentiaries, with the troops and gunboats of the allies, immediately evacuated the town and returned to their ships. Before finally leaving the Gulf of Pecheli, Baron Gros resolved to take the opportunity of visiting the Great Wall of China. He thought he would ascertain if the statement is correct, according to which it commences at the sea-coast near the entrance to the Gulf of Leotoung. On the 11th of July, at seven in the morning, the ambassador, his secretaries and attachés, embarked on board the " Prégent," an elegant little steamer (to be used as an advice-boat), which had just arrived from France. The place where the " Audacieuse " was anchored was supposed to be from ninety to one hundred miles from the spot where the Wall was said to reach the sea. We did not reach our destination the first day. Towards evening the weather was rather dull, and we could barely see the shore far in the distance. It was necessary to cast anchor at a considerable distance from land. On the following morning by daybreak we weighed anchor, put on our steam again, and soon came in sight of the Wall. It had the appearance of a long range of buildings of uniform height, crowned with battlements, and forming a barrier across the plain from the sea to a chain of mountains running parallel to the shore, at a distance of about two miles inland. An hour afterwards it became perfectly visible in its most minute details. We had before us the most interest-

ing and most picturesque scene in China. Along
the coast lay a spacious plain, covered with rich
meadows, and dotted here and there with villages
buried in the midst of trees.   Farther in the distance the landscape was bounded by lofty mountains,
some of which were abrupt and rocky, while others
were wooded and green to their very summits.   The
general effect was magnificent, and perhaps only to
be equalled among the Alpine valleys of Switzerland.
The Great Wall gave it an additional charm.   Ter-
minating in the sea, covered with bastions and
pagodas, and clambering over the wildest and most
precipitous crags, it imparted a character to the
whole landscape calculated to stir even the most
sluggish imagination.

' At the foot of the Wall, on the Chinese side, we
could see the white tents of two Tartar encampments,
the horses belonging to which were wandering at
large in the surrounding pastures. The landscape,
in the golden light of the dawn, was charming. It
was a glimpse of the pastoral life of the Mongol
hordes, and it gave us, on a small scale, a very good
idea of the land of pastures described so well by the
Abbé Huc.

' Seen from the Chinese side, the Great Wall re-
sembled a huge earthen mound crowned with battlements built of brick.   Everywhere it had an old and

dilapidated appearance.   In some places it had been altogether destroyed.   On the Mantchoorian side, on the other hand, the Great Wall seemed constructed of bricks resting upon a basement of stone. It is flanked by square towers throughout its whole length.   These are placed at the distance of about two bow-shots, in order that the enemy may be everywhere within range.   It descends into the sea in two parallel piers or jetties, which slope so gently that one can ascend to the top from the water flowing between them.   The largest ships may approach within two miles of the Wall, and, indeed, it is the very place at which visitors should in future disembark.

'Unfortunately we did not know this at the time, and cast anchor on the Chinese side of the wall. The beach at this place is level, but a heavy surf made it difficult to land, and prevented the ship's boats from approaching without the risk of being stranded upon the sand.   The beach was covered with Chinamen, who had come trooping down from the neighbouring villages.   M. Marquès, the interpreter to the mission, and Count d'Ozery, the commander of the " Prégent," got first on shore to talk with the authorities, and to ascertain if they would have any objection to our landing.   A mandarin, riding a white horse, and followed by two other personages also mounted, had come from the camp to ask who we were and what we wanted, and to ascertain from what quarter of the heavens we had dropped. On his being assured by our interpreter that our intentions were pacific, he declared that there was no objection to our coming on shore.

'We disembarked in consequence of this information; the process was not the least amusing part of the expedition. The boats in approaching the shore ran the risk of being capsized. They, however, escaped this danger. Baron Gros went on shore first, carried shoulder high by three stout sailors, who had stripped to the skin on purpose. The Vicomte de Contades, as well as the attachés to the embassy, and several officers of the "Audacieuse" and of the "Prégent," followed him, carried in much the same manner either by one or a couple of seamen. Not a few unlucky members of the exploring party, borne aloft in this fashion, were caught by a huge wave and hurled headlong with their bearers into the brine. At last, after a quarter of an hour spent in coming on shore, we all met, some dry, some dripping, upon the beach. We then set off into the interior with an escort of a dozen soldiers, their bayonets having been carefully protected from the water. We proceeded straight to the Wall. At first we had to cross several small water-courses, which run into the sea; then we went to some distance inland to get clear of the marshy tract which adjoins the shore. The closer we approached the Wall, this promised land which we were not destined to reach, the greater became the stir among the Tartars, who, mounted on horseback, pointed and gesticulated, and showed in every way that they were thrown into a state of high excitement by our proceedings. They soon after divided into three bodies. One of these remained on horseback before the camp, thus intercepting our route in the direct line to the Great Wall. The others came riding up to our left, and jumped off their horses among the tall herbaceous plants which covered the plain. The third party, composed of mandarins of the white and gilt buttons, came cantering up to meet us. They asked us whence we came and whither we were going, and told us that they could not allow us to proceed farther along our present road. Their chief they said was absent, and they could not take it upon them, without his permission, to allow us to go on, We expostulated, but in vain. They made amends for bad logic by an immense deal of tchin-tchin. What was our astonishment when we found that these people, encamped almost at the gates of the capital, were not even aware of the fact that their government had been at war with France and England! The capture of Canton, the bombardment of Ta-kou, the peace concluded at Tien-tsin, were all alike events unknown to them. After a long parley a fresh negociation seemed to have succeeded. They allowed us to advance a little way. But, as ill-luck would have it, three or four hundred yards further on another body of horsemen rode up, who requested us to halt.

' With an escort of twelve bayonets and a revolver apiece we could easily have kept at bay three hundred Tartar horsemen, and have climbed up to the Wall in defiance of them; but the ambassador was of course anxious to avoid an encounter, or indeed a dispute of any kind, whereby he might compromise his position while on a mere excursion of pleasure and curiosity. After taking a sketch or two, and buying a few fans of the Tartar horsemen, we delighted the Chinamen who gathered round us with a glass of brandy. We showed them our watches, and gave them a peep through our spy-glasses, all to their great wonder and satisfaction. We then returned to the boats, to which several among us swam out; in this way avoiding the risk of having our clothes drenched again.

' These Tartar horsemen, instead of having bows and arrows, were armed with matchlocks slung to a shoulder-belt. Their powder seemed very coarse, while their cartridge-boxes contained small bits of

lead besides shot. Their horses were small, and generally white or piebald, and belonged to a breed which
seemed essentially primitive. The horsemen carry their
principal pipe and a fan in their big boots. They all
had a ring of jade-stone to be used in tying their bows.

'Before leaving these shores we went with the
"Prégent" to make for land on the other side of the
Great Wall, off the plains of Mantchooria. The
plains rolled away before us in all that rich brilliancy
of verdure characterizing countries which, covered with
snow during a long winter, are vivified by the return of
a hot sun. The Great Wall, with its black tiers of
masonry, stood out from the dank and bright sward.
We saw it where it first appeared springing out of the
waters and lying against its huge buttresses. We
could track it with the eye as it clambered to the
very summit of the mountains, and we could follow
it farther, in imagination, along the course of the
same range to a distance of a thousand miles into
Central Asia, through those half-civilized countries
which extend to the confines of Mongolia and the
Kou-kou-noor.

'After having contemplated this magnificent spectacle for a long while, Baron Gros gave the signal for
departure, and the "Prégent" steered for the Toki
Islands, where the frigate awaited our return. Next
morning, after a passage of fifteen hours, we were

again on board, having brought back with us the recollection of a charming trip to the most picturesque and grandest scenes in China. We regretted that the officers of the "Audacieuse" had not participated in the excursion, as they might have done, for we found that everywhere the soundings were such that vessels of the largest size might, in perfect safety, ascend the Gulf of Pecheli as far as Leo-toung.'— *Moniteur*.

On the afternoon of the 17th July we left the 'Audacieuse' at Woosung, where the Yang-tse-Kiang joins the Whampou, and proceeded to Shang-hai on board the 'Prégent.' We had scarcely left the frigate when the leak which she had sprung during the storms off the Cape suddenly increased to an alarming extent. The water in the hold, instead of rising about an inch in an hour, gained nearly a foot in the same time. In the course of twenty-four hours there poured into the frigate 194 tons, or in weight nearly 400,000 lbs. of water. With such a serious injury it was impossible to put to sea. It was necessary to get out of this difficulty. At first we attempted to have the frigate repaired upon the spot; but there was no dock or basin large enough for the purpose. The proprietor of one dock offered to enlarge his accommodation so as to enable her to get into it, but he asked a delay of three months, and 4000*l*. In consequence, all thoughts of this were abandoned, and it was decided that the docks of Whampoa, in the Canton river, should be resorted to without a moment's delay. With a pilot belonging to the mercantile house of Dent, who was thoroughly acquainted with every place of refuge along the coast, and accompanied by a large American steam merchantman hired for the purpose, we put on all our steam for Hong Kong, and arrived there in four days without any accident. We fortunately escaped, in this rapid passage, the typhoons which are so frequent at this period of the year. The leak is near the axis of the screw, close by the rope-press. The system of screws without a cylinder is shown, I think, to be a bad one by the experience of our ship. It was calculated that, in crossing from France to China, the helix had made 6,300,000 turns which were quite useless in propelling the vessel.

The admiral, who arrived a few days after us, soon left with the whole French squadron, he having received orders to place himself at the head of the expedition to Cochin China, where he was to command both the French and Spanish sea and land forces. The 'Laplace' and the 'Prégent' alone remained behind to accompany the 'Audacieuse' to Japan. The general rendezvous for the other ships was fixed for the island of Haïnan in the Gulf of

Tonkin. As we had no connection whatever with this expedition, we remained at Shang-hai six weeks. The season was a bad one for a residence at this place. The thermometer stood at 104° Fahrenheit, and cholera, fever, and dysentery, which accompany the hot season in this part of China, were prevalent and deadly. Violent storms and frequent typhoons alone broke the monotony of our existence, and it will not be wondered at if we cast a longing gaze towards the island of Japan, situated within a three days' sail from Shang-hai, where we had still to perform the second part of the mission entrusted to us.

CHAPTER IX.

The Manners, Customs, and Government of China.

WE have collected, in this chapter, various facts and novel pieces of information concerning the Middle Empire, which could not be introduced with propriety in any other part of the book. They are set down here just as they occur to the author, without attention either to the order of the subjects, or to that which they came under his notice.

China, properly so called, is divided into eighteen provinces; but Europeans are only acquainted with six of these, which adjoin the coast, viz., Kwang-toung, Fo-kien, Tche-kiang, Kiang-sou, Chan-toung, and Pecheli. Formerly all political events interesting to Europeans were concentrated upon the banks of the Canton river in Kwang-toung; now, the scene of action has shifted to the north to Pecheli, and at no distant day Tien-tsin and Ta-kou may be expected to take the place once held by Bocca-Tigris and Macao. The three central provinces of Kwang-si, Hou-nan, and Houpé are the principal theatre of the great insurrection.   Kan-sou, Chen-si, and Chan-si reach the Great Wall to the north.   Su-tchouan and Yun-nan adjoin.   Thibet, Kouei-tcheou, Kiang-si, Ngan-hoeï, and Honan complete our enumeration of the provinces of China.

The Middle Empire is composed, besides, of several countries or tributary kingdoms, viz., Mongolia, Mantchooria, and Corea, the Loo-choo Islands, Thibet, Tonkin, Cambodia, and Cochin China. The Loo-choo Islands and Corea send a tribute to Pekin every year. Some other countries do so every three years, and others again at intervals less frequent, as for instance every ten years. With regard to European countries separated by the great ocean from the countries under the dominion of the Son of Heaven, they render him homage only at fixed intervals, varying in duration.   This interesting information is drawn from the Book of Rites.

China, during a period extending back for four thousand years, has been governed by twenty-eight dynasties.   The three last of these were the Mongol dynasty, the national dynasty of Ming, and the Ta-Tsing, or Tartar Mantchoo dynasty.   The last Emperor was called Tao-Kouang, or Shining Wisdom. His son, Hien-Foung, succeeded him in 1850, at the very height of the great insurrection.   His reign has been marked, hitherto, by a long series of national calamities.

The Emperor, in the machinery of the Chinese government, is a mere name or emblem representing the nation. In the Council resides the supreme power. The Emperor is the index or wheel of the machine which is exposed. Everything is done in his name, but without his direct co-operation. There is a thorough centralisation and an admirable administrative organisation extending over the whole empire. The institutions are excellent; but there is a lack of the right men to work these institutions.

The district of Nankin is rich; that of Pekin is poor and sterile. The central government, accordingly, raises a tax in kind over the fertile provinces which lie along the course of the Yang-tse-Kiang. Every year thousands of junks, laden with rice and despatched by the local mandarins, leave for Tien-tsin at the commencement of the south-west monsoon. This is a tax or burden imposed upon all the possessors of junks. They have no right to any remuneration by way of freight, but they have the privilege, on their return home, of carrying on commerce on their own account, and they sell besides in central China the first fruits and products of Leo-tong.

The seven provinces after named used formerly to

send their tribute of rice to the city of Pekin, by the Grand Imperial Canal, in more than twelve thousand junks. The junks employed in this service were divided between the provinces in the following way :

Kiang-sou	.	.	.	3,000
Ngan-hoei	.	.	.	1,500
Tché-kiang	.	.	.	2,000
Kiang-si .	.	.	.	1,500
Hou-pé .	.	.	.	1,000
Hou-nan .	.	.	.	1,000
Chan-tong	.	.	.	2,000
Total	.		.	12,000

In recent times the inundations of the Yellow River have been a dreadful source of misery in China. They have completely destroyed and rendered impracticable the Great Imperial Canal, and all this immense inland navigation above referred to has accordingly been destroyed. The Chinese tribute junks are now obliged to take the route by the Gulf of Pecheli and the Pei-ho, which places their whole revenue within reach of European war vessels. A few gunboats have only to come on the 1st of April each year, to cruise about Cape Chan-tong or Cape Macartney, and they will effectually interrupt all intercourse between the wealthy provinces and the capital, intercept the junks, and secure their stores.

In a few weeks famine will make its appearance at Pekin, and the Tartars will be put on short commons of millet porridge. In finding out the course taken by the junks, we have found out the weak side of the giant, and England will not forget to profit by this discovery.

According to Sir John Bowring, Yeh during the last two or three years has beheaded seventy thousand rebels. From the 1st of January to the 1st of August, 1855, the executioners were hard at work. From two hundred to six hundred rebels had their heads chopped off daily. The 'Hong Kong Journal' mentions another locality, a dependency of the two Kwangs, in which Yeh executed, towards the same period, thirty thousand persons. This brings up the number of executions to a hundred thousand. It must however be said for the governor-general, that he would not own to more than seventy thousand. The remainder he declared to be a matter of pure invention on the part of his enemies.

The name of the present Emperor is Hang-Foung or Hien-Foung, according to the different dialects. It signifies Universal Abundance. The symbol which serves to express this name in the Chinese character is a mountain between two kings. Superstitious Chinamen discovered a bad omen in this conjunction of objects. What is meant, they asked, by a mountain between two kings ? Clearly enough it indicated, for the future, division, anarchy, and civil war. Now is this not precisely what is taking place at present? Of his three capitals, Hien-Foung now possesses only one. Nankin is in the hands of the rebels, while Canton is occupied by the barbarians ; and so a great part of the empire is in a state of rebellion against the present dynasty. The prediction has been fulfilled.

Every mountain and hill in China is covered with tombs. The hills we have described near Macao are a striking example of this, and so is the mountain of the Blue Cloud at Canton. All the elevations on Danes Island and French Island, and on the Pearl River at Canton, behind Gough's Fort, exhibit the same appearance ; and, indeed, such is the extent of ground covered by these tombs that China might be described as one great cemetery.

A mandarin is never allowed to exercise his functions in the province where he was born. To secure impartiality he must always be a stranger to the country in which his jurisdiction lies. If he be a military mandarin he is not allowed to take his mother with him to the scene of action, as her presence might soften him and restrain his warlike impetuosity on the day of battle. If he be a civil mandarin he is not allowed to take his father with him.

The latter might differ from him in opinion on some
case in which he had to give judgment, and, if under
such circumstances he were to stand out, he would
then oppose the dictates of filial respect and piety,
which command us to yield obedience to parents. It
was as a mark of special favour from the Emperor
that Yeh obtained permission to live with his father
at Canton.

The Chinese, even when they come in contact
with Europeans, always preserve some share of anti-
quated and foolish prejudice, and, to an incredible
extent, the ridiculous notion that their race is superior to all others in knowledge, ability, and wisdom'
and possessed of qualities enjoyed by no other people
on the face of the globe.   Père Deluc was talking in
my presence with his Chinese secretary, on the deck
of the 'Durance,' about the news of the day, and
more particularly about the approaching bombardment of Canton.   The English and French gunboats
were already placed in line, and the other ships were
anchored in the deep places of the river.   'I do not understand,' said the secretary, 'why the mandarins don't
send a few Chinamen underneath the ships to bore a
hole or two up through them, and sink them in that
way.' 'But,' replied the Père, ' you don't suppose they
would be allowed to do this ?   How would they get at
the ships ?' 'Why,' answered the secretary, nothing

daunted, ' don't you know that there are Chinamen who can live for a whole day under water? It would have been a much more serious affair for us had the Chinese set on fire all the junks and sampans lying in the upper part of the river, and allowed them in one vast blazing spluttering mass to float down the current upon our vessels. In the midst of the confusion produced in this way, many ships would certainly have been destroyed in spite of the fireguards attached to them. A single sampan with gunpowder on board, which took fire, caused a vast deal of alarm. There was no way to get at it or direct its course; and, indeed, the ' Phlégéton ' escaped by a miracle from getting entangled with it. Fortunately it was burned almost upon the spot where the fire broke out.

The most preposterous accounts of barbarian folly find currency in China. Here is the way in which the people in the interior of the empire interpreted the retreat of the English and Admiral Seymour, on the occasion of the lorcha 'Arrow' case, which occurred, it will be recollected, towards the end of 1856. The Chinese admiral had resorted, it appears, to a most ingenious device. One night when the ebb had set in he threw a great quantity of large turnips into the river. The red barbarians, hearing the turnips bumping up constantly against the ships' timbers, got up in alarm to look out, thinking they were attacked. They rushed wildly to their guns, and kept up a constant fire into the darkness upon imaginary enemies. The Chinese admiral waited till they had foolishly spent the best part of their powder and shot, and then, opening a real attack, as a matter of course he took and destroyed all their vessels. In this way history is written in China! The governor-general of Tcheli had recourse in his official report to a similar stretch of fancy in order to explain our victory on the Pei-ho to his countrymen. Just as we made our appearance in these seas, a high tide, he said, of the most unprecedented kind, had suddenly come surging in from the ocean, overturning the forts of Ta-kou, rendering useless the bravery of its defenders, and enabling the foreign devils, who rode unharmed upon the waters, to force the entrance to the river and to ascend through channels at other times completely closed against them.

The pagoda, or banyan-tree, the *ficus religiosa* of botanists, is an imposing tree, which has, in point of fact, a religious and solemn appearance. It is met with everywhere in China, resting against the walls of the pagodas and shading the courts of the yamouns. In country places, round the trunk there are small altars, with joss-sticks burning, and a few Buddhist images resting upon the roots.

It is the finest of the Chinese trees.   Its foliage is luxuriant and always fresh and green.   From Macao to Shang-hai, from Tien-tsin to the Great Wall, everywhere we met with the banyan-tree, which is the necessary appendage of every ya-moun and Buddhist temple, sheltering alike under its dense leafage the squalid bonze and rapacious mandarin.

It is nothing uncommon in China for a pirate leader to become a mandarin.   Among other in-stances of this, may be quoted that of the famous Apak, who, not many years ago, had seven hundred pirate junks under his command.   He has retired from active service, and leads a life of quiet and honoured ease at Ning-po.   He enjoys all the prero-gatives attached to the blue button.   The Chinese government, finding they could not put him down, entered into treaty with him and made him a naval mandarin.

In China the compass is not made to point to the north, but to the south.   It has five, not four cardinal points.   The left, not the right side, is the place of honour.   White, not black, is the suit of woe.   Eti-quette ordains that we should not take off the hat, but put it on, in presence of a superior, or of any one whom we wish to honour.   Books are printed and read, not from left to right, after our fashion, but from right to left. At dinner, fruit comes first, and soup last. As children learn their lessons aloud, all saying them over at the same time, it is the object of a Chinese schoolmaster not to keep a quiet school, but to make his little congregation as noisy as possible; and silence is punished as a proof of idleness. When a man is ennobled for a service done the state, honours so acquired do not descend, as with us, to his posterity, but, strange to say, ascend to his ancestors and ennoble them. They all become, by a retrospective action, dukes and barons, and so forth, while the children and descendants of the new-made noble remain undistinguished in the common herd. Pages might be filled with similar contrasts between the habits of Europeans and Chinamen.

The inhabitants of the Celestial Empire have never shown any great liking or esteem for the Europeans who have settled, in spite of all opposition, upon their seaboard. To give some idea of the style in which it has been their wont, even in our days, to speak of us, we have but to read the following proclamation, which was placarded over the walls of a Chinese town in July 1851.

' The faithful soldiers and chiefs at the right heart of the whole people of the empire of the great dynasty of the Tsings publish the present order for the information of the detestable barbarians.

'Detestable barbarians! disgusting barbarians! Try to see your images in a glass! Look at yourselves there. You are little better than brutes and beasts. You differ from them only in your faculty of speech. Our people speak words of reason to you; but you lay down laws. You are blindly and obstinately stupid. You won't understand—so there is only one way of dealing with you, and that is to strangle and murder every one of your hateful race. Ever since you came to the land of the Middle Empire to trade, you have acted in the most brutal manner, without one thought to the consequences of your conduct. Your opium has shortened the lives of our people— it has undermined their health; your vessels have taken violent possession of our trade and profits. Hungry as whales, always ready to devour, and pertinacious as the silkworm which blights the mulberry-leaf, you steadily continue your encroachments. Allow you to take one step forward, and you take two.

'You have usurped our lands, impoverished us by force. You have destroyed our tombs. You have built in the town innumerable houses dedicated to the devil; and now, forsooth, you want ground for a course to race your horses on; you want, there is not a doubt of it, to go as far as Sou-Kiang to build one of your churches there.

'Your offences, numerous as they are, will be more

numerous still. Your crimes already reach the sky ; but highest Heaven is now in anger with you, and we, the people, are ordained to destroy you with the artillery of the gods.

'You think that in acting according to set plans you will gain your ends ; you are preparing to play the part of the wolf and tiger among the brutes. But you little know your position. Do you know that our people look upon you as birds shut up in a cage, as fish caught in a net, as dogs trapped in a snare, as sheep pent in a fold ? Some fine day the fury of the people will burst forth spontaneous and sudden ; they will rush upon you ; they will cut your throats ; they will leave in the land not one trace of your existence. The present edict is published for your information.'

The following conversation, which has been often quoted before, took place in October 1849, at Pekin, between the Emperor Tao-Kouang and Pih-Kwe, then criminal judge of the province of Kwang-toung. It is equally characteristic of Chinese conceit and ignorance. I do not know how the document came into the possession of the European consuls who published it, but there is no doubt as to its authenticity. The Emperor opens the conversation.

'*Emperor.* Then Seu-Kwang-Tsin did not continue to employ any of the persons who had been in office under Ky-Ing. Of late years Ky-Ing has been almost frightened to death by these barbarian affairs. The people whom he employed in the administration of these matters greatly exaggerated their importance, so that Ky-Ing was always in a state of alarm; in consequence of his giving credit to all they told him, he has only thereby helped to magnify the great renown of the barbarians. You have put all this to rights. It appears to me that the barbarians have not the means of existence if driven from Kwang-toung.

'*Pih-Kwe.* The people of Kwang-toung become more and more convinced every day that the barbarians have no means of existence without this province.

'*Emperor.* That is quite the case. Who are the agents employed in the administration of barbarian affairs?

'*Pih-Kwe.* Commissioners Heu-Tsang-Kwang and Howqua.

'*Emperor.* Have the English barbarians been recently brought under subjection or not?

'*Pih-Kwe.* They appear to have been to some extent subdued.

'*Emperor.* Does the garrison at Hong Kong not number from three to four thousand men?

'*Pih-Kwe.* Not more than from two to three thousand men, the greater part of whom only exist on paper; more than half of the green soldiers (the Ceylon Fusiliers) have left in consequence of the insufficiency of the funds appropriated to their support. Trade is not in a good state either at Ning-po or in any of the other free ports.

'*Emperor.* I have heard it said that it is in a bad state at Ning-po, Amoy, and Shang-hai. This proves that prosperity is always followed by decay.

'*Pih-Kwe.* The English barbarians were in a very precarious condition last year in their own country, where they were visited by an epidemic; and at Hong Kong last year more than a thousand persons perished in consequence of the hot exhalations.

'*Emperor.* Prosperity is always succeeded by decay! What avails the power of man?

'*Pih-Kwe.* Divine favour for your Majesty is doubtless the cause of the humiliation of the English barbarians.

'*Emperor.* You are a man belonging to the banners, born and brought up at Pekin. You must know this saying of the old women—"a thousand, nay, ten thousand schemes of man, are not worth one scheme of God!' Do you think that the English barbarians, or any of the other barbarian nations, will cause fresh trouble in the south?

'*Pih-Kwe.* No. Even the English have nothing new

T

to gain by causing strife. When these barbarians revolted in 1841, they depended entirely upon other nations which subsidised them with the purpose of opening up commerce. In the present year the countries subjected to English rule are ready to rise in rebellion.

' *Emperor*. It is evident from this that these barbarians make commerce their principal occupation, and strive incessantly to get new territories.

' *Pih-Kwe*. Quite so. They belong, in short, to the same class with brutes, dogs, and horses. They are utterly incapable of entertaining any elevated idea.

' *Emperor*. They are sometimes ruled by a woman, sometimes by a man. It is evident that they are quite unworthy of serious attention. Do they fix a certain term of office, like us, for their authorities, in the case of Bonham* for instance ?

' *Pih-Kwe*. Some of their officers are changed every two years, others every three years; and although it is their king, nominally, who sends them, they are in reality dependent upon the corporation of their merchants (the East India Company).'

The Chinese now speak of Europeans with a little less disdain. The name of barbarians has been dropped from their official language in respect of the treaties of Tien-tsin, but I suspect that it will be

* Sir George Bonham, Governor of Hong Kong.

long before international politeness banish from their conversation and every-day life the harsh ignominious expressions still used in talking of us. In the eyes of the Chinese we must continue, for years to come, to be considered a people more powerful than they are in war, and in possession of more deadly weapons of destruction, but far inferior to themselves in all that relates to a peaceful and civilized life. In short, we now appear to them as pirates on a great scale.

Instead of striving to open up China, European diplomacy might endeavour to prevent all egress from it. The empire swarms with population. Everywhere the Chinese people are spreading beyond the natural limits of the country. To the north they are gradually advancing into the Land of Meadows, pushing slowly before them the Mongol Tartars. In Mantchooria the Emperor in vain essays to guard the frontier of his paternal kingdom from his southern subjects, in order to preserve a place of refuge, should he, in the course of events, be driven from the Chinese throne. The inhabitants of the empire give little heed to Imperial decrees where the means of existence are concerned, and the Mantchoo civilization is disappearing piecemeal before the gradual and peaceful progress of the neighbouring people. From southern China there is a constant stream of population flowing. Thousands are embarking daily on board the emigrant ships. Everywhere round the shores of the Pacific, Chinamen are now settled as colonists. There are great Chinese communities in California, Australia, Java, Manilla, Pulo-Penang, Singapore, and Hong-Kong. Wherever they go they form the most industrious section of the population, and often by their skill and patient industry they are a source of prosperity to all the places where they settle, but they are at the same time the most turbulent and dangerous subjects a government can have, as they hang close together and form everywhere secret societies, which are formidable to the legitimate authorities. It is not long since they were very near taking the Philippine Islands from the Spaniards. They gave the Dutch some time ago the most serious grounds for alarm in Batavia. They require to be placed under the surveillance of a very vigilant police at Singapore and Hong-Kong. In the colonies of the Pacific the result of all this is that a dread of the Chinese begins to make its appearance, and their immigration in large numbers is now everywhere discouraged. In the colony of Victoria the local legislature have passed a law entitled the 'Chinese Emigration Act,' specially intended to diminish the importation of Chinese colonists. Under its terms, ships are not allowed to take on board more than one emigrant for every ten tons of the ship's burthen, and the captain or person in command is liable to a fine of ten pounds sterling for every passenger above the statutory number. At San Francisco, on the other hand, a tax of fifty dollars a head is levied from all Chinamen who land as emigrants, and Chinamen settling there are besides compelled to pay a monthly tax of six dollars a head, paid by no other class of foreigners. From New Zealand they are completely excluded. At a public meeting in that colony, a resolution was passed to the effect that any one assisting to introduce Chinese Coolies should be declared a public enemy. The last news we have, however, on the subject of Coolie emigration is from California. No regulation hitherto put in force having diminished the influx of the Chinese population towards the gold-fields, and the yellow race threatening in a few years to exceed in numbers and wealth the whole population of European descent settled along the coasts of the Pacific, the legislature of California have, it is reported, formally prohibited the introduction of Coolies into that country.

By dint of extraordinary sobriety, wonderfully laborious habits, and great aptitude for business, these emigrants in a very few years contrive to scrape together a considerable capital, with which they return to the Land of Flowers, impoverishing the colony to the extent of their fortune. They do not even allow their dead to remain on foreign soil, and accordingly we find large American clippers constantly engaged in conveying from San Francisco to Hong Kong the red coffins of Chinamen who before their decease have expressed a wish to be interred near the tombs of their forefathers. The fecundity of the Chinese race is prodigious. In this respect there is no other to be compared with it. Wherever the traveller goes, whether it be on board the junks, among the fishing-boats, or through the streets, the number of children always attracts his attention. Everywhere there are crowds of little ones. The prevalence of infanticide, the wholesale butchery of the rebels, and the constant stream of emigration from the southern seaports produce no effect in diminishing the population. The last census it is said fixes the Chinese population at 415,000,000.

Chinese civilization has lasted for the last four thousand years. Seven hundred years before the birth of Christ there was a Chinese literature. Several of the principal literary monuments of China belong to this early period. The national existence of our European states must appear to the Chinese a thing of yesterday when contrasted with the duration of their own empire. The mandarin language is that used by the learned; Cantonese, Fokinese, and various other dialects, are spoken by the people in

different parts of the empire.   The mandarin dialect
is to some extent in the countries of the far East what
Latin is in Europe.   Knowing mandarin, a person
can make himself understood throughout the whole
empire, and even in Corea, Tonkin, Cochin-China,
and Siam.   At Pekin the people speak pure mandarin.

I hear our officers who served in the Crimean campaign constantly making the remark, that the architecture of China reminds them very much of that of
the Turks.   The Chinese village which stood right
in face of us at Whampoa, consisting of houses built
upon piles, with painted balconies, and places set
aside under each for the reception of the tankas,
reminded them involuntarily of the shores of the
Bosphorus.   The tankas recalled the caiques, while
the minarets seemed copied from the same pattern
with the pagodas, which we saw in the distance.   The
narrow streets were as tortuous as those of the
Turkish towns.   The very appearance of the writing
bore an outward resemblance at least to that in use
among the Moslem.   But if there are between the
two races traits of resemblance, pointing to a common origin, they now differ most essentially in character.   The Turks are grave, reserved, and taciturn,
while the Chinamen are noisy, talkative, and undignified.   There may be something venerable in a long

Turkish beard, but I will defy any one to look at a Chinaman's tail and keep his countenance.

There is a whole population in China which is not entitled to inhabit the land, and which lives entirely on the rivers and canals. This is an inferior race, a conquered people, kept in this state in respect of a dim historical reminiscence which goes back to the earliest age of Chinese civilization. This outcast population explains the crowd of boats, junks, sampans, and hovels built on piles along the streams, which attracted our notice when we arrived in China, as they rose and fell, or were washed by the waves thrown up by the steamers. All the compradors who supply the ships with provisions belong to this class of boatmen. Some of them are very rich, and indeed possess on the waters of the Canton river magnificent houses, which are elegantly and sumptuously furnished ; but such is the force of tradition and prejudice in China, that they are not allowed to settle or acquire property on land.

In some parts of China wheelbarrows with sails attached to them are in use. When a good breeze blows from behind, or from one side, human labour is very much lightened by this means. This fact may at first appear a traveller's tale, but it is not such. These barrows are largely used in China for purposes of locomotion. The missionaries, for the sake of eco-

nomy, often prefer them to any other vehicle, in spite
of the fatigue of managing them. Often while we
stayed at Shang-hai and Tien-tsin we saw these singular conveyances arrive from off a journey. The
wheel is placed in the middle of the machine. The
traveller sits on one side, and his luggage is placed
opposite to him by way of counterpoise.

The great Chinese insurrection has now diminished
very much in importance. It has lost its leaders, the
kings of the four cardinal points. The famous King
of the East, the ablest of the four, the very soul of
the insurrection, who aspired to universal dominion,
has been assassinated by the others, who were jealous
of his influence. Besides, the rebels have been defeated in Nankin. Disputes among themselves, however, have committed greater ravages in their ranks
than the artillery of the mandarins. Tsien-Kiang,
the celebrated Canton demagogue, is still the chief
judge in their camp, but their ablest general has for-
saken their cause for that of the Imperialists, in consequence of a tragical event which we must record,
as it has been set forth by veracious testimony. This
ambitious general was displeased, it appears, at not
being appointed king of the fifth cardinal point. He
had received, however, from the leaders of the insurrection the promise of being exalted to this sublime
rank, if he could only gain for the rebels one great

victory over the Imperialists. When this promise of
advancement had been made to him he resorted to
every expedient to attain the end in view. He pre-
tended to abandon the rebel cause, and went over to
the camp of the enemy with the object of course of
betraying the latter. The old general of the Emperor,
however, was not to be taken in. He had not grown
grey among soldiers without some experience in
Chinese roguery. He at once took alarm at this case
of sudden conversion. Suspecting its true cause and
object, he received the rebel soldier enthusiastically.
He solemnly adopted him as his son, and heaped
favours upon him. Then, underhand, he lost no time
in spreading the rumour through the rebel camp that
the general had really gone over to the mandarins.
It was well known that he was dissatisfied, and that
he had long looked upon himself as an ill-used man.
The news of the reception he had met with in the
rebel camp gave strength to the suspicion against
him. The rebel chiefs, too, gave credence to the
rumours in circulation. Chinese justice soon followed.
His father, mother, wife, and children were apprehended. They were taken to the front of the camp,
and there, amid parade and the music of the pipe and
tomtom, they were cruelly beheaded. The general
was driven to distraction. He swore that he would
exact a signal vengeance for this barbarous deed, and

thenceforth he became one of the mainstays of the Imperial throne. Strange to say, this rebel chief has been appointed since this time commander-in-chief of the Imperial army. It was he who invented the new system of warfare now followed by the Imperialists. He burns and lays waste the whole tract over which he passes, so as to place the rebels in the midst of a desert. In this way he succeeds in starving them, and in point of fact he has put a limit to their success and progress towards the northern provinces. Numerous battles have been fought in the neighbourhood of Yang-Tcheou, the key to the Imperial Canal; and the result has been that this place remains in the hands of the mandarins. The insurrection has been stopped in its advance towards the capital for several years, and the Imperial authorities re-occupy several provinces to which the rebels had extended their rule. They still possess Nankin, the capital of the national dynasty of the Ming; but Pekin continues to be the residence of the Mantchoo Tartar dynasty, and the Emperor Hien-Foung has the support of the population generally, a frightful confusion having everywhere resulted from the overturn of his government. Unfortunately there is no revenue. The court is in desperation for money, and unable to supply the soldiers with the means of existence; the latter make depredations everywhere. The Emperor cannot call in to his assistance the Tartar hordes. This would be a useless expedient, or one at all events to be resorted to only under very desperate circumstances. The Mongols would be scattered under the hot sun of the plains. The Mantchoos could give little assistance. They are miserable tribes, scanty in numbers, and with no arms but bows and spears. The two powers, the rebels and Imperialists, remain then in a state of hostility and in presence of each other, living at the expense of provinces which successive governments have done their utmost to ruin and depopulate for ages. From time to time news is brought to the European ports that cannon have been heard on the shores of the Yang-tse-Kiang. The cannon have been fired, but it is all a device of the mandarins. They require to get up an occasional victory, in order that they may send a high-sounding bulletin to the court of Pekin, to support a fresh demand for money. The military authorities take good care not to crush the insurrection entirely. This would be killing the hen that lays the golden eggs. In point of fact, all the money which is sent by the government to pay the troops finds its way into the purses of the mandarins, and very little ever goes farther. It would evidently be a great mistake in the excess of zeal to put an end to a business so profitable to themselves. We may explain the religious and Christian character of the rebellion, at its origin, in the following manner.* The great Chinese national insurrection took place on the confines of Kwang-toung and Kwang-si, among the mountains of the Miao-Tze, independent tribes whom the Chinese government has never succeeded in bringing under subjection. Now there were formerly among the Miao-Tze many Christians who had sought refuge in the mountains. They had fled from Tartar rule, and remained supporters to the last of the cause of the son of the latest emperor of the dynasty of the Ming. The general of the Pretender's army in Kwang-si was a Christian. The Pretender himself was a Christian as well as his family. He was defeated and killed by treason in Kouei-lin, the capital of the province. There were confused and vague recollections or traditions of these events, and hence the vague sort of Christianity which characterized the insurrection at first, but which was soon combined with polygamy under the sway of the King of the East.

There is a considerable traffic in cattle between Mongolia and China, properly so called. By the gate of the Great Wall nearest to Pekin there enter annually twenty-five millions of sheep. The whole number of sheep entering the Celestial Empire annually may be estimated at sixty or seventy-five millions. In the northern provinces, near the great pasture-lands, sheep may be had at a wonderfully low price, while south of Shang-hai and Ning-po they are not to be purchased for any sum. The southern provinces, covered with rice-fields, are destitute of grass-lands where sheep can feed.

The family of Confucius is still extant. It inhabits the province of Chan-toung, and possesses great privileges. It forms the only hereditary nobility in China. Koung-Fou-Tseu, its founder, died in the year 479 before Christ. This family is certainly an old one, but it has degenerated, not having for a long period produced any man of the smallest consequence.

On attaining the age of eighty, Chinamen are entitled to wear yellow attire, this being the colour of the Imperial family. This is an honour conferred on old age by law.

Corea is a kingdom which is tributary to China. Every year it sends an embassy to Pekin. But the authority of the Chinese over this people is purely nominal and honorary. No Chinese has any right to reside in Corea, nor has any Corean a right to reside in Chinese territory. There is so little connection between the two governments that Admiral Poutiatine on one occasion saved the crew of a Chinese junk who had been shipwrecked, and who were about to be massacred by the Coreans without opposition on the part of the native authorities. The natives of Corea call their country Kerai. It is a gold region. There are three mines known to exist in it, of which two only have been explored. They are defended by evil genii according to the mandarins, who, being as yet far behind in political economy, dread an over supply of the precious metal, and get up this legend to scare the people. The Russians made themselves masters a year ago of the course of the Ousouri and Soungari, tributaries of the Amour. They have come into close proximity with Corea, and the independence of this country is thereby seriously menaced.

All the yamouns in China belong to the Emperor. They cannot be sold, nor does any prescription affect property in them. The mandarins, only retaining office for three years, think more of making money than of adorning their official abodes, and hence the state of disrepair into which all the public buildings of China have fallen.

Corruption is universal in China ; by dint of money and bribery everything may be effected, everything found out in all parts of the empire, and in every sphere of Chinese life. It is all a matter of calculation. The rich merchants of Sou-tchou-fou had bought up the secretaries of the High Imperial Commissioners from Pekin, and they knew as well as we did what was going on at Tien-tsin. Before we returned from Pecheli the tao-tai of Shang-hai had procured the Chinese text of the English treaty, and imparted its contents to M. de Montigny. With the crowd of literati and petty mandarins who always flutter about the Chinese authorities, it is quite impossible to keep a state secret.

There is still at Pekin a church standing, which is of larger dimensions than the cathedral of Tong-ka-tou. Taken in former times from the missionaries, the edifice has since been devoted to no particular purpose. A cross surmounted the dome till within the last five or six years, when it was taken down under the pretext that the symbol was unlucky, and might attract the rebels. If the court of Pekin would consent to restore this church to our missionaries, they would thereby give us a striking proof of their good faith and sincerity, in the abandonment of the old anti-European policy.

There are in China rich mines of gold, silver, and quicksilver ; but the government prohibit them from being worked under pain of death, alleging that it would be removing hands from agricultural labour. In a country like the Celestial Empire, which has an immense population to support on a limited area, everything, they hold should, be sacrificed to the cultivation of the soil and the production of food and clothing. There is another motive for this prohibition. The Chinese government conceded some time ago the right of working the mines to certain parties specified in the contract. The persons concerned in this joint adventure had no sooner made a little money than they were attacked by a band of armed men, who attempted to rob them of it. The mining adventurers resisted, and the consequences were highway robberies, assaults, fights, and pitched battles in infinite succession. This sort of thing could not continue long, so the court of Pekin, to bring the disorders to a close, completely prohibited the working of mines over the whole empire. What mining is still carried on is consequently fraudulent, and concealed from the authorities. At Ning-po, however, a Coolie has made a fortune by secret mining, his operations having been conducted with great skill and boldness, in defiance of legal ordinances. There are a great number of coal-mines in the neighbourhood of Pekin, but they are worked after the fashion of the patriarchal ages, without regard to the future. The mines of Formosa, in the hands of Chinese companies, now supply coal to the European steamers.

In the country places, all over the Chinese empire, the traveller may see everywhere red coffins standing in the middle of the fields. These are dead bodies which await burial. The family to which they belong,

U

not being rich enough to purchase a suitable place of interment and to bear the expense of a solemn funeral, delays until some others of its members die, when one ceremony will suffice for all of them. If the father dies, then the family waits till the mother expires, and indeed often until the death of the eldest son; for a solemn funeral is a ruinous affair, often swallowing up the best part of the savings of a lifetime.

The European coasting-trade has of late increased very much. Whenever a European vessel takes to this traffic, fifteen junks at least are driven from the field. There are several reasons for this; the chief of which are, that European ships are roomy, can go to sea at all seasons, and can be insured. Junks, on the other hand, have a very small tonnage. They must wait for the monsoons, and are not protected from risk by the system of marine insurance, which is altogether unknown to the Chinese. The coasting-trade is that in which the French would be most likely to succeed in China. M. de Montigny has already organised a whole service of Chinese barks, carrying the French flag, and having each a French sailor in command. They ply between Shang-hai and Ning-po. These barks convey letters, passengers, and goods, and have secured the confidence of the Chinese to such an extent that they are more trusted than any other vessels of the same kind, whether under Chinese or Portuguese colours. The French flag is held in high respect in the Chinese waters.

All Europeans settled in the free ports of China willingly bear testimony to the honourable manner in which business on a great scale is conducted by Chinese merchants. They even admit that the great Chinese banking-houses are often safer than the great European houses. But this is far from being the case with retail trade.

In Mongolia there are from eight to ten thousand Christians, but they are all Chinamen. The Mongols are receding gradually before the peaceful invasion of Chinese immigrants. The Chinese settle now beyond the Great Wall, buy land there, and till it. The Mongolians, unwilling to abandon their wandering life for settled occupations, are receding farther and farther before the agricultural communities into the north of the Land of Pastures; exhibiting in this respect some resemblance to the Indians of North America, who are gradually receding and disappearing before the tide of civilization. The Mantchoos have been influenced in a different way by the Chinese. Indeed they have become Chinese in all respects, and in dress and language there is nothing to distinguish them from the inhabitants of the Celestial Empire. In passing through Moukden, the capital of Mantchooria, we might imagine ourselves to be in a town of the two Kiangs or of the two Kwangs.

The missionaries often spoke to us of the frightful ravages caused by the use of opium in China, and of the rapid progress which this deleterious practice is making every year in the empire. Opium was at first exclusively used by the mandarins, to beget a certain energy of manner, and as a stimulant better fitting them either for toil or pleasure. At first they offered it to those who called upon them, as a rare and curious delicacy. It was brought out as a mark of respect, and the visitors were accordingly obliged to partake of it. Gradually this habit spread among the wealthy classes, the literati, the nobility, and all persons who by their position were brought into contact with the mandarins. Opium even found its way to the people under the name of polite tobacco, and was smoked at first from motives of vanity, and then from love for the thing itself. Now there is not one district in China which is not infected by the habit. It has found its way alike into princes' palaces and poor men's cottages. The Chinese government attempts in vain to remedy the evil—every one is practically opposed to interference. In vain has the punishment of death been decreed against all who smoke the drug. The wives of the Emperor violate the law within the very walls of the palace. It is a fertile source of revenue to the mandarins, and hence the futility of all attempts to suppress it. In fact, the persons who keep divans, or houses for opium-smoking, manage to protect themselves from justice by making handsome presents to the authorities, who wink hard in consequence. It is asserted that the tao-tai of Shang-hai makes nearly forty thousand pounds a year in this way. The craving for opium is irresistible when the habit of using it has once been acquired. To abandon it a man must possess a character of no common energy; and indeed the habit can only be cured at the risk of life, for the stomach when deprived of this sustenance contracts, thereby causing the most acute agony. The Chinese begin when about twenty years of age to smoke a pipe a day. Great smokers get the length of as many as eight pipes, but then they fall victims to the habit within five or six years. Those who smoke from two to four pipes a day, however, may live for twenty or even for thirty years. Opium is smoked in a pipe about nine inches long, perforated at its extremity with a small hole into which the bit of opium is introduced, mixed with essence of roses. The smoke is inhaled in four or five long draughts. Each pipe produces at first a sort of headache, and then, it appears, a delightful state of extacy. The smokers, after they have reached this stage, are removed to a great sleeping-

room and laid down upon mats side by side, and on
their backs. The sleep so induced continues for four
or five hours, after which the smoker remains for two
or three hours in a state of utter weakness and
prostration. Opium tends to brutalise those who use
it habitually. They can be recognised by their be-
sotted look, and by their lean and haggard faces.
At first opium is smoked on the sly, unknown to the
relations and family of the smoker. To escape notice,
the victim repairs to smoking saloons, places generally kept by females of doubtful virtue. When he
has had his draught and sleep, he goes home discon-
tented and peevish to his wife and children, and
conducts himself towards them in the most vicious
manner. This for a while is all the harm done. Very
soon, however, he becomes quite unfit for shopkeeping
or labour, and can think of nothing but his new
passion for opium. Ruin soon stares him in the face.
His lands are mortgaged, his furniture and dwelling
sold, and then his wife and his children are disposed of; often much to their satisfaction, as it is
hard to endure the perpetual brawl which this habit
introduces into a household. When with the help
of pawnbrokers and money-lenders all his means have
been eaten up, the unhappy victim enlists into the
army, gets employment from a secret society, or
joins some band of freebooters or insurgents. This

is the frightful evil which now gnaws at the prosperity of China, and demoralizes her people. It is humanitarian England, so noisy, vigilant, and susceptible about the negro slave-trade, which unscrupulously causes all this misery. One cannot pass Woosung, and see those great ' receiving ships,' sinking to the water's edge under their freight of opium and bristling with cannon, without a feeling of indignation. Here right is reconciled with the interest of the strong; the shameless and unprincipled love of gain is triumphant!

In defence of the traffic a few figures have been quoted which tell their own tale. According to Mr. Alcock, the Consul-General of Great Britain at Canton, the English import into China, and distribute among the Chinese, seventy thousand boxes of opium annually. Now one box of opium was worth, in August 1858, at Shang-hai, 480 taels. Taking the value of the tael at six and sixpence, we have the enormous sum of 10,920,000*l*. Now this commodity is only exchanged for silver ingots. Opium, then, withdraws from China more than ten millions of pounds of sterling money annually, which are immediately restored to the general commerce of the world. This traffic makes the Chinese yield up a part of the treasures which they are constantly absorbing and secreting in useless hoards. In exchange for silk and tea, the Chinese only receive a very small proportion

of our products, indeed a portion imperceptible in its
influence on the general trade.   They won't have
our goods, they will take only money.   Opium, in this
way, supplies the means of maintaining an equilibrium
in business, and prevents commerce with the Middle
Empire from becoming to an injurious extent dis-
advantageous to Europe.   The opium traffic has,
then, its economical advantages.   This is argued in
self-defénce, on commercial principles of undoubted
soundness, by the heads of all the great business
houses in China, which owe their splendour to the
existing system.   Besides, the Chinese, it is added,
are themselves to blame.   They have it in their
power to give up using opium.   No one can force
them to buy it.   Political economists may discover
some strength in these arguments, but we rejoice to
think that France takes no part in this traffic, and
owes no share of the prosperity she enjoys to the
demoralization and degradation of a whole people.
A man of Lord Elgin's noble and elevated character
could not fail to express warmly his detestation of
this evil.   But what efforts of an individual will avail
against commercial habits which have acquired
tenacity and have proved a source of so much wealth?
Not being able to put down this trade, however, he
has attempted to render it less criminal.   Henceforth,
trade in opium is subjected to customs duties, and,

after these have been settled, boxes are not to be considered contraband. It will now be imported and sold in all open ports. Uniformity in profits will thereby be restored among the foreign merchants, hitherto those engaged in legitimate trade only having paid duties, while the others paid none.

Secret societies have existed for centuries back in China; they are still numerous and formidable. The leading ones are those of the White Lily, the Red Nuphar, Heavenly Wisdom, the Triad (the heavens, earth, and man), and the White Cloud. Kwang-toung, Kwang-si, and Fo-kien are infested with them. They are also numerous at Hong-Kong, Manilla, Singapore, and Macao.

Tien-tsin is situated at a distance of about fifty miles from the capital city of Pekin, which stands in the midst of a dreary and sandy plain. The winters are bitterly cold; the summers are very hot, the weather being rendered more oppressive by the dust which fills the air. The climate is very trying to the lungs, and on this ground the Russians who belong to the college have requested that they should only stay six instead of ten years at the Chinese capital.

There are neither tankas nor tanka-women in northern China. They are entirely confined to the Canton river. No son of a boat-woman can become a mandarin; and if, concealing this prohibition, any of them should pass the examination and in this way obtain a button, he will be degraded so soon as the truth comes out.

The ordinary rapidity of Chinese couriers is about three hundred lis, or about thirty leagues a-day; when the despatches are urgent, or 'despatches of fire,' as they are called, the couriers who convey them should make five hundred lis, or fifty leagues a-day.

There is much ado made in France about the extent to which all the liberal professions are overstocked. The same thing exists to an incomparably greater extent, however, in the Middle Empire. In 1821 there were thirty-two thousand unemployed doctors or licentiates—a dangerous fuel for the secret societies and insurrections. The number of unemployed professional men must have increased since.

There are occasional earthquakes at Shang-hai, in an alluvial district formed of mud and sand; a curious fact, which, even admitting the truth that the volcanic region of Japan is close at hand, is not satisfactorily explained.

The Chinese army is composed of six hundred thousand men, who are scattered over the surface of the empire: a very small number of troops for a country of such extent. The Mantchoo army is composed of two hundred thousand men, of whom one hundred thousand are organised in the capital and in the northern towns. The Chinese Tartar troops, however, do not form a regular army like those of Europe. They are rather a militia, intended to support the provincial authorities and to maintain order in the empire. The soldiers are not lodged in barracks. Each lives in his own house, and they only meet on certain occasions under an order from their chief. As they are very badly paid, they generally add some other occupation to that of soldier. Most frequently they are day-labourers.

CHAPTER X.

ALL hope of the speedy return of the 'Audacieuse'
having been abandoned, and the bad season approaching rapidly, Baron Gros decided, in the beginning of September, to leave Shang-hai and set sail
for Japan, in order to accomplish the second part of
his mission.   He had at his disposal only two vessels
of the Imperial navy, the sloop of war the 'Laplace,'
the advice-boat the 'Prégent,' and a small trading
steamer, hired for the same purpose, named the
'Rémi.' The remainder of the French fleet had
received orders to join the admiral in Cochin China.
The ambassador, M. de Contades, M. de Chassiron,

and the Abbé Mermet, our new interpreter, took up their quarters on board the 'Laplace.' We were accommodated in the 'Rémi.' We had on board with us an intelligent and intrepid traveller, M. Casimir Leconte, who had explored in succession every country under the sun. During forty years he had travelled about incessantly, and yet he had never met with either storms or accidents of an alarming kind. He had never been sick. He had broken every limb and sprained every joint on the causeways of Paris; but he had never met with a mischance of the kind far from home. We put our trust in his star in adventuring with him upon the stormy seas of Japan; and we expected, not without reason, that his pleasant conversation would serve to relieve the tedium of the voyage, which it certainly did.

On Monday, the 6th of September, at ten o'clock in the morning, with fine weather, a clear blue sky, and a gentle wind from the north, we left the shores of the Whampoa. We were all well pleased to exchange the suffocating and unwholesome atmosphere of Shang-hai for the fresh sea-breeze. The captain of the 'Rémi,' his two mates, and the men who are in charge of the engine, are Europeans; the remainder of the crew is composed of Malays, Hindoos, negroes, and Chinamen. We were struck with the measured and melancholy singsong with which the

Malays accompany the tug and strain of their muscles as they haul in the anchor or hoist the sails. Our ship belongs to the house of Rémi, Schmidt, and Company. It is let at the rate of 5500 piastres a-month, or more than 40*l.* a-day, no uncommon sum for such service in these seas.

Our cabins are small but clean, and the saloon is well ventilated. But the ship has, unfortunately, other inhabitants, in the shape of rats, white ants, red ants, and cancrelas, which night and day give themselves up to all sorts of pranks and antics, to our supreme discomfort. A large vessel belonging to Jardine's firm, going directly to London with a cargo of tea, left the yellow waters of the Yang-tse at the same time with us.

Our engine is weak; the 'Laplace,' not to let us fall behind, gave us a tug for some time. However, they found it inconvenient. They dropped us in a few days; and leaving with the 'Prégent,' they fixed Simoda as the rendezvous. Slowly but steadily we advanced over the ocean. We had a head-wind, no doubt, but the weather was fine. It was like the beginning of October in France. The sky was clear, the horizon serene. A strong swell from the north-east, which set in against us, stopped our progress. However, we passed Van Diemen's Straits in safety, through the numerous islands which stud these seas;

and on the 9th of September we quitted the China Sea for the open ocean. On the 14th, at ten o'clock, after a passage of nine days, we cast anchor at Simoda. The 'Laplace' and the 'Prégent' had arrived the night before.

The port of Simoda is small and narrow : it would scarcely hold more than five or six ships at once ; but it is safe and well sheltered, excepting to the south-west, where it is a little open. The town is a mere village, protected from high tides by a dyke. The country is beautifully picturesque, exhibiting an admirable variety of hill and dale. Rounded knolls are covered with a luxuriant vegetation descending to the water's edge ; firs spring from the rocks ; and, amid wild and picturesque scenery, rich rice-fields, ranged in terraces, run along the hills. There were delightful dells with brooks rushing down their hollows ; and abrupt slopes and crags of volcanic rocks catching the sunshine at every angle, and giving wonderful variety to the scene. We were delighted with the country. Everywhere we met working people who had a gay and happy appearance ; and saw beautifully clean houses, with a look about them of the utmost comfort and prosperity.

If cleanliness is to be taken as a criterion of happiness in a people or in an individual, then the Japanese should be happy. They are very cheerful ; and seem

pleased when we make up to them. The women do
not run off as they do in China when they see a
European. There is no crowd of ragged Coolies
standing about. The costume of the men of the
poorer classes is very simple, consisting of a wide
dress with a belt, every part of it being exquisitely
clean. The reader may guess what the effect of all
this was, on persons who had just arrived from a six
weeks' sojourn in the midst of that hideous human
ant-hill, a Chinese town, and from the flat and tame
banks of the Whampoa.

At the bottom of the roadstead floated the American
flag, over the residence of Mr. Townsend Harris, the
consul-general of the United States, settled in Japan
in virtue of the treaty of Kanagawa. In spite of all
the noise that was made about it, Commodore Perry's
expedition has not struck very deep roots in the
country. The name of Admiral Poutiatine is much
more popular. It was in the road of Simoda that
the celebrated shipwreck of the Russian frigate, the
'Diana,' took place. It is the only case on record
of a ship perishing by the effect of an earthquake.
The land rose and fell on this occasion. At one moment the ship had sixty feet of water under her, and
the next, those on board saw her anchors lying high
and dry on the upraised bed of the ocean. An immense wave suddenly sprung up to seaward, and came

pouring into the roads. It overwhelmed the town, and inundated the whole valley. The admiral and his men jumped into the sea and swam ashore. Fourteen only were drowned. The shipwrecked carpenters, when all was over and things had returned to their usual state, set about constructing a small vessel in which the crew might return to the banks of the Amour. But a large American ship, which was sent out shortly afterwards from Shang-hai, furnished them with a safer mode of conveyance—and the small Russian schooner was presented to the Japanese, and still forms a graceful ornament where it rides at anchor in the road of Simoda.

During our stay in this port we received the warmest and most cordial reception from the Japanese. The governor of Simoda, his Excellency Nemorano-Nedanwano-Kami, came on the first day of our arrival on board the 'Laplace,' to visit the ambassador.

At noon, on the third day we had been in Japan, we went on shore to pay him in turn our official visit. He came forward to meet us at the entrance to his house, and received us with perfect grace, surrounded by his principal officers. A splendid luncheon was spread in the large reception-room. We took our places to the left side, on seats; and the governor and his six officers sat down on their heels, after the custom of the country, on the side opposite to us.

x

The Japanese interpreter, on his knees, transmitted the words of Abbé Mermet to the governor. Tea and saki, hot rice-brandy, fish, pork, and eggs in forty different forms, were served in plates and cups of red, brown, and black lacquer. Japanese cookery appeared to us, in a general way, to resemble Chinese cookery, but to be infinitely superior to the latter in the tempting appearance and cleanliness of the dishes, as well as in the way in which they were served up. Those who waited upon us carried two swords; and at each new course we were struck by some little refinement of luxury and elegance which we had not seen practised at the dinner of the Chinese mandarins. First, there were dwarf trees, cut into the shape of flowers and animals; then there was a large fish in a dish of water, imitating a pool of salt water, with seaweed floating in it; and lastly, there came superb flowers, constructed out of lobster-flesh and sliced turnips. The governor told us, with evident satisfaction, that these flowers were the work of his officers; which certainly gave us a high idea of the neat handiness of these gentlemen, although it somewhat lowered our opinion of the importance and serious character of their occupations. That the principal functionaries of the state are free to spend their time in making artificial flowers out of carrots and turnips and lobster-flesh, proves that the social machine is well

ordered, and works smoothly without watchful supervision. In the midst of all these *nouveautés*, it was
a surprise to stumble upon a real *gâteau de Savoie*, in
slices cut to perfection, and unexceptionable in flavour.
This importation dates from the Spaniards—that is
to say, it is two centuries old ; and it continues to
retain its Spanish name.

The official receptions over, we turned our whole
attention to the bazaar of Simoda, which is deserving
of special mention in this place. The reader is aware
that, down to our own times, it was an offence pun-
ishable with death in a Japanese to sell anything to
foreigners. This was a monopoly reserved by the
government. Warned, beforehand, of the arrival of
the ships of war belonging to the four nations, the
Japanese authorities had accordingly collected, in an
immense tent, all the products of the country which
were likely to interest foreigners. There were displayed Japanese lacquer, employed in every way ;
long rows of inkstands, boxes, and tables, of all
colours and sizes. The price of each object in *itchibous*, the coin of the country, was written in Arabic
numerals underneath ; and a small wooden box, made
expressly for each article, enabled the purchaser to
pack it on the spot, and remove it on board. The
Parisian ladies would have waxed enthusiastic over
so many marvels of taste and elegance. The ambas-

sador, his secretaries and attachés, the officers, the
very sailors were delighted with the exhibition. All
day long there was nothing but going and coming
from the shore to the ships; and when we left, it
was calculated that there had been spent about
1200*l.* on purchases of lacquered articles at Simoda.

Our intercourse with the inhabitants was very
familiar. We went on shore forenoon, afternoon,
and evening, at any hour. We were frankly received everywhere. We visited the pagodas, which
are very curious and well worth seeing; and while
sauntering about, would drop into the houses of en-
tertainment, to get a cup of tea. In the evening
we joined those who sang and danced in honour of
the moon; and really enjoyed the amusements of
the people. They showed every anxiety to please
us, and often supplied us with boats gratuitously to
get back to our vessel. Our entertainers said to us,
laughingly, that we would not meet with the same
attention at Yedo, the people there being of a more
serious turn of mind. We afterwards had an opportunity of appreciating the truth of this remark.

After staying five days in this charming country,
the ambassador gave us the signal for departure.
Up to the last moment the deck was crowded with
Japanese, who came on board to get a glass of champagne or liqueur, and then visit the engine and other

From a Native drawing.

Drawn on Left Block by Geo.

VIEW OF FUSI—YAMA

parts of the ship. On these occasions they took long notes on their fans of what they saw. In all this their conduct was very different from that of the Chinese. During my whole stay in the Celestial Empire I never saw a single Chinaman come on board except to sell goods. The Japanese are anxious to get instruction. The Chinese disdain whatever does not belong to the customs and literature of their own race.

On the night of the 19th of September we left the Bay of Simoda, in order to proceed to Kanagawa and Yedo. The evening before the governor had sent two of his officers in full dress to the ambassador, to announce to him officially the death of the civil Emperor of Japan. This important news had arrived that very morning from the capital. All the day we had our flags hoisted on account of the death of the taïcoun. I do not know whether the Japanese have noticed this demonstration on our part, which of course they won't understand until it is explained to them. At the entrance to the Bay of Yedo we were overtaken by the 'Laplace' and 'Prégent,' which did not leave for four hours after us. We saw from deck a crowd of barks, junks, villages, and towns, above which rose, in all its majesty, Fusi-yama—the mountain, par excellence, of the Japanese. A bright sun irradiated the hill sides. At three o'clock we cast anchor four miles from the extremity of the bay where the town is situated.   Before that part of the town which is called Sinagawa we perceived five ships of war of European construction, of which two were steamers; one being a gift from the Dutch, the other a gift from the English.   The civil Emperor died twenty days ago of gout in the stomach; he was only thirty-five years of age.   The government considered it prudent to conceal his death, in this adopting the traditional policy of the court of Yedo.   His successor, who is his adopted son, is only thirteen years of age, and is not yet recognised.   It is a council of regency which governs.   For forty days the Japanese must allow their beards to grow, as a sign of mourning.   It is whispered that the new taïcoun is rather of a blood-thirsty disposition; he has just begun his higher studies, but Confucius and his commentators are not much to his mind.   The laws compel him, however, to study under a master, who, although addressing his pupil on his bended knees, does not for all that require to mince matters with the royal youth when scholastic discipline is to be enforced.

The 'Laplace' was besieged for eight-and-forty hours by a crowd of Japanese officers dressed in rich silks, with attendants wearing two swords apiece, going, coming, and moving about through the ship. Seven governors of Yedo came at one time on board;

but the cold politeness of these distinguished officials made us regret the frank good nature of the inhabitants of Simoda. The firm resolution come to by Baron Gros, to go on shore, to live in the city of Yedo, and to negociate his treaty there, excited the strongest opposition on the part of these functionaries, and gave rise to interminable discussions. The death of the Emperor would prevent, they said, the French embassy from being received with all the distinction which the court of Yedo would have liked to confer upon it, had it not arrived at a time of mourning. If they wished honour done them, they must, according to Japanese custom, wait forty days. Baron Gros said that he would dispense with anything of the kind. Our presence in the town, they said, would cause trouble; it would collect crowds who might do us some harm. The ambassador said it seemed to him to be the duty of the Japanese authorities to prevent anything of this kind from happening. Cholera was then raging at Yedo; three thousand persons had died, and three hundred were dying every day:—why should we expose our lives by coming into the town at such a time? Baron Gros replied that we were acquainted with cholera, that it also existed in France, and that we were not at all frightened about it. Such were the principal arguments of the Japanese. The ambassador was obliged to enter into all this miserable cavilling, Lord Elgin and Count Poutiatine having already gone through the same process, At length, after three days of tiresome delay, we were permitted to disembark at the city of Yedo. At noon on the 23rd, Contades, M. Mermet, and Flavigny went on shore to see the house which the Japanese authorities had set apart for us, near the palace of the Emperor. They found it clean and spacious, in a suitable quarter, not far from the sea, and we fixed the 26th as the day for coming on shore. As the funeral of the taïcoon takes place on the 24th, we consented to delay for two days taking possession of our new abode, which was a bonze-house or convent.

On Sunday, the 26th of September, at eleven o'clock in the forenoon, we met on board the 'Laplace,' and put off in three ship's-boats to take up our quarters at last in the capital of Japan. As the ambassador left the 'Laplace' and passed in front of the 'Prégent,' the sailors, manning the yards, gave three cheers for the Emperor. No cannon were then fired, as a mark of respect for the taïcoon. The day was close and hot. It took us an hour to get to land. We passed under five forts built on piles, and constructed after the European fashion according to plans supplied by the Portuguese. They are in very good repair, and their defenders seemed numerous. Our luggage had been despatched in the morning from the ships on board junks supplied by the Japanese authorities. We approached the land with difficulty. The tide was beginning to recede, and our boats could not reach the landing-place. The ambassador was obliged to get into a fishing-boat to reach the shore, and then he had to climb up a ladder after leaving it to reach the level on which the city stands. In this act he did not badly represent western civilization mounting the breach into the antique civilization of Japan. We were in a fortified enclosure, in which were drawn up a hundred men wearing two sabres, who were to escort us. At the door of this enclosure we found the ambassador's chair, now an object of historical interest, and our chairs or norimons awaiting us, and carried by Japanese porters. We declined to squat in these elegant lacquered boxes, and, in order to have a look about us, walked after the chair of Baron Gros. For some time we passed through streets which were very much crowded, but the celebrated canabo mohi, or triangle-bearers, preceded us and opened a way. These functionaries, who are peculiar to Japan, stopped at each door, that is to say, at every hundred paces. Their gowns, chequered with yellow, green, black, or red patches, gave them a most fantastic appearance. They carried a large iron triangle, to which were attached at the top iron rings, which jingled when it was struck upon the ground. It terminated below in a sharp point, which they let fall upon the feet of the mob to keep them back. The crowd on seeing them approach drew back and allowed us to pass. We soon arrived at the official town, or the quarter set apart for the lesser bounio, their families and suites, during their stay of twelve months in Yedo. There is something of the sadness, severity, and gloom of monastic establishments about this quarter of the town. The houses, although their architecture is more highly ornamented, have the look of prisons. They have immense oaken doors with large iron locks, which are always kept closed and bolted. Behind the grated windows we could see a whole population of men, women, and girls, staring at us with no small curiosity. On one side of the street live the bounio and their family, on the other their domestics. In nothing did what we saw resemble China. The streets are wide, clean, and well ventilated. They are even macadamised and bounded on each side with a stream of limpid water. The houses are not heaped one above the other as in the Chinese towns. Everywhere traces are apparent of the supervision of an active and vigilant board of health. After walking half an hour we came to our house, which was situated at the foot of a wooded hill, on which

there was a Buddhist temple which overlooked the
bay and the whole town. Scarcely had we arrived
when the six great functionaries, appointed plenipotentiaries, came to the convent on a visit of
compliment to the ambassador. Then followed a
dinner sent by the taïcoon, a sumptuous and solid
repast, similar to that at Simoda; of which, however,
we were obliged to partake while the interview was
going on. The taïcoon at the same time sent us
a few baskets of pears, chestnuts, grapes, and other
fruits, with a message that he would provide the same
quantity every morning while we continued to stay in
the city.

The capital of Japan covers a space of one hundred square miles, and contains two millions and a
half of inhabitants. There are in Yedo a number
of small wooded heights covered with joss-houses,
whence there is a fine view over the remainder of the
town. Everywhere in the town we came to the
edge of large gardens and parks, in which the Japanese authorities sauntered about with their families, for they never go into the streets except on
business. In Japan, as in China, the authorities seldom make their appearance among the people, and
when they do so it is in full dress, and accompanied by
a cortège. Accordingly the Japanese could scarcely
believe us when we told them that the Emperor

Napoleon III. went out every day in a phaëton without any attendants, driving the conveyance himself; that he rode through the streets on horseback attended only by an aide-de-camp; and that he spent his time in attending to public business. The idea of a prince moving about familiarly among his subjects was altogether at variance with their prejudices, but the fact of a sovereign being hard worked in the administration of state affairs seemed to them to be altogether absurd. They remarked ingenuously that it must be more tiresome than pleasant to be taïcoon of the French.

The taïcoon of Japan leads quite another life. When he goes abroad all the streets must be cleared; then every one must go within doors, and motion must cease, and every sound be hushed in the town; the few persons who witness the scene must remain still, their heads bowed to the ground, and the slightest infraction of this posture is punished with death. The inhabitants of Yedo, however, are seldom troubled by the presence of their sovereign. He does not leave the enclosure of his palace more than five or six times a year, in a norimon or Japanese palanquin, for the purpose of worshiping the images of his ancestors in a temple situated two or three miles from the town. He is so completely hedged round by etiquette, his life is so much bound up with the rites, that at last he has become a sort of demi-god, hid from men, and by far too loftily exalted to take any interest in the affairs of this world. The gotaïro, who is his prime minister, and the councils accordingly govern the state. The taïcoon, who has been called the temporal Emperor of Japan, is the lieutenant of the mikado, or ecclesiastical Emperor. Originally appointed to relieve the mikado from the burden of business, he has thrown it in turn upon his prime minister. In our times the taïcoon is gradually becoming a second mikado.

At six o'clock in the morning the day after we took up our abode at Yedo, M. Mermet, Maubourg, and I set out on a long walk towards the palace of the Emperor. We found that the way to get to it was to go in the direction directly opposite to that pointed out by our guides. We crossed two great enclosures with broad ditches or moats full of running water, and lofty embankments, which were kept in very good order, covered with greensward and shaded by dark green trees, the branches of which drooped to the ground. Storks with beautifully clean plumage stalked about over the grass. We passed every now and then, as we proceeded, guard-houses, lacquered inside, and occupied by men with two swords, who sat upon their heels. The silence of these spacious official streets was only broken at times when a group of daïmio, or Japanese princes, passed on horseback, or to an interview with the taïcoon, all in full dress and escorted by a numerous cortège. Before each, twenty men with two swords marched pompously down the middle of the street. Then came the daïmio, with a lacquer hat of many colours and a pearl-gray dress, mounted on his horse of state. The trappings of these animals were quite feudal, and carried the mind back to the middle ages. In Japan horses are never shod; their hoofs are covered with straw, like the feet of the men. They are much larger and much stronger than those of the Chinese breed; they are fed exclusively on rice-straw, and resemble a good deal our old Limousin stock, which has been stupidly allowed to die out. Horses are not used for draught purposes; they are employed solely for the saddle. The carts at Yedo are drawn by bulls, and in all Niphon there is not a single carriage. It is not every one who is allowed to ride on horseback in the capital of the taïcoon; it is a privilege reserved for the great functionaries of state. To return to the cortège of the daïmio : these personages are followed by the same number of men with two swords as that which precedes them; then come several Coolies, who carry large boxes of black wood stuck at the end of a stick of bamboo. The higher the daïmio is, the greater is the number of boxes. I was told that dresses for all occasions and all weathers—for heat, for cold, for sunshine, and for rain—were stowed away in them, and that the daïmio make it a rule to have part of their wardrobe borne in state behind them. Whether this is the case or not, the Coolies form a singular part of the cortège. We followed a procession of this kind for some time. We were just entering the third enclosure of the palace, when our three guides suddenly barred the way, and made us understand by signs that, if they allowed us to proceed further, they themselves would be subject to the unpleasant process of decapitation. We had no fear for their heads, but we knew that the Japanese government is very severe on those who infringe the rites, and we did not wish them to be reprimanded on our account, so we reluctantly consented to retire.

The evening before, in the historical chair which had figured at Tien-tsin, Baron Gros had made his entrance into the town, carried by eight Japanese Coolies decked out as Chinamen. Now it appears that it is a thing quite unknown in Japan for a native to appear in Chinese garments; it is an enormity—a violation of all propriety. It is more—it is a crime. On this occasion the unfortunate Coolies were not considered the only guilty parties. Six hundred Japanese officials, who had not prevented

the offence, were sentenced to a hundred days'
imprisonment!   Here, then, was a total of sixty
thousand days' imprisonment, all on account of this
unlucky palanquin.   The ambassador was much an-
noyed when he heard of this proceeding, and took care
to get the prisoners immediately liberated.   But if a
wholesome respect for Japanese legislation had been
taught the two hundred officers sent by the taïcoon
to guard and watch us, they had also been alarmed
to an extent painful to us, lest we should be found
wanting in respect for those rites to which the government attached so much importance, without
their having it in their power to keep us right.

Yedo is divided into two distinct districts; that
which surrounds the palace is the official quarter.
It is, as we said, sad, calm, and solemn.   The other
is full of life and bustle.   One can scarcely imagine
them to form part of the same place.   They look
like two towns separated a hundred miles from
each other.   The official town is filled with the families of the daïmio, the bounio, the governors, those
functionaries retained as hostages by the government, and those who are spending their alternate
year in Yedo.   It was dull enough to saunter
through the wide and silent streets.   What a difference there was in this respect when we went into
the business quarter!   The moment we set foot in it

there was a general hubbub. The children shouted, and the full-grown men and women came racing up from every quarter of the compass, as if their lives depended on their celerity in making a ring round us; there was a noisy crowd formed at our heels before we could escape, and we never proceeded along the street without the attendance of a clamorous mob of not less than five hundred persons. This sort of thing was not much to our liking, and, after spending an hour or two in being stared at in this way, we were always glad to abandon our exploration and escape to our residence.

Our quarters are not very comfortable. We are separated from the outer air by mere partitions of rice paper, and during the night it is bitterly cold. The Japanese with whom we come in contact are very goodnatured; after having ministered to our wants, they do their very best to make themselves agreeable. In this attempt they expend a great deal of ingenuity. Many of them can already bid us good day, and good night, in French, and can count with our numerals as high as a hundred. To gratify their anxious desire for knowledge, we have converted the joss-house into a sort of school-room, and have opened classes for the alphabet; our pupils do us credit. If we were to stay a month longer at Yedo French would be the only language spoken at this bonze-house.

Y

The evenings are rather dull. At eight or nine o'clock all the gates which separate the various quarters of Yedo are shut, and the movement in the streets is stopped till next day. We then get out on the roof of the bonze-house, to breathe the fresh air, look about us, and see the comet; after this we retire to a hand at whist with Commanders Kerjegu and D'Ozery, and in this way we contrive to spend the time.

There are five hundred wrestlers at Yedo, men of herculean proportions, who let themselves out on hire to exhibit their feats of strength. We thought at first of engaging them for an evening, but it afterwards occurred to us that the diversion was rather undignified, and we therefore abandoned our intention.

The conferences were conducted with great despatch. Baron Gros having been good enough to appoint me secretary, I attended them with his Excellency and the interpreter, the abbé Mermet. The ambassador presided, and the six Japanese ambassadors sat before him, round the table, in the order of their rank. Each of the latter entered into the discussion with arguments of his own, and we had more than once occasion to admire the acuteness and ability they displayed. I must give their names, which, although they may be elegant in Japan, sound

From a Nature drawing.

JAPANESE WRESTLERS

Day & Son Lithrs to The Queen.

harsh and crabbed enough to French ears. Here
they are: — Midzounó Ikigougonó Kami, Nagaï
Hguembano Kami, Ynouïé Schinanonó Kami, Hori
Oribenó Kami, Iouaché Fingounó Kami, and Kamaï
Sakio Kami. The plenipotentiary last named was
remarkably quiet. Indeed he never opened his
mouth even in the midst of the most animated discussion. He listened, but never expressed an opinion. We
set him down accordingly as a personage of no great
ability. What was our surprise then when we found
out what his functions were! He was a most important personage. We saw his card one day, and
from it we learned that he took the title of Imperial
Spy, or, literally, man on watch to report to the Emperor.

Espionage is firmly rooted in Japanese manners. It is legal and constitutional. It forms part
of the administrative arrangements of the state, and
has been elevated to the rank of a principle in the
home policy of the empire. It is a mode of government with the court of Yedo. It may be said without exaggeration that one half of the population of
Japan are employed as spies to watch over the other
half. Our hundred iacounin, or men with two
swords, were pleasant fellows enough no doubt, but
for all that they kept jotting down upon their fans
all that took place, however trivial, while we were

walking or talking in our rooms, to give an account of what had taken place doubtless in the proper quarter. But the iacounin had to be watched themselves, so we had six new persons added to our guard to look after them, and see how they conducted themselves towards us. There were, in short, spies upon the spies.

On Saturday, the 9th of October, the signature of the treaty took place, and, nothing keeping us any longer at Yedo, the ambassador fixed next day for our return on board. We bade adieu to our six bounio. They promised to meet us again in France. Nagaï Hguembano Kami, the second plenipotentiary, told us that he had been already appointed ambassador to the court of the Tuileries. The Japanese government are besides to send other missions to London, St. Petersburg, and Washington. We asked Nagaï how he meant to come to France, whether he would take the route by Suez or the Cape, by the regular passage-boats, or come in a French vessel of war. ' I will go,' he said, ' on board a Japanese man-of-war, manned by Japanese seamen, and will land at the harbour of Toulon, with the red globe of Japan flying from the mainmast.' When we discussed an article of the treaty which required the Japanese interpreters to learn French in five years, Nagaï, with an evident desire to be polite, said, with a smile, to M. Mermet, that he knew that our language was the most generally understood of the European dialects, and that over the whole continent well-bred persons made it a point to speak it well.

We parted on the best terms, and, another dinner having been sent by the taïcoon, we ended as we had begun. We each received besides from the Emperor a present of some rolls of silk of various colours, in token of goodwill and peace. The Japanese silk is not so fine as that of China, but it does not yield to the latter in its brilliancy or the brightness of its colours.

On Monday, the 11th of October, the French embassy left Yedo to return on board. From an early hour in the morning there was an unwonted bustle in the joss-house: after packing and paying our bills, we took a hurried breakfast, and then the removal commenced. A hundred Coolies had been sent us the night before with all the necessary apparatus. It was not without some alarm that we saw all our little traps handed over to these men, who disappeared with them in the crowd. The under bounio, who was head of the bonze-house, surrounded with his iacounin, came as we were leaving to bid the ambassador good bye. We followed Baron Gros on foot, without getting into our chairs or norimons. The drapeau tricolor was carried before us, and flaunted before the astonished gaze of the citizens. The gates were closed, and ropes were stretched across the streets to keep back the crowd, so that we passed on without obstruction. We arrived at the landing-place, where better arrangements had now been made, and by midday we were again on board ship. Five cheers for the Emperor welcomed back the ambassador to the deck of the ' Laplace.'

Next morning, by daybreak, we weighed anchor and bade adieu to Yedo. On leaving the bay we encountered a high wind which carried us in four days to Van Diemen's Strait, and in five to Nangasaki.

We found the ' Laplace ' and ' Prégent ' there, they having arrived the same morning, as well as a large Russian frigate called the ' Askold,' which had been dismasted in a typhoon, and two American steam frigates, the ' Powhatan ' and ' Mississippi.' There were a number of Japanese boats in the road, some set to watch what was going on, others busied in carrying out provisions to the ships. Even after seeing Simoda we admired Nangasaki, which seemed fully entitled to the reputation it enjoys. The country is not so picturesque perhaps as at Simoda, but there is a wider and opener landscape. Among the trees and on the heights above the landing-place we saw cannon bristling, and here and there long sheets of canvas were stretched out over a framework in such a way as to imitate batteries.

There are now at Nangasaki two handsome little steamers, the 'Nipon' and 'Yedo,' which the court of the Hague have disposed of to the Japanese government. The captain of a frigate, an aide-de-camp of the King of the Netherlands, brought them from Europe, with orders to instruct the native seamen in the management of the machinery. His commission will not terminate for two years yet. He speaks in the highest terms of the assiduity and intelligence of the Japanese who are put under his charge. It is an easy matter to make excellent seamen of them, but it is not possible to train proper officers in a day, and it is officers who are chiefly required to secure the efficiency of the Japanese navy.

Besides M. van Kattendycke, we found at Nangasaki M. Donker Curtius, the president of the Dutch factory and commissioner of the King of the Netherlands to Japan. M. Donker Curtius has been twenty-one years in India, and five years at Nangasaki. He has not been once in the interval back to Europe. He is married. His wife and five children live in Holland, for hitherto the Japanese have not permitted the Dutch to bring their families with them.

We passed our time very pleasantly in the midst of the little Dutch colony. M. Donker Curtius told

us that during the summer months it is as hot at
Nangasaki as at Batavia ; but that during the winter
snow falls, with an occasional frost. They have no
butcher's meat. In Japan there is neither sheep,
goat, nor pig. The Japanese, like the Chinese, live
almost exclusively on rice, fish, and fowl. Oxen are
employed exclusively for tillage. To kill them would
be considered a sort of sacrilege. During the winter
quails, wild boars, deer, and game of various kinds
are to be had. At this period the price of a pheasant
at Nangasaki is about twopence halfpenny.

The Japanese princes shoot over their estates. In
doing so they sometimes use matchlocks and dogs.
They more frequently, however, employ bows and
arrows, archery being considered a nobler sport, and
requiring greater quickness and dexterity in the
sportsman. They are fond of scientific studies. One of
them, Prince Satsouma, puzzled the Dutch officers with
inquiries about some recent applications of science, of
which the latter had not heard. He wanted to know
how photography had been employed in barometric
observations; and the Dutch naval men whom he
cross-questioned had not heard, or had forgotten, that
an apparatus in which photographic paper is employed has been for some time in use at Greenwich
to record the variations of the barometer, thermometer, and hygrometer. It did not appear how this

fact, which was quite a recent one, had found its way to Satsouma from the banks of the Thames.

At Nangasaki one is allowed to walk about quite freely. Frenchmen, Americans, and Russians are met with everywhere in the streets. In order to get on shore we passed over the famous island of Decima, a sort of artificial breakwater which is celebrated on account of its having been for two centuries the abode of the Dutch merchants, who allowed themselves to be cooped up there rather than lose the right of trading with Japan, so highly did they value the privilege. Now the guard-houses are empty, the gates are removed, and every one is freely allowed to go into the town.

The importance of the trade between China and Japan has been very much exaggerated. There is scarcely any intercourse between the two countries. The Japanese despise the Chinese too thoroughly to have much communication with them. Only four or five Chinese junks visit Nangasaki annually. The subjects of the Middle Empire have a large space set apart for their use to the right of Decima, but it is enclosed by a strong palisade, and they are not allowed to go beyond it. A great part of their imports, it is said, consist of European articles, so that in this respect they compete with the Dutch.

On Friday, the 22nd October, it was arranged that

we should leave. The governor of Nangasaki, in a pleasure junk, ornamented with streamers and banners, and tugged along by a dozen small boats, came on board to take leave of the ambassador. At eleven o'clock the three vessels weighed anchor and left the harbour. The 'Prégent' left us to proceed to the archipelago of Liou-tchou and Hong-Kong, with books, letters, and European newspapers for the missionaries settled in these parts. We lost no time in getting to Shang-hai, where four couriers were awaiting us. We expected to have had a favourable wind with plenty of sea-room, but instead of this we were almost becalmed for a couple of days. At the end of the third day, however, we came in sight of Woosung and the banks of the Whampou; and after an absence of six weeks we cast anchor once more before that part of the quay at Shang-hai which lies opposite to the French grant.

CHAPTER XI.

Manners, Customs, and Government of Japan.

DURING our short stay in Japan we had an opportunity of making some observations upon the manners, customs, and government of this distant country ; and of obtaining a glimpse of an extraordinary civilization which has come to maturity without any contact with the rest of the world. These observations are very imperfect no doubt, but as they, nevertheless, possess some interest, we do not hesitate to bring them under the notice of our readers without any attempt at methodical arrangement.

A poetical legend informs us that Japan was colonised at first from China. In a remote age there lived an Emperor of China who was so violent and cruel that he became an object of dread to his whole court. The monarch took ill, and beginning to lose his strength he bethought himself of a medicine which was generally believed to exist, whereby a man could make his life last for ever. One of the court doctors, who wished to save his head by getting out of the way, undertook an expedition in search of the precious drug. 'The herb of immortality,' he said, ' does exist, I know. It grows beyond the seas, in the valleys of Kiousiou; but it is of a nature so subtle and delicate that, to lose none of its value and virtue, it must be gathered by chaste and pure hands. Give me three hundred youths and as many maidens, sound and stout in body and mind, chosen from the best families of the land, and I will cross the seas with them and come back in a week or two with the precious herb, which will enable your Majesty to reign long over us.' The cunning doctor deceived the monarch. He set forth, but he never returned. He settled, indeed, with his companions in the green Kiousiou, and from him and them descend the noble race of men who for centuries have peopled the Japanese archipelago.

Unfortunately, facts ill accord with this pretty legend. The Japanese, with skins as white as our own, cannot be the descendants of the yellow sons of Han ; and indeed they repudiate all idea of common descent with the Chinese. Their civilization, which in many respects is identical with that of the Chinese, is in others totally different from it. No doubt the writing is the same; the worship of Boodha and reverence for Confucius are common to both countries; the same sort of pagodas are constructed, and the same services are celebrated in them by bonzes who resemble each other in their shaved heads and long grey gowns; the junks of both countries are constructed after the same fashion; rice, fish, tea, and brandy form the food of the people at Yedo just as they do at Canton; the Japanese Coolies utter the same cries in the streets at Nangasaki which are made by the Chinese Coolies when they put bales of tea and silk on board European ships in the harbour of Shanghai. Then the literature of the archipelago is not national. It is entirely Chinese. The head-dress of the Japanese is similar to that of the Chinese under the old dynasties, before the introduction of the tail. But here the resemblance ends. The Japanese, who are of a noble and proud disposition, and who remain under the influence of military and feudal instincts, differ altogether in character from the sneaking, submissive, and cunning Chinamen, who despise the art of war, and devote themselves, body and soul, to the drudgery of commerce. The Japanese know the point of honour. To take his sword from one is an insult. He cannot restore it to the scabbard without having first steeped it in blood. The Chinamen burst into a laugh when they are reproached with running away from the enemy, or when they are proved to have been telling a falsehood. They have not the smallest feeling of shame under such circumstances. The Chinese are dreadfully dirty; the Japanese are cleanly to a miracle. The Japanese are prone to good fellowship, intelligent, and keen to learn; the Chinamen despise whatever does not belong to their own country, and hence display none of the qualities above indicated in their contact with foreigners. In all respects then the inhabitants of Japan are a superior race to those who people China; and may be inferred to have sprung at an early period from the great Mongol family, and to have emigrated by Corea.

The Chinese consider Japan as a country tributary to the Middle Empire. Nevertheless at Nangasaki they are not allowed to go beyond the walls of their factory, which is surrounded by a high paling. At Yedo we were obliged to put a stop to our Chinese servants' going on shore in consequence of the practical jokes provoked by their dresses and tails, which were a source of great fun to the natives of Japan.

The Japanese generally call their country Niphon, and, in poetical language, the Country of the Rising Sun. Their archipelago is composed of four large islands and a number of small ones. The four large islands are Yesso, Niphon, Sikok, and Kiousiou. Niphon, the largest, contains three great political religious and commercial capitals, viz., Yedo, the residence of the taïcoon; Meako, the residence of the mikado; and Oosaka, the commercial capital. The empire of the taïcoon extends, including the Bonin and Liou-tchou group, over more than three thousand and eight hundred isles and islets. The archipelago is exposed to violent and frequent earthquakes, and for this reason all the houses are of wood and only one story high. At Yedo, however, the walls and doors are built of huge blocks of unhewn stone fitting into each other in a sort of Cyclopean masonry. There are several active volcanoes. Fusi-Yama, the highest mountain of Japan, rises to the height of twelve thousand feet above the level of the sea. It is not, as has been said, covered with perpetual snow, for when we saw it there was none. The heat of the season had melted it. Terrible typhoons burst forth every summer in the Japanese seas, which are perhaps the stormiest on the face of the globe. It was St. François Xavier who said that, in his time, out of three ships going to Japan from France, one only had a chance of getting back again. The equinoctial gales of autumn are the most severe, and the consequence is that the Japanese junks remain at anchor in the creeks of the coast from the 5th to the 25th of September. On the 26th they all put to sea at ònce. We were at Yedo when this happened, and we saw the vessels, when the time came, putting out and covering the whole bay.

The climate of China is hot, and moist, and un-healthy. The climate of Japan, cold in the north, hot towards the south, but always dry, is, on the contrary, very healthy. We have already remarked that the Dutch consider it to be as hot in the island of Kiousiou as it is in Java during the hot weather; but in winter it snows. The harbour of Hakodadi, which has been opened to commerce, will be useful for our seamen stationed in the China seas, who are apt to lose their strength in the hot atmosphere of the south-west monsoon, and who will now be able to come and recruit in the bracing climate of Yesso.

It takes only three days, in good weather, to cross from Shang-hai to Nangasaki, and eight days to return from the coast of China to Yedo. However, there is scarcely any intercourse at present between Japan and China, the archipelago having been as much closed against the Chinese as any other foreign nation. Not more than four or five junks at most cast anchor annually at Nangasaki. Japanese silk, which is very abundant, is not so fine as that of China. Japanese tea, also, is inferior in flavour; it is even slightly bitter. The Japanese, however, maintain that it is a better article than that produced on the continent, and hence very little of it is imported by them. Drugs are enormously expensive over the whole of

Niphon, and it is said that the principal articles brought by the junks are Chinese medicines.

The Japanese ladies receive a certain amount of education at schools which are set apart for females. They have not been led to believe that foreigners are devils, and in this respect differ from their Chinese sisters. The married women are distinguished from those who are still single by the hair being pulled from their eyebrows and their teeth dyed black by a drug composed of iron filings and saki. They walk about freely in the streets, and are not pent up in the depths of the yamouns like the Chinese women.

There is no gazette published in Japan, everything like publicity is prohibited. Things are not so bad in this respect in China, where the ' Gazette de Pekin,' a long official journal, is published daily and circulated throughout the empire. Japanese history is about the most tiresome affair which it is possible to conceive. It consists of a dreary account of the events in the daily life of the taïcoon, and tells all about his ailments, his constitutional walks, and his visits to the flower gardens. The only history of Japan, in the true sense, is that of Père Charlevoix.

The Japanese of every class are fond of the hot bath, which is so frequently resorted to, and fills such a large part in their daily life, that it has a

strong influence on all their habits.   They say that
it is preferable to sleep as a means of quickening the
blood and resting the wearied limbs.   The hundred
iacounin in the joss-house at Yedo abandoned themselves so tumultuously to this exercise as to disturb
our slumbers during the early part of the night.
During the summer the whole process of washing
the person, it is said, is carried on in the streets;
and even the ladies, at this season, come out in front
of their houses to take a wholesome dip under water.
The first chill of winter, which had been felt when
we reached Japan, prevented us from witnessing this
amusing trait in the open air existence of the people
during the summer months, and deprived us of one
souvenir de voyage.

When the Japanese wish to designate the I, that
is to say their own personality, they touch their nose;
the tip of this organ being, according to them, the
seat of individuality.   There is nothing wonderful in
all this.   When a Frenchman wishes to be very impressive, and to indicate his ego, does he not press
his hand upon the stomach?

The monetary unit in Japan is the itchibou, a
pretty little coin shaped like a domino.   Three
itchibous are equal in value to a Mexican piastre.
The kobang, a gold piece, is worth four ichibous.
The Dutch of Nangasaki employ taëls in paper, and

the people make use of tchen or coppers for all small transactions.

China is a country of perfect equality. Everybody, with the solitary exception of the sons of tankaderas, or boatwomen, may, if he pass the examinations, become a mandarin and aspire to the highest honours. In Japan, on the contrary, feudalism prevails, the empire being governed by a military aristocracy. The Japanese are divided into nine classes, and, with a few exceptions, no one can leave the class in which he was born. Every attempt to do so is jealously watched, public opinion being decidedly hostile to it. To the absence of luxury and of all field for ambition, we must attribute the look of contentment and sociable gaiety which lies at the bottom of the Japanese character. Nowhere else are people to be met with who exhibit greater signs of happiness or who seem less harassed with care. The princes or daïmio, the nobles, the priests, and the soldiers form the four highest classes of the nation, and have alone the right to wear two swords. The subaltern employés and the doctors form the fifth class, and are allowed to wear one sword only. The merchants and wholesale dealers, the retail dealers, the mechanics, peasants, and coolies, tanners and curriers form the four lowest classes of the people, and are not allowed, under any circumstances, to wear a sword. All those who deal in skins are considered impure. Not being allowed to reside in the towns, they dwell in villages set apart for their use in the middle of the country. From them the executioners are chosen. It is to be presumed that these officers of justice have a deal to do, for the penal law of Japan is very rigorous, and attaches the punishment of death to very slight offences. Any person who commits manslaughter, however involuntarily, or who receives a criminal to hide him from justice, is forthwith beheaded. It is to be hoped that contact with Europeans will gradually temper the severity of Japanese legislation.

The only sciences cultivated in the empire are medicine and astronomy. There are two observatories in the island of Niphon, one at Yedo and the other at Meako. We were at Yedo at the time of the great comet seen in the beginning of October, 1858, and we did not perceive that it caused the slightest signs of astonishment or alarm. At Shang-hai, during an eclipse of the moon which took place in the same year, there was not the same tranquillity. The military mandarins marched forth and discharged their arrows at the dragon which was eating the moon; and in every junk and pagoda a tremendous thundering of gongs was got up to scare away the monster. In point of fact, after hard work for an hour and a half it was alarmed, and moved off, leaving Dian, without farther molestation, to pursue her course, more radiant and more beautiful than ever. The Japanese physicians read Dutch works on medical science, and really know what they are about. We had a visit from two of them at the joss-house at Yedo, whither they came to consult our young surgeons about the treatment of cholera, which had just made its appearance in the town.

The Japanese are very tolerant, or rather they exhibit the greatest indifference about religious concerns. Several forms of worship have existed side by side in the islands for centuries; Bouddhism, and the religion of Confucius, which are importations from abroad, and the Sinto, or Kami worship, which is the primitive religion of the country, divide the adorations of the masses. As a consequence of the tolerant spirit of the Japanese, the Spanish and Portuguese missionaries had only been a few years in Japan when they converted and baptized two hundred thousand natives. There had been, previously, no example of any religious conversion of like magnitude. In speaking of it, Saint François Xavier said, ' I will never stop if I speak of the Japanese; they are the delight of my heart.' Now times are changed. For two hundred years back there has not been one Christian in Japan. They were exterminated by the Emperors Taiko and Yeyas. In the end of the year 1640 thirty-seven thousand perished in one day in the castle of Simabara, when it was taken by assault after a determined resistance. In our own times there are three or four French missionaries scattered over the Loochoo Islands, which are tributary to Japan and China, who await anxiously the day when they will be allowed to follow in the footsteps of the great apostle of India. Their zeal hitherto has been without reward.

A whole army of satellites are employed, night and day, in preventing all intercourse between them and the islanders. The missionaries are forbid to retain the same servants above a certain time. All the houses which overlook their abodes have had the doors and windows turning in that direction built up, and new openings made on the other side. When they go out into the country they find that, by instructions from the authorities, everybody avoids them. The only answer they get to any question they put is, 'I don't understand you.' Those who are acquainted with the working of the Japanese government, and the dread it has of the European powers, will not be at a loss to understand this conduct. The fact is, that, in the eyes of the taïcoon, the missionary is a foreign agent, a mere spy, sent out to discover, for European information, where Japan may be easily attacked in the event of an invasion. The Japanese in this respect are just where they were two hundred years ago; they have not made the smallest progress. The celebrated reply of a Spanish captain to the Emperor is said to have brought down the great persecution. Taiko was talking one day with the commander of a Spanish ship, which had recently arrived from Europe. 'How is it,' he asked, 'that the king your master has contrived, with such a small kingdom, to conquer so many different countries?' 'That is easily told,' replied the Spaniard, inconsiderately; 'why, priests first go out, and convert the idolatrous natives by their virtue and eloquence. Then, while the converts are favourably disposed towards them, and the whole coast is cleared, the court of Madrid send out a few companies of soldiers to the country, and declare it to be annexed to the Spanish dominions.' This unlucky speech made a great impression on the Japanese king. He readily apprehended what truth there was in it. He took alarm, and determined in his mind that Christianity should be put down. He set himself with perseverance to the task. The Spanish and Portuguese priests were driven from his states. The converts were obliged to choose between death and recantation; and the result was, that in a few years nothing remained of the glorious edifice which had been so rapidly called into existence by Saint François Xavier. The revolution which destroyed Christianity in Japan was, it is evident, purely political, and in no degree religious.

There is no permanent army in Japan. All the persons wearing two swords, who compose the suite of the princes and governors in time of peace, become soldiers in time of war. They are brave, undoubtedly; but, with their present weapons, it would be difficult for them to cope with Europeans. It is said, however, that, conscious of their backwardness in this respect, they have been reading up in strategic science. Japan has got into close quarters with Europe, and is a prey to a species of invasion panic. The Japanese know that, with bows and arrows, they cannot offer any formidable opposition to Minié rifles and bombshells, and they are working hard, accordingly, to make themselves masters of the naval and military sciences as they now are understood in Europe. Before they can organize an army, they must reform their costume, giving up sandals, bag-trousers, and long sweeping dresses. They are quite prepared to do all this. The Japanese do not, like the Chinese, entertain the idiotical notion that they are superior to all the rest of mankind. They consider themselves to be in advance of the Chinese; but they form a very just estimate of the relation in which they stand to the Western nations.

In Japan it is no longer the custom, as it used to be, to make light of ripping open the abdomen; and now-a-days, a suicide in this empire, like a suicide elsewhere, cuts his throat, or gets a dear friend to chop his head off for him. The old custom has evidently died out. Just as we have in Europe dancing-masters and fencing-masters, there are, nevertheless, still in Japan masters who teach the old suicidal process. Indeed the knowledge of it forms part of a liberal education, and is very much prized by the young nobles. It is often a means of escaping infamy, and anticipating a public execution by a voluntary death. The following anecdote, which has been told before, but which will bear a second telling, is characteristic, and must belong to a very early period.—Two gentlemen in the royal service met on the stair of the palace. The one was going down with an empty dish; the other was taking a full plate to the royal table. By accident their two swords knocked against each other. The gentleman who was stepping down stairs considered himself insulted; drew his sword, and ripped open his stomach. The other hurried up stairs, put his plate on the royal table, and rushed back to his friend, whom he was glad to find still in life. He begged the dying man to excuse him for not having performed the deed at the same time with him, alleging that he had his duty to fulfil. This said, he drew his sword—made the fatal gash, and fell beside his friend on the palace stair. There was, at the bonze-house at Yedo, a Kodamaya who had made himself disagreeable. We accused him, whether rightly or not, of increasing the prices of curiosities which we went to purchase. As we left Yedo, Flavigny made a sign to him, whereby he indicated, by drawing his finger over his stomach, that the Kodamaya could not do better than commit the rash act. But the rascally iacounin, instead of drawing his sword, took a hearty laugh, in which he was joined by the bystanders. Our young colleague was twenty years behind.

The palace of the Emperor at Yedo is surrounded by a wide ditch, full of limpid running water, with banks beautifully kept, covered with rich turf and Japanese cedars, the long branches of which droop to the ground. It has quite the appearance of an English park. Commanders Kerjegu and D'Ozery took a stroll round it one day. It took them fully an hour and a half; and they estimated, from the distance they walked, that the palace and grounds of the taïcoon are about five miles and a half in circumference.

There are, both at Yedo and Simoda, great numbers of fishing eagles and black crows, which are never disturbed by the Japanese. One of our party having fired at one of the latter at Simoda, an old bonze .came rushing out, with a lighted pipe, to offer a sacrifice to the soul of the departed crow. Luckily there was no harm done, which seemed to give great satisfaction to the poor priest.

The bay of Yedo swarms in every direction with small fishing-boats, dragging nets in which are caught great quantities of fine fish. The Japanese government, faithful to its protective policy, rigorously fixes the shape and size of junks, and enforces such regulations as prevent them from leaving the coast and adventuring into the open sea. Formerly, natives of Japan who had the misfortune to be shipwrecked on the coast of China, or to be driven by stormy weather as far as Formosa or the Philippine Islands, could only be brought back to Japan by Dutch ships; and when they got home they were subject to suspicion all the rest of their lives, or, as we should say, they remained under the surveillance of the high police. The existing law of Japan, on this subject, is somewhat softened, but even now it is a bad affair for a Japanese to have been picked up at sea, and brought home to his own country in a European ship.

The Japanese are quite aware of the horrible

ravages committed by opium among the Chinese, and the government of the taïcoon has accordingly insisted on having a clause inserted in all the four treaties, whereby the importation of this drug into Japan is prohibited.

The government of Japan, like that of Siam, exhibits the remarkable anomaly of two sovereigns reigning at once legally and in virtue of the constitution of the country. At Siam there is a first and second king, who exercise supreme power at the same time; in Japan there is the civil emperor and the ecclesiastical emperor, the taïcoon and the mikado. The taïcoon, whom Europeans call erroneously the Emperor of Japan, is merely the delegate or lieutenant of the mikado, who is the true King of Niphon, the representative of the old dynasties, the descendant of the gods, and who, being by far too mighty a personage to concern himself with the affairs of this world, throws this burden upon the shoulders of a subordinate. The taïcoons at first were the *maires du palais*, the stewards, the great officers of a degenerate dynasty, who, instead of sending the last of the Japanese Merovingians to a monastery, after shearing his locks and putting a cowl upon him, have locked him up in a superb temple, and converted him into an idol; having succeeded in persuading the demi-god himself, and the whole nation, that this was the situation most in conformity with his divine origin. The new dynasty in this way mounted the throne, and usurped supreme power, while all the time professing the utmost respect for the elder line of monarchs, and recognising in them the absolute sovereignty of the archipelago. On this fiction rests the whole edifice of the political constitution of Japan. The mikado continues to reside at Meako, the old capital of the Son of the Sun, surrounded by a magnificent court, and made the object of much outward respect by his powerful vassal. His idle life passes away in the midst of his great palace, which he is prohibited from leaving by a rigid and unalterable system. His court is the rendezvous of poets, musicians, artists, and astronomers. The rice which he eats is picked for the royal table grain by grain. He never wears twice the same dress. He never drinks twice out of the same cup. The one he has used is immediately broken lest any rash mortal should dare to touch it with his profane lips. Formerly he was obliged to sit for hours upon his throne, there being a mysterious connection between the immobility of his person and the stability of the empire. If he moved or turned his head, that part of Japan which lay on the side of the new posture was menaced with great misfortunes. But it was found that absolute immobility was too much for the human nature even of a mikado; and, provinces innumerable having been threatened with calamities, to put an end to alarm a wise expedient was hit upon.   Accordingly, the crown alone is now placed upon the throne, and while it remains unmoved the stability of the empire remains secure. The new arrangement seems to have been attended with the happiest results. For two hundred years Japan has enjoyed profound peace, and no war civil or foreign has troubled its tranquillity.

When the mikado had been disposed of in this way, the new dynasty turned its attention to the daïmio or princes, whose ancestors in the old heroic times were proprietors of the soil of Japan, and had each a small court in their own provinces, where they had the command of numerous vassals. The independent and warlike disposition of this class became the cause of serious apprehensions to the court of Yedo, and a Machiavellian policy was adopted and steadily adhered to, with a view to humble them and annul their power.   Louis XI. and his advisers were completely thrown into the shade by the old statesmen of Japan.   After centuries of intrigue and perfidy, the provincial princes, one after the other, were forced to succumb.   They preserved merely the appearance and outward form of power, and be-

came what they now are, submissive subjects of the
taïcoun. An agent of the court was appointed to
reside within the jurisdiction of each, and intrusted
with its administration. They were obliged to pass
one year out of each two at Yedo, and during this
time there was no means which was not put in force
to diminish their wealth. Even now, princes whose
domains adjoin are not allowed to live at the same
time on their estates, unless they are on bad terms;
and then the supreme power strives to foment the
quarrel, and to provoke new causes of discord. The
wives and daughters and whole families of the
princes remain at Yedo as hostages, and are held
accountable for the acts of the head of the house.
An army of spies surrounds them, and gives an
account of their smallest actions to the court. In
this way, gradually, and without any violent shock,
by the simple effect of a traditional course of policy
perseveringly adhered to, there now remains in
Japan a mere vestige of feudalism, while political
and administrative centralization are in process of
being established in the empire.

But everything in this world comes to an end.
Dynasties, like empires, sink into the decrepitude of
years. This haughty lieutenant of the mikado, this
all-powerful taïcoon, the chief of the armies, and
the energetic governor of the archipelago, allowed

himself in turn to get entangled in the inextricable toils of etiquette and vanity. He too was persuaded that the government of the empire was a great burden, and that an easy and idle life was more consistent with the dignity of his race. Accordingly the administration of his kingdom was thrown upon the gotaïro, the hereditary prime minister, who for several generations has taken up a position close by the throne. The taïcoon passes his whole time in observing ceremonies and giving receptions. He never passes beyond the palace walls more than three or four times a year, when he goes to worship the images of his ancestors. It is not at all likely that he will ever see the elegant yacht which has been sent to him as a gift by the English government in their ignorance of the present political state of Japan. It may come to pass in the course of time that the gotaïro, the hereditary *maire du palais*, will acquire the title of a sovereign as well as the power of one. He will then found, to the exclusion of those at Meako and Yedo, a third dynasty at Oosaka.

The lieutenant of the mikado, or the civil emperor, is both taïcoon and siogoon; siogoon, inasmuch as he is a military chief and commander of the armies, and taïcoon in his capacity of chief justice and civil administrator of the empire. All the books which refer to Japan speak of him under the name of siegoon, but, in consequence of the military capacity displayed by the hereditary prime minister, we only heard him spoken of as taïcoon during our stay in Japan. The word siogoon has, in consequence of all this, become a term quite without meaning, representing a state of matters which no longer exists.

The name of the gotaïro, or present hereditary prime minister, is Hii-Camonno-Kami.

Some towns, such as Simoda, Oosaka, Nangasaki, and Hakadadi, have been entirely removed from the rule of princes, and are now, under the name of imperial towns, directly under the control of the court of Yedo, which appoints their governors. There are always two governors for each of these places. They reside alternately in the capital; the one remaining at the seat of government while the other is at the capital, and *vice versâ*. They are subjected, like the princes, to a close surveillance, and their families, like those of the princes, are retained at the court as hostages. This being the case, it is easy to understand the great extent of the official town at Yedo. We had a glimpse of many of the fair faces, condemned by the jealous policy of the government to a sort of perpetual imprisonment; and, as we saw them watching us with the greatest curiosity from behind the wooden window bars, we could not help pitying their lot, although it must be admitted that the utmost contentment beamed on every countenance, indicative only of that imperturbable gaiety which seems to be inherent in the Japanese character.

Van Diemen's Strait is situated to the south of the province of Satsouma. The Prince of Satsouma is the most powerful vassal of the court of Yedo. He is the only one who preserves any influence, and for whom the taïcoons continue to show respect. The family of the taïcoon intermarries with that of the princes of Satsouma. The Loo-choo Islands are a dependency of Satsouma. While we were staying at Yedo we heard that the reigning prince was of a cruel and tyrannical disposition. "Better serve the devil than the Prince of Satsouma" had passed into a maxim there. At his court it was said that the old national custom of ripping up the stomach was still adhered to. The taïcoon who had just died was highly spoken of, and said to be very moderate when compared with his vassal. The Dutch at Nangasaki, on the contrary, zealously defend the Prince of Satsouma against his calumniators. According to their account of matters he is run down at Yedo because he will not allow a spy to remain at his court. He relentlessly chops off the head of any note-taker whom he happens to catch within his bounds. He is determined to have his laws obeyed, and he takes the only course in his power to secure submission. Several of the Dutch naval officers met the prince at Kagosima. He came on board and went all over the ships, examining everything, putting a great many questions, and talking to everybody with great affability. His dress was of a plain cotton material, and there was nothing to distinguish him from the persons belonging to his suite save his exquisite politeness and extensive knowledge.

The central government of Japan is conducted with great energy, and now exercises absolute authority in all parts of the empire. We could collect very little information concerning it, any question put on the subject having a tendency to inspire alarm. Attached to the civil emperor, who reigns but does not govern, is the hereditary prime minister, or gotaïro, who does govern. He is assisted by a great council, composed of six members, and of another council, composed of fifteen members, and entrusted with legislative functions. There are besides four ministers. The ministry of war or national defence includes more than fifty members, and is considered the most important of all, loss of national independence being the chief dread of the Japanese. The ministry of the imperial domains has entrusted to its care the imperial towns detached from the terri-

tory of the princes and the province of Yedo. The
ministry of foreign affairs, composed of six members,
takes the management of all that relates to the intercourse of Japan with foreign nations. The ministry
of police comes last. This must be the most actively
employed of these bodies, as its members are obliged
to read innumerable reports sent them by an army
of spies scattered all over the surface of the empire.
We must have put them to no small trouble ourselves if all that was jotted down on fans concerning
us was sent to head-quarters for perusal.

Latterly the Dutch governor has attempted twice
to induce the court of Yedo to abandon the old
policy of excluding foreigners. In 1845, more especially, an aide-de-camp of the King delivered to the
taïcoon an autograph letter of King William II. of
Holland. This letter called the attention of the
Japanese government to the subject of opening
China to foreign commerce. It pointed out to the
Emperor the danger of wishing to preserve strict
isolation at a period when the increasing traffic
on Chinese waters was on the point of extending to
Japan, when steam-power had abridged distance,
and when the development of European commerce
and industry imperiously called for new fields of
mercantile enterprise. In this letter the taïcoon was
recommended to enter into amicable commercial

relations with other nations as the only means of avoiding perilous disputes with them. But the court of Yedo remained deaf to this friendly counsel. The demolition of the Ta-kou forts may have produced a good effect on the government of the taïcoon. However, it must be admitted that, although fear may have had some share in prompting the Japanese to adopt the arrangements entered into, they were in a greater degree attributable to the good sense and clear insight of the government; these qualities leading it to concede with a good grace and spontaneously what might otherwise be wrested from it by a strong hand.

CHAPTER XII.

Typhoon in the Chinese Seas.—Stay of Kouei-Liang and Houa-
Cha-Na at Shang-hai.—Revision of the Commercial Tariffs.—
Lord Elgin ascends the Yang-tse-Kiang or Blue River.—Ship-
wreck of the 'Laplace.'—The author brings home the Treaty of
Yedo to France.—Return of the Embassy.—Conclusion.

On returning to Shang-hai we heard bad news. A
violent typhoon had spread its ravages all along the
China Sea. Fourteen ships had been cast ashore in
the road of Swatow. A great number of junks were
destroyed. Several English gunboats had lost their
masts. The Russian steamer by which Admiral Poutiatine had come to Hong-Kong had put in at Woosung completely disabled. The English newspapers
asserted that the 'Rémi,' caught in the hurricane,
had been swamped at sea. Happily this turned out
not to be the case. The French embassy indeed had
passed through the midst of the tempest without any
injury, their vessels being at anchor during the whole
time of the wind. We found that the High Imperial
Commissioners had arrived at Shang-hai, with a suite

of six hundred persons. The mandarins of the town gave them a grand reception, and the whole population was thrown into a high state of excitement by the arrival of these illustrious personages within the walls of the city. The conferences for the revision of the tariffs immediately began. M. de contades, assisted by M. Edan, chancellor to the consulate, represented the interests of French commerce, with a view more to the future than the present. We went in great state, escorted by the disembarkation corps of the 'Laplace,' to visit Kouei-Liang and Houa-Cha-Na, and the latter, accompanied by the governor of the two Kiangs, the fou-tai of Sou-tchou-fou, the tao-ai of Shang-hai, and several other authorities, came to visit us in return. The élite of Chinese society met in the drawing-room of M. de Montigny, but we cannot say that we were dazzled. Neither the refined language of the court nor the graceful manners of the capital made much impression upon us. We were afraid that these great personages would avail themselves too freely of the request courteously made them by M. de Montigny, to take some little article of European production as a souvenir of their visit. The long train of rod-bearers, executioners, literati, and palanquin porters, covered the quay, while the sound of the gong announced the arrival and departure of the representatives of the

Son of Heaven. We found the Tartar Houa-Cha-Na as gloomy as he had been at Tien-tsin. On the other hand, the countenance of Kouei-Liang was irradiated by a smile of satisfaction, and, between his glass of champagne and cup of coffee, both of which were new luxuries to him, he took occasion to talk very graciously to his entertainers. The tao-tai of Shang-hai stood out from the throng, distinguished by his good looks and easy manners. He was quite at home at the house of M. de Montigny, and he explained to the illustrious functionaries the merits of each dish, and the use of all the articles on the table. The commissioner of the two Kiangs talked with wonderful volubility, and put some very intelligent questions to Baron Gros. Chance placed me next Houa-Cha-Na, in whose inanimate face I could discover no trace of either interest or astonishment at the new scene before him.

Lord Elgin, having concluded the revision of his tariff, left us in the early part of November to ascend the Yang-tse-Kiang, and visit the three ports opened under his treaty in the upper part of the river. His lordship took with him two steam frigates and three English gunboats. Till this time European ships had never ascended the river higher than Nankin, and it was not known to what distance it was navigable from its mouth. After exchanging a few shots with the rebels of Nankin, and obtaining complete evidence of the dreadful devastation caused by the insurrection, and visiting the deserted towns and uninhabited country, which had been the seat of the war, Lord Elgin returned to Shang-hai; the farthest point he had reached in his expedition being Wou-tchang-fou, in the province of Houpeh. He left behind three ships, which had stuck fast in the mud above Nankin. But he had solved the problem of the navigation of the Yang-tse-Kiang, having ascended this river to a distance of two hundred leagues from its mouth.

Meanwhile Baron Gros was less fortunate. In crossing from Shang-hai to Hong-Kong, the 'Laplace,' on board of which were the French Embassy, had a narrow escape from shipwreck on the isle of Tai-shan, near Chusan.

Hong-Kong, December 12.

' The French war sloop, the " Laplace," left Shang-hai on the 27th November, for Hong-Kong, to join the " Audacieuse," and thence to proceed with her to Tourane. At one o'clock on the afternoon of Sunday she ran aground on the banks which lie to the north of the island of Tai-shan. The ship was then proceeding at the rate of nine miles an hour. The foggy weather, and it may be an error in the reckoning, caused by the currents, were the cause of this

unfortunate accident. However, as there was no
shock felt when the vessel was stranded, it was evident
that she had got into a bank of mud, where there
were neither rocks nor sand. If it had been otherwise, the "Laplace" would have been totally shipwrecked.

'Her situation was, however, precarious. The
ship, strained in every timber by the sea, which
broke over her, plunged about violently. Her helm
was knocked in, a part of her anchors and her small
boats were lost, and three seamen, who had courage-
ously offered to take a rope preserver on shore,
perished in the attempt without the possibility of any
one going to their rescue.

'At eight o'clock in the evening the commander
announced that he had given up all hope of saving
the ship, and accordingly every one prepared to get on
shore as he best could, with his most precious articles.
However, the wind fell towards the evening. A
ship's boat too, more fortunate than the first, gained
the land with an officer and some men of the crew.
They hastened immediately to send letters to Shang-
hai and Ningpo, making known the position of the
"Laplace," and asking prompt assistance.

'Those on board the "Laplace" remained in great
distress from the 28th to the 30th. The ship kept
knocking against the bottom. It was getting gradu-

ally closer to the shore. At length, on the 1st of December, the weather cleared up, and then the native junks made their appearance in great numbers, although during the storm we had fired our signal of distress in vain. They took on board the artillery, ammunition, and ballast of our stranded ship. An anchor, the only one left us, was then dropped out at sea, and the ship, lightened in the way we have described, was dragged into deep water without her hull or engines being in any way injured.

'On the 2nd of December the "Nimrod," and the gunboat the "Opossum," belonging to the British navy, arrived,—the one from Ningpo with the English consul, and the other from Shang-hai with the French consul. The latter brought the news that the "Inflexible" would be up the same day to assist the "Laplace." Having ascertained beyond all doubt that the ship was safe, Baron Gros resolved to embark with the members of the Embassy on board the "Nimrod," in order to go to Shang-hai, where he arrived on the 6th. Thence he proceeded by the packet "Aden" to Hong-Kong.

'In coming in sight of this harbour, the ship, in order to give notice of the fact that the French ambassador was on board, hoisted the tricolor from the mainmast. Admiral Seymour immediately sent the captain of his flagship on board. At the same time all the vessels in the road hoisted their colours and welcomed the ambassador with the usual salute of nineteen guns.　Baron Gros, after having gone on board the "Calcutta" to thank Admiral Seymour for the prompt assistance afforded him by the British navy, went on shore, where he met with a warm welcome.　He was received at the landing-place by the governor *ad interim*, surrounded by the troops of the garrison under arms, and, after a salute from the forts, he was taken in the governor's carriage to the club-house at Hong-Kong, where apartments had been provided for his reception.'—*Moniteur*.

I was not present on this occasion.　Entrusted by the ambassador with the duty of conveying the Treaty of Yedo to France, I had left Shang-hai on the 7th of November, on board the Peninsular and Oriental Steam Company's steamer the 'Aden.'　At Hong-Kong I came across the 'Audacieuse' again; and, after bidding farewell to the officers of the frigate, the missionaries, and the English authorities of the colony, I continued my rapid journey across the Indian Ocean and the Red Sea.　On the 27th of December I arrived at Marseilles, and immediately afterwards at Paris, where I was graciously received by their Majesties and Count Walewski.　Some months later, Baron Gros, returning by Bombay and Suez, also reached Marseilles, with the other members of

the Embassy, after two years of rough service. Much
had been accomplished within this period, and Baron
Gros had good reason to be satisfied with his success.
Let us shortly enumerate the results of the Chinese
treaty. The magistrates of Si-lin-hien, who had murdered Père Chapdelaine, had been disgraced and declared incapable of exercising any employment under
government—a measure which, it had been arranged,
was to be published and inserted in the 'Pekin Gazette.'
An indemnity had been granted to the Frenchmen
and the protégés of France whose property had been
pillaged or burned by the populace of Canton. The
Chinese government had become bound to pay the
French, for the expenses of the war, the sum of two
millions of taëls, or about sixteen millions of francs.
The course of the Yang-tse-Kiang, the greatest of the
Asiatic rivers, was no longer to be closed against foreign
commerce. Six new ports had been opened: Kiung-
tchaou and Tchaou-tchaou (Swatow), in the province
of Kwang-toung; Tai-van and Tan-shwi, in the island
of Formosa; Tan-tchao, in the province of Chan-toung;
and Nankin, in the province of Kiang-nan, were about
to become European colonies. Frenchmen were now
entitled to proceed freely to the places of production,
to make their purchases on the spot; the only condition attached to this privilege being that they should
obtain a passport, legally delivered by the consul, and

countersigned by the local authorities.   The representative of France had acquired the right to proceed to
the capital at certain times to settle affairs there in
person with the principal personages of the empire, and
this intercourse was to take place on a footing of perfect equality.   Every word that, up to the date of the
treaty, had been written, proclaimed, and published
in China by order of the government against the
Christian faith was abrogated and recalled.   The
13th Article of the Treaty of Tien-tsin stipulated
that, the Christian religion having essentially for its
object to lead men to virtue, the members of all
Christian communions were to enjoy entire security for
their persons and property, and to be entitled freely
to practise their religious ceremonies;   moreover,
ample protection was to be given to missionaries travelling in the interior of the empire.   This clause was
added to the same article : *No obstacle will be raised by
the authorities of the Chinese empire to the right which
every one in China is admitted to possess of embracing,
if he thinks fit, the Christian faith, and of following its
observances without being liable to any penalty inflicted
for his so doing.*   This was liberty on the widest scale
—freedom in religion, freedom in trade, and freedom
in intercourse.   The old errors of the court of Pekin
had yielded to a new creed, the times of the all-
powerful governors of Kwang-toung seemed to have

passed away, and European complaints were no longer exposed to the risk of being intercepted in a yamoun at Canton without ever being heard of in the head-quarters of the government.

The empire of Japan had also been opened to European civilization after two centuries of complete isolation. The commercial monopoly of the government had been put down, and the law abrogated whereby the citizens of the empire were forbidden, under pain of death, to sell goods of any kind to foreigners. Free trade had been proclaimed in place of the old system of exclusion and protection. Yedo, Oosaka, Hakodadi, Kanagawa, Nangasaki, Hiogo, and Ne-e-gata had been opened. The French were not authorised to settle at Yedo until the 1st January, 1862, and at Oosaka till the 1st January, 1863, but in all the other ports they were allowed immediately to build houses and open shops or warehouses, with the right to move about, within a distance of ten ris, or about twenty-five miles. The Consul-general of France was entitled to travel into all parts of the empire, and the capital of the taïcoon was fixed upon as his residence. The practice of trampling upon the cross on certain solemn occasions was abolished. The French subjects in Japan had the right conceded them of freely exercising their religion, and with this view were permitted, within the space set apart for their residence, to build churches and chapels, and to enclose churchyards. Religious freedom was, no doubt, still withheld from Japanese subjects, but an immense stride was taken towards a more liberal policy, and the echoes of Niphon may soon ring once more with the sounds of the church-going bell. The Japanese government had learned to dread foreigners less in coming closely in contact with them, and they had obtained ample proof that it was neither the lust of conquest nor commercial gain which had brought the representatives of France to those seas, but the necessity of protecting the political influence of the empire and the honour of the national flag in the extreme East.

Such was the state of matters when Baron Gros and Lord Elgin, returning to Europe in the middle of 1859, transferred to M.' de Bourboulon and Mr. Frederic Bruce the management of French and English interests in China and Japan.

THE END.